Praise for *House of Havoc*

"What your mother never told you, count on Marni Jameson to do so in this survival guide for living with your spouse, kids, dogs. I promise, it will help save your sanity."
> —Betty Lou Phillips, *award-winning author of* Inspirations from France and Italy, Villa Décor, *and other home design books*

Praise for *The House Always Wins*

"I know of no other book that's such an entertaining read while teaching what to do and what not to do to make your dream house a reality. As Marni so wisely advises, take your time—and I would add: put this book at the top of your to-do list."
> —Sarah Susanka, FAIA, *architect and author of the* Not So Big House *series and* The Not So Big Life

"A memorable book with useful tips surrounded by a funny, relatable story."
> —Newsday

"Filled with (home improvement) tips we can all use, not to mention nearly a laugh a page."
> —Los Angeles Times

"Jameson, whose uproarious voice recalls Erma Bombeck's, dishes out home advice in witty essays . . . You don't necessarily have to be in the middle of a remodel or redecorating project to appreciate the laughs in *The House Always Wins*, but anyone on the rocky road to making a house a home will find Jameson an especially charming companion."
> —BookPage

"Jameson's book is bursting with so many practical insider tips— some from experience and some from interviews with experts— that it's worth reading even if you only plan to renovate one room at a time with a modest budget."
—*Hartford Courant*

"A plan of attack with a sense of humor"
—*Dallas Morning News*

"Jameson packs her narrative with advice elicited from professionals . . . which makes for a practical as well as amusing tale."
—*Library Journal*

"Readers gain the benefit of Jameson's experience—along with laugh-out-loud anecdotes—in this informative home-improvement guide."
—*Publishers Weekly*

"Pragmatic humor is no longer an oxymoron."
—*Booklist*

"By detailing real-life scenarios and experiences, Jameson shares her point of view in a humorous yet straightforward fashion . . . she offers how-to tips, design options, strategies, time-saver pointers and expert advice on common remodeling issues."
—*Chicago Tribune*

"Humorous and practical"
—*Metro New York*

"By detailing real-life scenarios and experiences, Jameson shares her point of view in a humorous yet straightforward fashion . . . the funny interactions with her spouse, irritated neighbors and others provide enough color for you to keep turning the pages."
—*Orlando Sentinel*

House of
of
Havoc

Also by Marni Jameson

The House Always Wins

House

of

Havoc

How to Make—and Keep—a Beautiful Home Despite Cheap Spouses,
Messy Kids, and Other Difficult Roommates

MARNI JAMESON

Da Capo
∞
LIFE
LONG

A Member of the Perseus Books Group

Designed by Trish Wilkinson
Set in 11.5 point Goudy by the Perseus Books Group

Library of Congress Cataloging-in-Publication Data

Jameson, Marni.
    House of havoc : how to make and keep a beautiful home despite cheap spouses, messy kids, and other difficult roommates / Marni Jameson.
        p.   cm.
    Includes bibliographical references and index.
    ISBN 978-0-7382-1311-8 (alk. paper)
    1. House cleaning. 2. Storage in the home. 3. Interior decoration—Amateurs' manuals. I. Title.
TX324.J35 2010
648'.5—dc22
2009039129

First Da Capo Press edition 2010

Published by Da Capo Press
A Member of the Perseus Books Group
www.dacapopress.com

Da Capo Press books are available at special discounts for bulk purchases in the United States by corporations, institutions, and other organizations. For more infor-mation, please contact the Special Markets Department at the Perseus Books Group, 2300 Chestnut Street, Suite 200, Philadelphia, PA 19103, or call (800) 810-4145, ext. 5000, or e-mail special.markets@perseusbooks.com.

1 2 3 4 5 6 7 8 9

*For my personal havoc raisers—Dan, Paige, and Marissa,
and the furry ones, Theo and Oliver—without
whom my house would not be a home*

Contents

PART ❋ SIX

Specialty Spaces and Making
Your Home Stretch

PART ❋ SEVEN

House Hygiene

PART * EIGHT
Taming the Wild Kingdom

PART * NINE
The Future Is Green, but What If You're Yellow?

Foreword

AFTER OVER A decade of working on design television and many more years of working in the interior design industry, I have learned the following: Home design speaks to everyone on some level. We all have homes and we all have opinions on our homes.

People gobble up design information and always seem to want more. They love to see the results of good design (and bad, actually). They love thinking about it, love doing it, and love the topic in general.

However, these same people tend to become stuck when designing their own homes. It's easier to watch others design on television, or delight in the before-and-after pictures in a magazine, than to dive in and make those big changes. People want to do what we as designers do, but they don't know where to start. To get to that well-designed home, they first have to overcome an enormous hurdle—clutter and havoc.

Marni Jameson has come to the rescue. When many people throw up their hands, Marni rolls up her sleeves. She knows that before you get to the pretty stuff, you have to deal with the chaos. She knows that a beautiful bowl of lemons on the coffee table doesn't look so beautiful surrounded by a half-eaten sandwich on a paper plate, a pair of socks, and yesterday's newspaper. You can't see beauty through chaos.

None of us wants to be scolded about the state of our homes. And we don't need fancy designers telling us what's wrong with our lifestyles and households. What we do need are tips for simplifying our lives and our home habits, and, once we have moved past the havoc in our homes, simple and inexpensive solutions for making a beautiful space.

That's what makes Marni such a valuable companion. She's the girlfriend who's been in your shoes, made mistakes, and figured it all out—and she shares it all in this book, while somehow managing to leave you laughing. Finally, here's someone who has both the DIY chops and the advice of the very designers and experts who can get you to that better designed life and home—and make it beautiful, too!

Above all, Marni gives you clever information you can really use. Guided by Marni's unique insight and personality, you can turn chaos control from a chore into—dare I say—fun. And in the process, you can make the rooms you live in look a lot more like those gorgeous rooms that you see on TV and in magazines.

I recently visited a friend to help him clear his home of chaos and clutter. This friend—a television host we'll call "Clive"—tends to let life's mementos and clutter build up. I lovingly placed an early copy of *House of Havoc* on his coffee table and told him that what he needed was not really me, or any designer, but this book. Let's just hope he can find it under that half-eaten sandwich!

—Lisa LaPorta, *designer and host of HGTV's* Designed to Sell *and* Bang for Your Buck, *and KILZ® Brand Spokesperson*

Preface: Living with THEM!

ONE EVENING, while reading a slick magazine about the good life, I felt irritation well up like a case of hives. As I turned pages featuring articles on making your own scented candles, drying herbs for your fall tea, alphabetizing your favorite recipes, and crafting a journal out of sea grass, I thought, not for the first time, about how wide the gap is between the picture-perfect home portrayed in the media and my home.

I thought about my tornado of a day. I'd dealt with a broken washing machine, maneuvered around school projects that had claimed the kitchen table, extracted a ketchup stain from the carpet, and stopped a pillow fight the dogs were having on the living room sofa, in between working, paying bills, and feeding my tribe of a family.

No wonder I felt annoyed. Here I can barely get the kids out the door on time with clean clothes, and I felt like a slacker because I didn't put origami napkins in their lunch boxes.

However, I also recognized that my cynicism was cover for something else, for what I really wanted from my home and felt missing. Despite my mocking, I did want a more gracious lifestyle, more order in my home, and a more beautifully decorated haven for my family—but how? How when I live with a thrifty spouse, careless kids, and run-amuck pets in a time-crunched world where meeting the basic demands of work, home, and family matters commandeers all my attention?

How when I live at home with *Them!?*

That's the question I began exploring in my weekly syndicated home design column. As I delved into that murky space where life and home design collide, I looked for small, affordable, realistic ways to make big improvements at home. I read organizing and design books, then interviewed lifestyle and interior design experts, peppering them with my selfishly motivated, burning questions.

The result is this girlfriend's guide to mastering the art of living more beautifully with others. It's a handbook for those who want to take their house back, and create calm out of chaos, heaven from havoc, and beauty on a budget, while feeling better about the fact that their home isn't perfect. As in my column, I share everyday domestic scenarios, then serve up practical, tested tips that have made my home a better place to live, and will help yours, too.

You won't find any gee-whizzy, this-woman-needs-to-get-a-life kind of advice. (Like you, I have plenty of life.) I've included what worked for me, and have left out any advice that made me want to scream. I won't tell you how to make an origami napkin, but I will share how to buy perfect towels the first time. I won't frustrate you with over-the-top, pricey decorating ideas, but will teach you how to make dreamy drapes with a glue gun for cheap. I will not dole out vapid design advice: "Rooms should evolve over time, reflect your sensibility and heritage, and have their own pedigree of purpose." But I will pass on useful design direction (i.e., keep table accessories larger than a cantaloupe), so you can fix up your home yourself with the confidence of a pro.

You also won't find any advice that doesn't pass the *Them!* test. If the advice won't fly in a havoc-filled home, it's not here. That's because at my house, good relationships trump good design. Whether I'm grappling with gender wars, kids' rooms, school projects, daily clutter, unpredictable pets, or a shoestring budget—and I do all that in the coming pages—my goal is to live better and more beautifully with *Them!*

Photos illustrating many of the ideas featured in this book may be viewed at www.marnijameson.com.

PART * ONE

At Home with Havoc

As long as you live with others—kids, spouses, dogs, or other difficult roommates—you live with havoc. The first step to attractive, harmonious cohabitation is to understand your enemies. The second step is to meet them halfway.

Havoc and I,
We Have a Deal

I DIDN'T REALIZE that havoc and I would become permanent roommates until Marissa, my youngest child, was in kindergarten. Until then, I thought the fact that my house looked chronically vandalized was just a phase, like teething or potty training.

See, before children, you could have dropped by any time and my house would have looked pulled together and company ready. But my first child arrived the way every baby does, like a small explosive: Laundry—Kaboom! Dishes—Kerpow! Toys—Kablam! Soon, an orderly home became as common as a full night's sleep. And the chaos didn't end when the kids stopped spitting up and were out of diapers. It merely changed. Next I was dealing with mud on the stairs, bike tracks on the walls, candy in the carpet, and home birthday parties featuring Silly String contests and chocolate fountains.

I realized havoc wasn't leaving the day I pulled into the school parking lot to take Marissa to kindergarten. Just then she remembered she was supposed to have brought five things that started with the letter *s*. I quickly weighed my options—plead mommy Alzheimer's or scurry back home. Then I saw the answer in front of me. Scattered around the car—which before kids was always immaculate—were sunscreen, a straw, sunglasses, a shoe, and a sock. Bingo! We'd hit our quota without counting the soccer ball and my daughter's sandwich. I actually could have covered several letters of the alphabet.

As we put the s items in a "sack" I found under the seat, I couldn't help noting that the car was just an extension of my house, which was an extension of my life—Havoc. Life was not getting less hectic now that my kids were in school. And it wouldn't be less hectic once they were able to "help," or drive, or move out. Now that they're both teenagers, I'm still dealing with havoc, only the laundry piles are bigger. Family life, in all its stages, is messy. But do we have to live like this?

That day in the school parking lot, I drew a figurative line in the dust. I made myself a mandate: I would figure out how to live more graciously and more beautifully in a family-friendly home. I would develop systems and household habits that would keep our home running smoothly without feeling like boot camp. I would learn how to buy household goods—like sheets, towels, dishes, and glassware—right the first time, so I could live each day with more quality and less clutter. I would figure out how to make my home look like a million bucks while staying within my seriously tight budget and not giving my hardworking husband higher blood pressure. I would create a picturesque background for family memories without shortchanging the memories themselves. I would live more simply, in a prettier, greener home, with less stress and more joy.

That was my vision. This book is about how I got there.

We're in This Mess Together

First, I had to make a deal with havoc.

I accepted that havoc is a much larger force than I would ever be—and that's saying something. But, we agreed, if havoc would grant me the illusion of household control, I would stop trying to abolish it. I would let it live and play at the periphery of my home—in check.

I would stop deluding myself into believing that I could conquer it, and instead would follow the advice in that prayer, "Accept the things I cannot change." This meant finding an honest place between reality and that ideal that home design and organizing experts perpetuate.

First, I tried their way. When I started taking my house back, I bought a passel of home design and organizing books. (Wrong! Only buy one book. Buying a dozen creates clutter!) Just buying them made me feel virtuous, the way buying a diet book does, like I was doing something about the problem. Next, rather than incorporate their advice seamlessly into my life, I did what journalists do when they don't want to deal with their problems firsthand. I interviewed the authors and experts, and dispatched the best nuggets of wisdom in my weekly column. When I actually test-drove the advice to see what stuck, I felt guilty when it didn't.

Although I did uncover a lot of useful advice that really worked, I also uncovered many pieces of advice that didn't. Some were outright preposterous. I started this journey of learning to live beautifully with *Them!* and with havoc by putting some of those wrongheaded notions up front, so you know what this book won't be about. Here are my major findings about what's wrong with the advice out there, and a bit about what's right:

Major Finding #1: The more you read organizing and household management books, the more you wonder why there hasn't been a public outcry against these experts.

Here's just a sampling of what they dictate: Grocery shop only once a week—with coupons and a list. Have a place for everything and put it there. Handle every paper only once. Make your kids think housework is fun. Do a little laundry each day. Keep closets neat and pared to only items you have worn over the past year. Whenever you buy something, get rid of something. Have a streamlined filing system so you can put your hands on every family member's birth certificate, Social Security number, passport, and first-grade report card in under three minutes.

See what I mean about an outcry? Either these experts are lying about the fact that they really do all this, or their families have run from their houses screaming.

Major Finding #2: Organizing rules sound great for those who are single and celibate, which, trust me, you will be if you practice them.

For those of us who live with others, havoc is a constant. Households have havoc raisers. At my house, we have the sprawler: My oldest daughter, Paige, has never encountered a piece of unclaimed real estate she didn't overtake. She has at least one garment in every room, and her schoolbooks can be found everywhere this side of the Mississippi.

My younger daughter, Marissa, is the creator. She likes projects, the stickier the better. She cooks. She crafts. She does not clean up. She cries artistic freedom, which explains why there's cookie dough on my ceiling.

And we have Mr. Oblivious. My husband, Dan, was one of five kids, born within seven years. Forced to choose between sanity and decorum, his mother chose the former, so the house became a sort of functional bedlam. Not only is Dan used to chaos, but he also thrives in it. I, meanwhile, find comfort in order, unlike anyone I live with. My mother was an army nurse, so you get the picture. Beds will have hospital corners! All this proves that, like most families, we have no more in common than a few strands of DNA and an address.

But, because I yearn for a clean, tranquil, well-organized home where I can artfully coexist with *Them!* I continue to look for that sweet spot between what experts recommend and behaviors that won't give everyone I live with facial tics. For example, although I advocate for a clean home, I would never tell you that your floor needs to be clean enough to eat off, because, seriously, who is going to eat off your floor, except maybe the dogs, who, frankly, lick a lot worse by choice?

Major Finding #3: If you're the resident neatnik living with slob who maintain that they are okay with dirt and disorder ("Mess? What mess? We don't care if the house is a mess."), you have these choices:

- **Crack the whip.** At the risk of inviting a mutiny, tell everyone to step it up or you will cut off food and Internet access.

- *Be a martyr.* Silently (I'm so not good at silent) and slavishly clean up after everyone, so you get the house your way.
- *Live and let live.* Adopt a can't-beat-them-so-join-them attitude. Let the house go to heck, and get used to it. (I have a friend who has a sign on her front door: "Before you come in, let me explain. I have two dogs, three cats, four kids, and a job." Understood.)
- *Hire help.* Weigh the costs of a housekeeper against the pluses of less arguing, less stress, and lower family-therapy bills. (See Chapter 46.)
- *Do a little of all the above.* That's what I do. I kick my family into action occasionally and do more chores myself because having a nice home, apparently, is my own quirk. I let some standards slide, and periodically ignore unmade beds, buried closet floors, and sinks I could write my name in. And I have housekeepers come once every two weeks, bless them. These compromises work for my havoc-raising brood.

Major Finding #4: *To keep havoc respectfully in its place, you don't need to obsess to the point of being a fun-sucking domestic dictator, but you do need a plan for taming the following five areas in your home, areas we'll discuss in detail in the chapters ahead.*

- *Time:* Every family member can have a planner, but you also need a master family calendar. This way everyone can see that the trombone recital lands the same night as the soccer play-off, which falls the same evening as your annual business meeting.
- *Stuff:* We all deserve a public flogging for our consumption habits. Having too much stuff is bad for our cupboards, wallets, planet, and peace of mind. Figure out why you acquire, accumulate, and can't let go, then deal with it. (We have ways of making you purge.)
- *Space:* Manage it wisely. Decide what should go where and what doesn't belong at all. I'm not saying all your drawers need

pristine dividers separating pens from paper clips. I am saying
don't put your toothbrush in your underwear drawer with the
screwdrivers.

- **Meals:** Creating a menu plan and stocking items you need for
  the week makes a sickening amount of sense. It saves time,
  stress, and money. At my house, I make daily store runs, and
  Dan does the occasional big shopping, buying stuff that doesn't
  add up to a meal. However, we know there's a better way, and
  are working on this.
- **Housekeeping:** Tomorrow really doesn't have any more time
  than today. (Isn't that rude?) So invest time daily to keep housework from growing like the monster under the bed. Every day
  bust some clutter and some dirt. Then commit a couple hours a
  week to deep clean. Most days I try the nightly sweep. Before
  bed, I blitz the house, toss the newspaper (there will be one tomorrow), put remotes in their bin, clear dishes, wipe counters,
  put kid stuff in kid spaces, and clear my desk. So tomorrow I
  start the next day with a jump on havoc.

*To win a war, as I mentioned earlier, you must know your enemy. If that
war is on your home front—and family members are foe—you need to
learn to think like kids, men, and pets. Here are some battle tactics. We
start with a look at your standards, give them a reality check, then move on
to ways to live together more beautifully without being voted off the island.*

The Nice Thing About Kids Is They Take Your Life Apart a Piece at a Time

I WOULD LIKE the record to show: I am not the problem. I hang up my clothes. Clear and clean my own dishes. Push in my chair. Fold my towel. Wipe the counter when I'm done using the sink. I keep my surroundings hygienic. I move my laundry through before it sets down roots. In short, I'm not the messy roommate around here. My children, on the other hand . . . and I've had to learn how to coexist.

Though I resisted compromising my standards, eventually it became more important that my kids were happy than that everything around us was just so, which meant I held my tongue when I found a cup of earthworms in the refrigerator.

In my fussier days I cringed when my family left the family room looking as if the Tasmanian devil had come through with his henchmen. I'd grumble as I picked up toys, straightened sofa pillows, and cleared bowls of popcorn remains. But one evening my dad was over, and my perspective changed. After the kids were in bed and I stood surveying the upended room with exasperation, Dad put his arm around me and said, "Isn't this beautiful?"

Just like the kids—and most men—he didn't see any mess, just all the fun we'd had. Now when I encounter kid-created chaos, I try to see the joy behind it rather than the burden.

That said, I did not give up on creating beauty and order at home. The challenge became how to make design choices that made our hectic home lovely and livable.

If You Can't Beat Them, Hide Them

Faced with choosing between my love for fine, delicate furnishings and my family, uh, well, I've felt torn. Let's see, would I rather live in a pristine world where white things stayed white, silk was not a controlled substance, and underwear stayed folded, or with three barely evolved humans in conditions no better than an army barrack?

Anyone who has a family knows that the following three realities cannot coexist in one house: kids, a white couch, and low blood pressure. Forget it. Before we had kids, Dan and I bought a white linen, down-stuffed sofa, which was gorgeous in its brief prime. But once we acquired children (not to mention dogs!), the couch was no match for our household.

Mud, paw prints, throw up, newspaper ink, bike tracks, crayon, coffee rings, and mascara (from crying over all the above!) left their marks until the sofa was pretty much a biohazard. I had it cleaned so many times the fabric finally came apart, like me. But before I threw in the rubber gloves and all-purpose cleaner, I called a family meeting. I stared them down—Dan, the girls, the dogs—and said, "Don't you care how the house looks?"

Blank looks all around. Tails curled under.

It hit me: If we were going to peacefully coexist, I could either relax my standards and buy more family-friendly furnishings, or raise kids who bite their nails to their knuckles in frustration.

But how? I flashed back to my college days, when I waitressed at a Coco's coffee shop. We had these hideous wenchlike uniforms: peasant blouses with poufy skirts. But the skirt fabric—a sturdy cotton print— was brilliant. You could spill anything on it—coffee, mustard, grease, ketchup, fudge—and never find the stain. Ever. Goop just got sucked in and disappeared, as if it hit the black hole of the fabric universe. The patterned fabric was more durable than a storm cellar, more forgiving than the pope. That's what I needed in my home.

Today, the white furniture, fragile fabrics, and light carpets are gone. I've moved on to slate and distressed wood floors, impervious leather sofas, and earth tones in every color of dirt and grime.

Then I consulted a slobproofing expert. Interior designer Debbie Wiener has taken slobproofing her home to the next level. A wife and mother of two teenage boys, Wiener has stopped stressing about her house and started making it work for her slovenly brood. Her awakening sounded a lot like mine: One day her sons and husband broke the door off the armoire while wrestling. Next, Wiener almost came unhinged.

"Then I saw they were laughing and having fun," she said. "I was the only miserable one. I asked myself, what's more important, that they're happy or that my home looks like my idea of perfect?" She was singing my song, of course. So I asked her how she redesigned her home. Her answer was to choose her decorating materials for livability. The place still looks great, but everyone can relax. "What I really care about is that they're happy to be home."

❋

Here are some of Debbie Wiener's top slobproofing tips. You can find more at www.slobproof.com:

- **Think camouflage.** Go for more strong color and patterns. Having beige in the house is like having another kid. If you choose color over neutrals and prints over solids, you've made a huge leap.
- **Make floors match your dirt.** Skip the white travertine. Go for floorings made of slate, mottled stonelike pavers, and wood, the more distressed the better. When picking carpet, think how the color will look in six months under the doggie bowl.
- **Put rugs at entries.** That's your first line of defense. Rugs should have colorful patterns, and include the color of your pet's fur. Wool is particularly durable.
- **What not to wear on furniture.** When choosing upholstery fabric, hold a swatch up to the light and pull on it. If you can see through it or it stretches, forget it. Thus, avoid fragile fabrics like silk, linen, and chintz. Opt for cut (not looped) chenille, leather, and heavy woven fabrics. We both love Crypton. (See section on slipcovers in Chapter 5.)

❋ *continues*

continued

- **Get drapes off the floor.** A room with an active family is no place for floor-length curtains. Wiener prefers shades that sit inside window moldings, accented with valances. Side panels in landings, master bedrooms, or formal living rooms could work, but not in kid zones.
- **Go darker on walls.** Darker paint hides more dirt. Use a sheen you can scrub.
- **Add some glass.** If you hyperventilate when someone puts a drink on your wood table without a coaster, spare yourself. Have inexpensive glass toppers cut to fit wood end tables and coffee tables.
- **Lose the lamps.** In active rooms, put all lighting in the ceiling. "Nothing I do will prevent the men in my house from throwing a football around on game days," says Wiener, who took the offensive and removed all floor and table lamps. She doesn't have to worry about anyone tripping over cords, smashing lamps, or staining lampshades.
- **Know the power of pen.** Arm yourself with a dozen Sharpies in assorted colors and White Out. With those, if walls, fabrics, or furniture get dinged, you can touch up scuffs and blemishes in a jiff. And no one gets hurt.
- **Get them to pitch in.** Next time your house looks as if it were ransacked by buffalo on a beer binge, try this: Put a laundry basket in the upended room. Have the kids dump in everything that doesn't belong in that room—shoes, cups, Frito bags, the cat, each other. This clears the room and makes putting items away easier.
- **At least try to have a boundary.** Adopt this rule: What happens outside stays outside—or at least in the garage. Create a zone in your garage with open shelves, cubbies, and peg board, to host sports gear. Make a sign: "Park all soccer shoes, knee pads, roller blades, helmets, ski poles, balls, racquets, bats, blood, and mud here, and no one gets hurt.—The Management."
- **Take this to heart.** Just as dirt builds immunities, chaos breeds creativity. Disorganization encourages resourcefulness, and relaxing the rules fosters flexibility. Show me one kid who feels more loved because his parents cleaned more, and I'll show you a kid with bowel problems.

Before we talk about other ways to make your home more family friendly, I first need to talk about men. One of the big frictions in many homes comes down to fundamental differences between the male and female species. For instance, why don't men smell the kitty litter until it can walk or see the toast crumbs until the counter is sandier than the beach? There are reasons for this.

Gender Wars:
What Men Don't Get

I ENTER THE house cautiously. I have been out of town for three days with my younger daughter, Marissa, and left my older daughter, Paige, home with her dad. Dan is like most men, another species. The combination of man plus teenager is hard on a house, the way steel wool is hard on a manicure.

I tiptoe in, and am slow to turn on the lights. An avalanche of dishes fills the sink. Grit coats the counters. The mail looks as if it dropped in by airplane. Shoes pepper the floor. And that's just the kitchen. Paige greets me with desperate eyes. "Did Dad feed you?" I ask.

"He grilled burgers last night."

"That's good."

"We ate on the sofa because the game was on," she says. She knows I'm not a fan of TV eating.

"Well, once in a while," I say.

"When I asked for something to eat on, he handed me a section of the newspaper."

"At least he thought of a place mat."

"Mom, we didn't even have plates."

"Napkins?" I feel my face scrunch in disgust.

"We shared the dishtowel."

"At least you didn't go hungry." I look at the dish-filled sink.

"Dad said we don't have to do dishes when there's a game on."

"There's always a game on!"

I share this scene with Michael Gurian, an expert on gender brain differences, and author of *What Could He Be Thinking?* (St. Martin's Press).

"Your husband's evening with his daughter was a perfect expression of how guys bond," he says, reassuring me that I'm not married to a Neanderthal. "Men bond shoulder to shoulder through activity. Women bond eye to eye by talking. Sitting next to each other watching a game was his gift to her." (Doesn't he know girls prefer jewelry?)

"He was not only showing her how to be more independent (read: survive in the wild) but also how to bond shoulder to shoulder with men, something she'll need to do later in life." (Over her father's dead body.)

"Okay, but how do you explain why men have no domestic standards?" I ask.

"Women notice more sensory detail than men do, because women have more areas of the brain devoted to that," he says. "When a woman walks in a room, she notices the shoes under the coffee table and that the kitty litter smells. Men don't. She sees dishes in the sink and doesn't like the disarray, the smell, and that it reflects poorly on her. He's oblivious."

"Are we male bashing here?"

"Nah. You tell men that they don't notice the dishes in the sink, and they'll say, 'Who cares?'" (And, yes, Gurian concedes there are neatnik male exceptions, so don't get your knickers in a twist if you're one, or live with one. Just consider yourself lucky.)

"In other words, when women see a counter covered with grease, they see a surface that needs cleaning. Men see a place to set the dead car battery."

"Exactly," he says. Men, on the other hand, notice movement better, and respond to action. "They walk into a sports arena, and they'll see the puck, and all the nuances in the players' moves. This has a lot of adaptive advantages." I try to think of one.

"So," I say, "if a woman picks up the shoes her man steps over and throws them, he'll notice?"

"Right, but that doesn't mean he'll put them away. And certainly, don't expect a guy to stop watching the game to do a sensory task like dishes."

Well, that sounds familiar.

As I said, knowing the enemy is half the battle.

❉

Here's what else gender expert Michael Gurian, who heads the Gurian Institute in Spokane, Washington, says is different about the sexes:

- *Women's brains take in more sensory data* than men's. They are biologically wired to see more, hear more, smell more, and feel more, he says. "This is why men don't understand why women can't relax if the house is a mess." This brain difference also explains why men don't notice gritty counters, and why more women get the dogs groomed.
- *Men focus on gross value,* while women focus on fine value. "Men get their identity from how big their home is and how much land they have. Women get their identity from the quality of the interior space." That's why, given a choice between a large bathroom or a small one with fabulous accent tiles, men opt for bigger, women for nicer.
- *Women trust feelings;* men trust logic. A woman will decide to buy a home if a bird is nesting in the eaves, and the cupboard knobs are just like the ones her grandma used to have. Men will buy if the seller knocks 10 percent off the asking price.
- *At home, men look out.* Women look in. This harks back to our predecessors' days when cavemen focused on the woolly mammoth hunt, while cavewomen focused on finding the perfect hearthstone to gather 'round. Which is why, 10 million years later, when a little extra money flows in for a home improvement, men want rain gutters and women want drapes.

To help women keep up their houses and their sanity while living with the other species, Gurian offers these tips:

- *Accept what you can't change.* A lot of the reason men and women don't see and behave in their shared world the same way is brain difference. You can't change men's wiring. However, the more men and women understand each other's wiring, the better they get along.

❉ *continues*

continued

- ***Respect the differences.*** Understand that men and women operate from a different set of standards. Women have female standards, which they think are basic. Men's standards really are the absolute minimum; they think women's standards are over the top. (This explains why I believe in folding underwear, while Dan considers that a royal waste of time.) "Both sets of standards are fine," says Gurian. "When kids see two ways of running a house, they're forced to analyze which works for them. If your mate interacts with the kids differently, and the children aren't in danger, let it go. It's a gift."
- ***Focus on the positive.*** Instead of focusing on making men do what they aren't wired to do, look at what they do bring to the table, besides sloppy habits. A man's role is to provide for his family, protect them, and help children become independent. If men do all that, it's really okay if they don't do the dishes.

Beyond matters of house hygiene, men and women also have major clashes over home decorating. Michael Gurian has explanations for that, too. See if this sounds familiar.

A Woman's Touch, Who Needs It?

"Why do you want to cover that beautiful floor?" This is Dan's standard response whenever I suggest buying an area rug.

"Because a rug will finish this room."

"The room is finished," he insists. Dan thinks a room is finished when the big screen and easy chair are in, or the doors are hung and the walls painted.

I huff off, frustrated again by the million and one differences between men and women—and that's just counting the differences in the universe of home improvement, where women are from Venus and men are from another solar system. Here are some more differences:

- Men don't get drapes. Show me a man who does, and I'll show you a man who got an extra X chromosome. Ditto for wallpaper.
- Men don't get custom bedding. They really don't understand why you can't just zip two sleeping bags together. But usually, if

a custom coverlet makes the woman happier in bed, he won't put up a fight.

- Men don't get centerpieces. "Why put something on a table that you just have to move every time you need the table?" they ask.
- Men don't get throw pillows. (See above logic and section on throw pillows in Chapter 18.)
- Men don't get big, conveniently located laundry rooms. Men would just as soon put the laundry room outdoors like an out-house. Women want it central, so lugging clothes around the house isn't their primary workout. Then again, men don't get the need to do laundry until the pile morphs into a giant polar bear that walks into the room and blocks the big screen.
- Men do get home theaters and surround-sound systems. Women, however, don't get why it's cool to have sound so realistic the whole room vibrates during a World War II scene—so you feel bombs dropping down your neck.
- Men want big grills; women want big bathtubs.
- Men love their garages, and will defend them to their death. Actually, death threats have occurred when a woman craving more space wanted to turn the garage into a gym or art studio.
- And men don't get area rugs. If you have carpet, men think putting a rug on carpet is redundant. If you have hard floors, like stone or wood, they know how much they cost, so refuse to cover them up.

None of this surprises Gurian, who says that as with housekeeping, the different ways men and women look at home improvement—or life—come down to the way the two sexes' brains are wired. In men, the dominant brain region ponders questions like, How big? How much? Does it have a remote? Women's brains allot much more space to the region that ponders, How many colors does it come in, and is it washable?

Absorbing all this, I've come up with a strategy to help women prevail on the home front more often: *Think like a man*. I try this on Dan, and reapproach the subject of that area rug. "I know you think a rug will cover up our beautiful floor," I say, "but think of a beautiful area rug like great lingerie." That got his attention. "It invites you to imagine what's underneath." He doesn't immediately fall for this, but at least I got him thinking.

Of course, men and children are only part of the house of havoc. We still have to find ways to understand and compromise with other difficult roommates.

Home Gone to the Dogs

Every dog is a lion at home.
—ITALIAN PROVERB

O̲N̲ ̲M̲Y̲ ̲F̲A̲M̲I̲L̲Y̲ room coffee table lies a beautiful book called *Living with Dogs*, by Laurence Sheehan. I love it because it makes me laugh. Every glossy page pictures pedigreed pooches and their Ralph Laurenesque lifestyles. Spaniels romp in verdant green meadows. Hounds hover respectfully while their mistresses cook in grand kitchens. Border collies lounge on immaculate down furniture and white coverlets. Not a muddy paw in sight.

Sigh.

Then I look at my house. All around me is the havoc my two precious pets—the beastly bichon brothers, Theo and Oliver—have wrought: scratched doors, chewed furniture legs, torn screens, and stuff dragged in from outside (recently a family of pill bugs in a muddy drain cover). To me, "living with dogs" means investing in lint brushes and Nature's Miracle.

Now, I love dogs. (Dan says that after he dies, he wants to come back as my dog.) Over the years my four-legged friends have taught me, among other things, qualities to look for in a man: unfaltering loyalty, eyes that worship, the ability to listen with interest, to always agree and never interrupt, to come when called, and to always be ecstatic to see me. (Maybe that reincarnation idea's not so bad.)

But dogs as design element? Obviously, as this book beautifully rubs in, there's an art to living with dogs that I haven't mastered. So I call this Sheehan, who lives in Massachusetts with Addie, an Australian shepherd; Buster, an English setter; and Carol Sheehan, his wife, also the editor of *Country Home* magazine—so you can imagine what their home looks like. "Significantly, our home is not in the book," he points out. Okay, so I like the guy, but surely he must have some clues.

"Over the years," he says, "dogs have migrated from the barnyard to the bedroom."

"That's why my bedroom looks like a barnyard?"

"As they've infiltrated our homes," he continues, "we've adapted." (Some better than others.) As he talks, Oliver—that little angel dumpling—has taken the rubber tip off the doorstop and is chewing it like gum. "They've worked their way into the very fabric of our lives." Theo—that little lamb muffin—is napping (and drooling) on the linen chair in my home office. Because Sheehan never mentions carpet care, I assume he must have wood floors.

However, the real key to successful canine cohabitation, he says, lies in disaster prevention. "When we go out, we leave the TV on and put out squeaker toys, so Addie and Buster don't get bored and into mischief."

"So it's like kids," I say. "You need to keep their minds off their natural inclinations or you wind up raising wolves."

"Exactly," he agrees. "What we do is nothing," adds Sheehan, who commissioned a top dog portrait artist to paint Addie for his wife's birthday. Nothing, that is, compared to the dog-o-philes in his book, like the Jack Russell terrier owner whose home houses 10,000 porcelain dog figurines, or the New Yorker whose apartment is a backdrop for her collection of 300 antique dog collars. (Some she wears!)

But, hey, what's a home if not a reflection of your passion? I may never be featured in a coffee table tome, but I know this: From the dog-shredded doormats to the nose-printed windows, my home is a passionate reflection of the people and pets who live here. If that means a few areas of my house have gone to the dogs, I wouldn't have it any other way.

❃

Here are a few other tricks Larry Sheehan uses to live with dogs in style:

- *Use a lot of slipcovers* and throws to cover furniture. (See next chapter.)
- *Choose sturdy, fur-friendly upholstery fabrics* that are washable, like twills. Use velvet and chenille sparingly, as they are hair magnets. Prints are generally more forgiving than solids. Crypton, which I talk more about later, is a synthetic stain-bouncing fabric, available at Jo-Ann's fabric stores, or online at www.cryptonfabric.com. Dog Gone Smart (www.doggonesmartbed.com) uses NanoSphere technology fabrics on dog beds and crate pads. The protective finish lets you rinse off soil and dirt with water. Tyler & Friends (www.tylerandfriends.com) makes some adorable products, including wallpaper, in designer doggie prints, though the fabric is not quite as durable. Leather makes another good pet choice. It wipes easily, won't snag, and leather lubricant can usually buff out scratches.
- *Choose flooring in a pet home with care.* Carpet is cozy, dulls noise, and, if it's the right color, can hide fur. But it traps odors and stains. Avoid loop carpets, like Berber, because claws can catch a loop and unravel the carpet. Hard floors are far easier to clean; wood is warmer than stone.
- *Don't lie with dogs (unless you want to).* I'm not promising that putting a dog bed in your room will instantly get your pooch off your bed and into his, but it's a start. Pick one the same shade as your dog's fur. Many styles are available online, and at stores like Petco, Target, Wal-Mart, and PetSmart. Snoop around pet boutiques, and you'll find elaborate dog canopy beds, dog sofas, and chaises in fun, pooch-friendly fabrics. Some end tables and nightstands out today double as dog crates in disguise.
- *Display doggie accessories,* particularly if they feature your dog's breed, with impunity. I love my pillow that has a petit-point bichon on it, and miss the bathroom I had in my last house, which I covered in wallpaper featuring different dog breeds.
- *Keep dog toys in a lined basket.* My dogs' toys were strewn around the house like booby traps, so when you stepped on one barefoot, the gooey texture and squeak took a year off your life, until I put all them all in a basket that Theo and Oliver can help themselves to.

❃ *continues*

---

continued

- ***Store dog treats in a stylish container.*** The Sheehans use an antique milk-glass canister; ours come out of a cookie jar with a bichon frise face painted on the wooden lid. Around the neck of the jar is a wooden dog bone tag with "Theo & Oliver" painted on it. Over the top, I know. Custom dog treat vessels may not be for everyone, Sheehan agrees, but they are for those of us who share a passion for pooches.

Perhaps the biggest toll our furry friends take on our homes is on our furniture. Mud, drool, and conquests of the hunt are hard on most fabrics, which is why homes with pets need some divine intervention.

Slipcovers as Divine Intervention

IN THE BEGINNING God created the heaven and the earth. Then he created a few more things, including men, women, and children. Right after he saw what slobs people were, he created slipcovers. To which the people said: Hallelujah!

Now that's divine intervention. Your sofa looks as if it's been center ring in a dog fight. Your clumsy cousin spills red wine on the dining room chair. That light floral chintz armchair doesn't seem seasonal now that it's fall. Don't pitch a fit or the furniture—slipcover!

Unlike Watergate, blemish concealer, and beach sarongs, these cover-ups really work. Slipcovers successfully mask ugliness, change with the season, go in the wash, and keep the woman of the house from screaming, "You eat that on my sofa and you'll go live with the wolves!" This is why I recommend slipcovers in lieu of vodka shots.

I came to this opinion early in life. My aunt had a beautiful home, but her living room might as well have had a cord across the door. No one was allowed near her lemon yellow sofas. "They are for company," she told us.

But what were we?

We were to stand at the door and look. Much as I've always wanted a beautiful home, I've also always wanted a house I could live in with this menagerie I call a family.

I discussed my thoughts about slipcovers as a household blessing with Elaine Ellis, owner of I Do Slipcovers, a busy workroom in Englewood, Colorado, where I brought two well-worn chairs for slipcover rehab. Ellis didn't seem to mind that I hoisted myself onto her worktable and started asking questions.

"There's a personality that goes with a slipcover," she said. "They're not for everyone. The slipcover person is more forgiving, accepting, and relaxed."

As she talked, I thought how I didn't fit the profile. I'm more tightly wound than a corkscrew. But slipcovers help me be more relaxed and forgiving. Without them, if the dogs put their muddy paws on the settee, or the kids eat cherry Popsicles on the living room sofa, or a party guest drips chocolate fondue on the easy chair, my hair might stand up like porcupine quills. If any of those accidents happens on a slipcover, I say, "Pish, I can wash it."

❃

If you're thinking of putting your furniture under wraps, here's what else to consider, says Elaine Ellis, who's been in the cover-up business for twenty years:

TO SLIPCOVER OR NOT TO SLIPCOVER

- *Not for every home.* If you like a tight and right, formal look, stick with upholstered furniture. Slipcovers also don't work in commercial settings, which are all about business. (But few people in this setting put their feet on the furniture.) However, they're great in less formal homes, particularly ones with rustic, country, or traditional styles.
- *Not for all furniture.* Slipcovers are ideal for well-made, often-used furniture. Don't slipcover cheap furniture. Invest the money in a new piece instead. (To test whether a sofa or chair is well made, try to wiggle the arm using both your hands. If the arm moves, the frame is poorly made. If it doesn't budge, chances are you have a well-made item.) Slipcovers also don't work on leather pieces, because the slipcover slides around. But leather is tolerant, so doesn't beg for protection. Slipcovers also don't fit barrel-back chairs well. If the piece has back cushions, slipcovers work best if the cushions are removable, not attached.

- **Refresh those cushions.** Don't worry if cushions are shot. A good slipcover maker can revive cushions by wrapping them in Dacron, having them refeathered, or getting new foam. But don't slipcover a piece with dead springs. Hint: When you sit down, you need to be airlifted out.
- **Know your options.** Slipcovers come ready-made, semicustom, and custom (cheap, medium, expensive). Off-the-shelf slipcovers won't fit precisely, but will refresh your furniture, and usually come with ties to adjust fit. For a semicustom cover, you send furniture measurements to a manufacturer who makes a slipcover. These will fit better. However, you'll get the best fit from a custom slipcover that a fabricator sews with the furniture in hand.
- **Details make the job.** If you can, spring for contrasting welt (piping), varied fabrics, and clever closures, such as bows and buttons. These make the difference between ordinary and custom.
- **When choosing a fabricator,** inspect her work. Inside seams should be serged (edges overstitched). Welting should be cut on the bias (diagonally), so fabric doesn't unravel. Outer seams should tuck into furniture crevices, so they don't show. Finally, a good slipcover should fit like a well-tailored blouse; it shouldn't pull, look stretched, or sag.
- **Find a slipcover studio** near you on www.slipcovernetwork.com, click on "Directory," and find experts in your state.
- **Consider a seasonal change.** Some women, who are far more organized than I, have two sets of slipcovers, one for warm months, and another for cool months. "You have to have space to store the off-season set," says Ellis. "You also should have them professionally cleaned and packed right when you remove them, so when you open them in six months they're not moldy, stained, and wrinkled."

  "So you can't just shove them under the bed?"

  "Like I said," she adds patiently, "they're not for everybody."

A slipcover is only as durable as its fabric. I did my homework to find a dog-friendly fabric that didn't feel like Tupperware.

When Furniture Fabric Has Gone to the Dogs

All day, while I work in my home office trying to turn my problems into your solutions, Theo and Oliver snooze on the large off-white linen chair in the corner. Although they're little phoofy dogs (think large cotton balls with beating hearts and wet noses), when they sleep, they drool like St. Bernards. When nature calls, they let themselves out the doggie door, then return to wipe their dirty paws on the chair. I've told them to use the doormat, but they ignore me like everyone else around here.

Off-white linen is not the best chair fabric for a newspaper writer with two dogs and a coffee habit. (Yes, I bought this chair before I knew the secrets of living with slobs outlined in Chapter 2.) Adding to this chair's decline, somebody briefly set food on the back of it, which left a scent so compelling the dogs licked the spot until they'd formed a football-sized hole in the fabric. As the chair became a mottled collage of every imaginable shade of filth, the layers of soil compressed.

This was no longer a chair; it was an archaeological dig. I tossed a large woven throw over it and tried to forget. But underneath, the chair was a good chair, well made and comfortable. We had a past together and, I hoped, a future. I could no more set this chair on the curb than sell my eyeballs. What would I tell Theo and Oliver?

Slipcover to the rescue.

My first instinct was to cover the chair with another linen. After all, what is life if not a series of repeated mistakes? But a stern fabric store manager rescued me from myself. "No you don't," she said. "From what you've told me about your dogs, you need a synthetic."

"How about sturdy cotton?" I asked hopefully.

"Nope," she said in that tough-love tone.

"What do you have in Teflon?"

Back home I did some research and found a fabric called Crypton, a name takeoff on Krypton, the substance that could take down Superman. "Our fabric resists spills, stains, mold, mildew, bacteria, and odors," the Web site bragged. Sure, I thought. The stuff probably feels like Astroturf. I ordered samples, which, though they didn't feel like linen, were softer than I expected. I spread the samples on my kitchen counter turned laboratory, scribbled on them with marker, poured cooking oil, coffee, and red wine on them, and ground it all in. This was fun, until Marissa busted me.

"What are you doing?" she asked horrified.

"Uh, research?"

"If I did that, you'd ground me for life."

"Here," I said, handing her a marker. "Get it out of your system."

Water and dish soap did indeed release the stains. Plus, the fabric didn't look rubbed out after the scrubbing, and it dried without a water ring. So now I had a dilemma: I'm a purist who loves natural fabrics. I'm also a pragmatist who doesn't want to pay to slipcover this chair again. Was my purity for sale?

I called an expert. Warren De Young, president of Kenneth McDonald Designs, of Costa Mesa, California, a leading supplier of interior fabrics to the trade, gave me permission. "We've seen a major industry shift toward using acrylic and other synthetic fabrics indoors," he said. "These fabrics used to go only on outdoor furniture or in commercial settings, but more are coming into homes because they're so much softer, wear so well, and last." I would even say they hold households together.

So I ordered the Crypton in three shades of faux suede, sage green for the chair, cognac for the trim, and celery for the accent pillow. I brought it to Ellis, who worked her magic.

❋

When choosing family-friendly fabrics, before you choose a color or pattern, first pick your material, advises Warren De Young, of Kenneth McDonald Designs. Consider not only how much use the piece will get but also its sun exposure. Then use this durability chart:

- *Fragile:* Silks and soft linens (such as Belgian linen) are lovely, but delicate. Save these for adult homes with no pets, and put them only in living areas rarely used, or use them for drapes.
- *Semifragile:* Chenille feels lovely, which is why it accounts for half of all interior fabrics sold, says De Young. But some chenilles have a loop stitch, which jewelry or pet claws can easily snag. Cut chenille doesn't have the loop stitch, so may be more practical.
- *Durable:* Cotton, heavier linens (such as Irish linen), cotton blends, cotton prints, denim, and velvet are sturdy and family friendly.

❋ *continues*

continued

- ***Tough:*** Synthetic fabrics (polyester, acrylic, synthetic blends) are the go-ahead-and-beat-me fabrics of the upholstery industry. All the fabrics mentioned above—silk, linen, chenille, cotton, and also suede—have a synthetic counterpart. These will be more durable, more fade resistant, and less expensive than a similar all-natural fabric. Leather is also a fabulous, rugged choice, and often looks better with age. "It's as durable as a cow in the rain," says De Young. The only thing it won't tolerate is any kind of puncture.
- ***Indestructible:*** Power fabrics, like Crypton (available online and at Jo-Ann's), have been used commercially for years and are now showing up more in residential design. In the end, that's what I chose to slipcover my office chair. It may not be right for every home, but it's right for mine, and for any home that must choose between fine fabric and Fluffy.

If you're wondering whether your family's use and abuse may have taken too much of a toll on certain pieces of furniture, and made them not worth recovering or repairing, look again. Before you usher a well-worn, and possibly worn-out, piece of wood furniture to the curb, first see if you can fix it.

Fix—Don't Toss— Abused Furniture

*I*F A LITTLE denial is good for the soul, a lot is good for the home. At my home, if I weren't in denial about the stained carpet, the disheveled bonus room, the frayed bedspread, or the dingy paint, I would be in a perpetual state of repair, replace, and spend. I would have even less time and money than I have now, which is hard to imagine.

But a point comes, say when you pull up the rotting blinds and they fall in shreds on your head, or someone sits in a chair and risks spinal cord injury, when you have to put home furnishing denial aside and face facts. This is how I found myself and my eight kitchen chairs in the furniture hospital.

My chair denial crashed to a halt when my cousin, a firefighter, felt a chair give way under him. He hopped up, and, with his bare hands, pulled the chair back from the seat, ushered the parts to the mudroom, and said, "I'm putting this out of service before someone gets hurt."

"Those chairs have gotten a little rickety," I said, apologizing.

"Rickety? They're an emergency room visit waiting to happen."

No wonder. Since I bought the chairs—French country pine with rush seats—sixteen years ago, they've become the most used and abused furniture in the house. They've been rocked back, leaned on, scooted in, and yanked out. They've provided support through meals, coffee breaks, hairstyling, counseling sessions, homework projects, board games, and taxes. They've been hoisted for the kids' lion-taming acts, stood on to change lightbulbs, and set on their sides to barricade the dogs. Eventually, their arms and backs became as wiggly as loose teeth. Except for Dan and the girls, who understand the chairs' weaknesses, I wouldn't seat anyone I cared about in those chairs, though I could see putting the husband of one of my girlfriends in one.

I considered fixing them. A furniture repair expert gave me an estimate. To take the chairs apart and reglue and clamp them would cost, please have a seat: $750. This was reasonable given all the work, but not reasonable given that's about what I paid for the chairs. Yet tossing and replacing them felt like betrayal.

Dan, who's often handy with stuff like this, fired a few nails in and squeezed in some glue, which didn't hold. Glue ran down the legs like nasal discharge, and dried. (We later learned his handiwork made the ultimate repair a lot harder.) I ignored the problem. We continued to live with the chairs, accommodating them the way you would an older relative with bad hips—until they almost put my firefighter cousin on disability.

That's when I called Mike Ackerman of Ackerman & Sons, a furniture refinishing and repair business that has been in business five generations, and that fixes chairs like mine every day. When I asked if someone in his workshop could show me how to fix my chairs myself, he invited me and my chairs over. Head carpenter Russ Jones showed me what to do. I rolled up my sleeves, befriended the cordless drill, and got to work. By the end of the day my chairs were tighter than a barfly at last call, reinforced for many more years of domestic abuse.

In general, living graciously with others boils down not to changing their habits but to accommodating them—beautifully. That is an art in itself. It also sometimes means deliberately designing to reduce, not add, to our sensory overload. Yet magazines often have articles suggesting ways to "design for the senses." Forget that! Hectic homes need to design for the un-senses.

Before you toss that wobbly desk or rickety chair, fix it the way they do at Ackerman's:

Gather these tools:

- A cordless drill or electric screwdriver.
- A dead blow hammer. It provides wallop without hurting wood.
- Sharp metal scrapers.
- Wood glue. (Don't use craft glue, silicone, contact cement, or Liquid Nails.)
- Wood shims.
- Pipe and slide clamps.
- A half-inch paintbrush.
- Rags and a toothbrush.

Follow these steps:

1. *Disassemble.* Take apart the weak joints. Remove seats from chairs. Don't take apart pieces still holding well. Remove screws and use the dead blow hammer to detach pieces. Check dowels. If they're broken, drill out broken ends and replace with same-size dowels.
2. *Scrape.* Use the sharp metal scraper to remove all old dried glue, being careful not to scrape too much wood.
3. *Glue.* Put wood glue in a small cup. Use the paintbrush to coat surfaces that will be rejoined, dowels, and dowel holes.
4. *Clamp.* Using pipe clamps or slide clamps (for smaller distances), put pressure on glued joints. Put a wood shim between the clamp and the wood to protect it. Tighten clamps until glue squeezes out the sides. (If it doesn't, you haven't used enough glue.) Wipe excess glue with a damp rag. Use a wet toothbrush to clean crevices.
5. *Dry.* Let the chairs sit clamped for several hours or overnight. Replace screws and seats.

Fast Fix: For furniture that's just a tad loose, try glue injections—it's like Botox instead of surgery. Clamp furniture first. Then carefully drizzle instant glue (cyanoacrylate, also called E-Z Bond or Zap-A-Gap) right into the joint. Reapply a few times as glue seeps in. Keep a rag underneath to catch drips; this stuff dries fast and will damage finishes and fabrics. Spray the joint once with an accelerator like Hot Shot, which flash dries the glue. Sit back and relax.

Designing for the Un-Senses

As I PORE over home design magazines, to which I'm admittedly addicted, I frequently find articles on "designing for the senses." These articles all report a variation on the same sensory advice: *Rooms should not only evoke pleasant visual experiences but also delight the other senses through sounds, textures, and scents.*

Then they offer advice like, "Light a scented candle after work and play a CD of crickets in a meadow." Which is such a major crack-up. They absurdly presume we all have master bathrooms decked out like spas, when they're really a blender swirl of blow dryers, wet towels, mascara wands, and roll-on deodorant.

Here's a typical sensory scene at my house:

It starts with the familiar sound of grinding metal. "Get the spoon out of the garbage disposal!" I yell from two rooms away. My kids are doing the dishes, which is an ambiguous blessing.

"How did she know it was a spoon?" I overhear one sister ask the other.

"She always knows."

"Experience," I yell, over the basketball game and my husband's hooting because the Nuggets are winning.

The disposal slows to a pitiful grind. The clanking stops.

A few minutes later, I walk into the kitchen and feel the familiar crunch of sugar beneath my shoes—another lovely sensory experience. The sugar bowl is on its side, cascading grit on the floor. I right the bowl, and grab the counter edge for balance while I inspect the bottom of my shoe. My fingers hit something gooey. A reasonable part of me doesn't want to know what it is. I get a whiff of Jiff, then know. But the peanut butter smell isn't enough to mask a more pungent stench coming from the laundry room. From twenty paces I can smell the urine- and manure-ridden horse blanket Paige has dragged home from the barn for a cleaning.

"How long are you going to leave that here?" I ask her.

"Until I'm done punishing you," she says.

I get no respect. As I go to put the smelly blanket in the garage, the house phone and my cell phone ring at the same time. Then the Girl Scouts knock with our cookie delivery, which makes the dogs bark and tear through the screen door I just had repaired.

"I'm going upstairs," one sister says. The other follows. Moments later music from different artists blares from each girl's room, which doesn't quite drown out the Nuggets or my husband.

Ah, home. It's a feast for the senses, all right.

I don't need more sensory detail at home. I need less. In my home— and I'm willing to bet yours—designing for the senses shouldn't be about adding scents, textures, and sounds but eliminating them. I'm not suggesting we ignore our senses when designing and living in our homes but that we come to our senses and shoot for domains that are clean, odor free, and quiet. At home, my senses only want one thing— a break.

Here are inexpensive ways to de-sensorize your home:

- *Sight:* Forget whether the room is perfectly furnished or color coordinated. (We'll get to that in Parts Four and Five.) For instant visual ambience, dim the lights and light a fire. Everything, even you, will look better.
- *Smell:* Whenever I see an air freshener in someone's home or car, I wonder what that person is trying to hide. Artificial fresheners are like billboards that say: My home stinks. Seek first to odor bust unwanted smells in your home, don't just mask them: Get hampers and trash cans with lids. Run baking soda down the disposal. (My drain guy recommends powdered Tang!) Refresh the cat box daily. Then add back natural, pleasant scents like potpourri, fresh flowers, pure lavender oil, a wood fire, baked cookies, or an open window. Or leave the smell of nothing, often the best smell of all.
- *Sound:* Most active homes are noisy enough. Some also have noisy neighbors and traffic. I can almost never have too much silence, which is why, when finishing our basement, I put an extra layer of soundproofing material in the basement ceiling to mute sounds from upstairs. It's good stuff. Had I known how good, I would have lined every wall. Our dual-pane windows were also a worthy investment. Carpeting, drapery, and upholstered furnishings also absorb noise, so consider adding those when seeking ways to reduce or muffle noise in and around your home.
- *Touch:* Yes, übersoft throws and suede pillows are delightful. But the first feel you get from a room is its temperature. Be sure your rooms are insulated well to retain heat when it's cold out, and have a fan or other means to cool off when it's hot out.
- *Taste:* We have a food rule at our house: Food stays in the kitchen, dining room, or, occasionally, the family room. But it doesn't go beyond, so not in bedrooms. This keeps the bug population down, and the dogs from foraging for snacks, which they return in liquefied form. Once that ground rule is set and observed, break out a little. Set bowls of nuts or fresh apples on coffee or side tables, where the dogs can't reach.
- *Un-Sensed?* Once you've un-sensed your home so that it feels like a monastery, go ahead and go wild: Light a eucalyptus-scented candle, throw a yak fur on your bed, and break out the chocolates.

PART TWO

It's All Under Control, She Lied

Order—not age—goes before beauty. In fact, beauty requires order. So before we talk about creating a great-looking home, we have to address how to have an organized home, one that runs smoothly and supports those who live within. As you can guess, I'm not after perfection. I'm after good enough to get by. My goals are two: Save time and sanity. With that in mind, I've gathered tips for the noncompulsive among you (compulsive types don't need my help) to better organize time, papers, home offices, kitchens, and photos. These habits and systems work for me, but be warned: These organizing tips may fool you and others into believing you're on top of the madness.

8

Take Your House Back

To misquote Leo Tolstoy (who said, "Every unhappy family is unhappy in its own way"): Every unorganized family is unorganized in its own way.

THE URGE TO take control often hits in January. After December— a season of Shop! Eat! Party! Let the house go!—the signs of the past season's gluttony are everywhere: the bills, the scale, the jammed cupboards. Around this time every year I commit for the umpteenth time to take my house back. I don't just need to hit the treadmill and freeze my credit cards, I must get organized, purge, and clutter bust to compensate for a whole year, maybe years, of slouching toward hedonism.

A year in a typical home often goes like this: We get a brief grip on our homes in January. We get that New Year's urge to start with a clean slate, and we declutter and reorganize—a little. Come spring we relax and let our guards down. By summer, we throw care to the wind. We start hoarding again in fall, then live like Roman gods from Thanksgiving to New Year's, when we resolve to end our bacchanalian ways and come clean.

Ah, the cycle of life.

But no matter when the urge to get a grip on your house hits, you have to know how to tackle the great destroyers of order: time-wasting habits, paper overload, and clutter. Here we go.

Time Lost

So the New Year came, along with my annual resolve to get organized, and I didn't know what to do. I'd lost my new annual calendar refill, and couldn't get past 10 A.M. I was rudderless. I blamed my family, the deliveryman, and the phase of the moon.

For fifteen years I've used the same daily calendar system. Its pages tell me who to call, what to do, where to go, and when to buy more vacuum bags. In short, my calendar book provides high-speed dial-up to my brain, which would otherwise wait all day for connections.

Every November my calendar reminds me to order the next year's calendar, and I obey. When the box containing my new refill arrived, I put it with the boxes that stored past years. But when I went to set up my calendar for this New Year, I discovered my past and future had vanished. I shook down my office, cleaned every shelf and cupboard. I shook down members of my family, who, seeing how I'd been ransacking the house, went to their rooms and said I couldn't enter without a search warrant. I shook down the dogs, the fish, and the refrigerator. (I've found stranger things than calendars in the vegetable bin.) I sent out a UPS tracker, which confirmed what I already knew: The package had arrived, and I was going nuts. Feeling out of control makes me do things that give me the illusion of control. Namely, I start cleaning like a Molly Maid on espresso.

After working over my office, I started on the oven. Next I swept the garage so hard the kids flew off into the street and didn't come back until after high school graduation. Then I overhauled the mudroom. That still didn't bring back my past and my future, but my office, the oven, the garage, and the mudroom looked great. I don't know what hurt worse, ordering the $60 system again, or losing years of my life.

"So order a new calendar and forget the past," Dan, ever practical, advised, as I made him raise his legs one at a time so I could look under the sofa cushions. "Who cares what you did last year?"

"I care! My future biographer will care!"

He made a funny choking sound. "Your—*ahem*—future biographer won't care that you brought snacks for the gymnastics team the month of June."

"Fine, make fun of my life. But how else will I track important facts, like how long I went between hair-coloring appointments two summers ago?"

"Like I said . . . ," his voice trailed off.

And so I entered the New Year in a tailspin of loss, aimless organization, and pitifully low family support. A week later, my second refill calendar arrived. That same day I recruited my reluctant family to take down holiday decorations. As the kids took ornaments off the tree and nutcrackers off the mantel, I took a poinsettia from its perch. Six weeks earlier, I'd set the poinsettia on the floor where it looked too low, so I built a perch and draped it with a holiday tapestry. As I pulled the tapestry off the makeshift base, I shrieked as if I'd found a severed head. There lay three stacked boxes, two containing boxed calendar years from the past, and one for the New Year! My past and my future under the poinsettia all this time.

I shared my lost calendar story with Cynthia Ewer, editor of OrganizedHome.com. "Imagine what you could have accomplished if you'd put that cleaning energy into creating time-saving, home-organizing systems that would be working for you well into March?" she asked. But then she threw me a bone. "The fact that you are so completely dependent on your calendar tells me you're using it correctly."

Unless, of course, you use it to prop the poinsettia.

✳

All right, so a calendar is where time, money, child rearing, career, and social life come together. It's crucial to driving a home. Besides using one faithfully, how else can we better manage our time around the house? I asked two time experts: Laura Stack, author of *Exhaustion Cure* (Broadway Books) and a mother of three, and Cynthia Ewer, who wrote *House Works* (DK Publishing). Here are some ways they suggest to find more time in your day:

- *Lower your standards.* Solicit help from your family, but remember not everything needs to be done your way. If you don't like the way your kids or spouse fold laundry, or load the dishwasher, zip your lips, or people will happily let you do the task yourself, says Stack.
- *Accept help.* When you've invited people over and they ask, "What can we bring?" Don't say, "Nothing." Say, "Do you have some specialty you'd like to share?" Likewise, don't be a martyr when people offer to help clean up. People like to help, and you get to visit while you work.
- *Let cooking do double duty.* If it's no more trouble to double the lasagna recipe when making dinner, make two batches and freeze one. Do the same for other entrées or cookie recipes.
- *Go hands-free.* Talking on the phone can be a huge time burn. Get a Bluetooth and catch up on conversations while doing mindless tasks: watering plants, sorting laundry, or emptying the dishwasher.
- *Wear it twice.* To reduce laundry volume, tell your family that wearing something once doesn't make it dirty. Likewise, unless someone's been sick or is having hot flashes, sheets can go two weeks between washings, and towels a few days. Next, do what your mom did—a load a day. That beats seven on Sunday.
- *Delegate.* Thanks to some great advice a reader, and former home economics teacher, sent me, I declared laundry independence day when Marissa was around nine. One day, after finishing and folding everyone's laundry, I told my family that from now on it was every man, woman, and child for himself or herself. They were all to do their own laundry. And they do. I just do mine and the household sheets and towels.
- *Put it on the list.* I waste so much time ricocheting to and from the store for two or three items because I don't plan. Stack puts a grocery list in the kitchen. Whoever uses the last of something writes it down. They know: "If it's not on the list, it won't exist." (See Chapter 12 on kitchen organizing.)

- *Create cleaning habits.* "Find the bare minimum of household tasks you need to do to make your home run smoothly," says Ewer. "Then turn those chores into habits." Here are a few that make sense to me:
  - ○ *Do all the dishes before bed.* If you have to move the dinner dishes to make breakfast, you're already behind. Even better, set up the coffeepot and set out the breakfast dishes for the next day.
  - ○ *Clean bathrooms weekly.* This way if you miss a week it's not so bad. Don't wait until you need to call in the toxic waste crew. (See housekeeper section in Chapter 46.)
  - ○ *Keep washed what has to be clean*—socks, underwear, and school clothes. Don't fall behind. Anyone who has ever dried his kid's underwear in the microwave knows the importance of keeping up. (Incidentally, microwaving underwear makes the elastic gooey.)

Another common household problem that wastes time and space is too much paper. If you don't have a system for staying on top of proliferating paper piles, you're headed for years of wasted time and frustration. This household habit is not negotiable.

Paper Control:
File This Under File This

THE SIMPLE REQUEST—"Mom, I need my birth certificate"—triggered the lost weekend. The minute Paige finished driver's education, that paper was all that stood between her and her driver's permit.

"Your birth certificate?" I repeat, stalling (thinking about where it might be instantly gave me a headache).

"As in proof I was born," she says, her tone implying I had the IQ of a flatworm.

"I'll just write a note telling them how old you are."

"Mom, the DMV needs real proof because they don't trust you."

And well they shouldn't. My brain rewinds years, to a time before car seats, tooth fairies, 2 A.M. calls to pediatricians, and endless drives between Brownies, ballet, and barns, and tries to recall where in the universe I stuck that little piece of paper that said I now possessed a live birth that would entangle me in more ways than I could imagine for the rest of my life.

"Okay, but you have to help."

She follows me to the garage. "My birth certificate's in the garage?"

"It's not personal. Mine should be in here, too. Somewhere."

"They had birth certificates back then?"

"You want to drive or not, young lady?"

I scan the crammed garage, where the file cabinet landed on moving day five years ago, and has since been buried so deeply we need an archaeologist. "There," I point.

"Seriously?"

Between us and a two-drawer lateral file lie two bikes, a broken lawn mower, an air compressor, a scooter, four pairs of skis, a set of crutches, and a bale of hay. We unearth the cabinet to find it's locked. "Swell," I say. "Finding the Da Vinci code would be easier than finding the key to this."

"I bet other families don't live this way."

"I guarantee you, parents of fifteen-year-olds all over are going through the same thing." I spy a sledgehammer. "Stand back." I swing it like a wrecking ball into the cabinet's locked face. It feels good. The lock smashes open. The top drawer rolls out, exposing my past: long-expired insurance policies, failed investments, projects from three careers ago, unfinished novels, old résumés, and other papers I once thought important.

"Ta-da!" I pull out a dog-eared file that says "Birth Certificates" and feel something like redemption.

"Proud of yourself?"

"Yes, actually," I say. However, the moment forces me to face the awful condition not only of my personal records but also of my office files. I then do what I always do when facing a domestic crisis: Shop! This time I bring home an ugly four-drawer upright filing cabinet in vanilla metal.

In my office, I dump contents from all cupboards onto the floor, five years' worth of resources and articles in every stage of revision and print. I burrow like a prairie dog, making little headway. Someone in my family walks by and throws me a tuna sandwich. After a weekend of sorting and wrecking my nails, I fill four recycle bins, and feel that cleaned-out feeling you get after the stomach flu. I then realize: Unless I want to go through this again (never!), my habits must change.

Kathi Burns, owner of addspacetoyourlife.com, convinced me that regular filing was worth the time and trouble. "Not filing burns a lot more time," she says.

"So I need to convert?"

"You think you should have to move a lawnmower to get to your birth certificate?"

***

For those on a constant paper chase, professional organizer Kathi Burns offers these filing tips:

- *Know your papers.* Every paper falls into one of five categories. Some people use color-coded files for each category, which seems neurotic. I divided categories by file drawer and location. Here are the groupings:
  - *Action* (stuff to deal with soon)
  - *Research and reference* (stuff you'll need later)
  - *Agreements* (insurance policies, contracts)
  - *Tax-related stuff* (receipts, W-2s, returns)
  - *Permanent records* (birth and marriage certificates, education, medical, and property records)
- *Create AAA filing systems.*
  - Active files for home and work go on your desk. Consider a small space-saving vertical desk file.
  - At-hand files of often-needed reference should be in easy reach.
  - Archive files can go in a closet or basement, not the garage.
- *Remove and replace.* When the new versions of certain documents—insurance policies and Social Security and investment statements—arrive, toss, or shred the old.
- *Thin it.* I'm a magazine junkie. Some I plan to read; others contain articles I've written. Burns lightened my life with this advice: Tear off the cover, tear out the article you want to save, toss the magazine. Wow. My magazine stack shrunk by 98 percent.
- *Trust technology.* Old habits compelled me to keep a hard copy of stuff stored on my computer. But if you have a good backup system, you're covered. Really. (Wait till you see the section on photos in Chapter 13.)
- *Ask before you hoard.* When tempted to save an article or brochure, ask whether you could easily find more current information online later. If so, let go.
- *Bust paper before it gets in.* Open mail over the trash. Shred credit card offers, pay stubs, and other sensitive docs. Take what's left and sort it into a file for either bills, mail that requires action, or calendar items. Don't set unsorted mail on the counter or it will mate, and reproduce. "Don't shove papers in a 'To File' file," says Burns. "That's as bad as a 'Miscellaneous' file."

You've Got (Too Much) Mail

I just learned that the average person spends eight months of his or her life opening junk mail. No wonder my abs aren't what they should be. Think of all the sit-ups I could have been doing. Those eight months don't even include the time we, on average, spend dealing with the 44 percent of junk mail not opened. (Those of you opening 56 percent or more need to get a life.)

Besides wasting time, unsolicited mail messes up the house. The average household, says *Natural Home* magazine, gets forty-one pounds of junk mail a year. I don't mean to brag, but mine gets more. I get forty-one pounds in mortgage refinance pitches alone. Yelling, "I'm not interested in refinancing my house! Now go away!" hasn't worked. So I was all ears when *Natural Home* told me how to stop junk mail—a public service so miraculous I'd consider it on par with finding a cure for cracked heels. (Ladies, now really, they look terrible. Get a foot file. And if you can't repair the cracks, please, put your shoes back on.)

At that, I wasted no time logging on to two stop-junk-mail Web sites. Over the next several months, the unwanted paper pounds disappeared, along with the clutter. That's my kind of housework. Before the junk mail subsided, about 90 percent of the clutter around here came in through the mailbox. Seriously, Monday I'd set a stack of mail on the kitchen counter. By Friday it had reproduced like vermin on Viagra, and by the following week it had overtaken every available surface in the kitchen and family room.

"Anyone seen the toaster?"

"Under the Eddie Bauer catalog."

Some days I felt like rigging my mailbox, so when the mail carrier dropped off my mail, it would fall straight into the recycle bin. Until my junk mail arrest kicked in, I needed to sort mail into four stacks: recycle, shred, look at later, keep. Shredding—those credit card offers—is a nuisance, but it beats having someone steal your identity. Although why anyone would want to be me when she could be someone with a much larger bank account, I can't tell you.

Never mind, by eliminating junk mail, a cleaner house is on the way, along with a greener mailbox. You'll see in Part Nine, I'm all for going greener so long as the change is convenient, doesn't cost more, and gives me a result as good as or better than the less green alternative.

❈

A greener mailbox is just a click away. Here are some more reasons to opt out of junk mail and cut your clutter:

- *Help the planet.* In an average year, the U.S. Postal Service distributes 100 billion pieces of unsolicited mail, 300 pieces for every adult and child. To produce that volume requires 100 million trees for paper, the equivalent of deforesting the entire Rocky Mountain National Park every four months.
- *Make less trash.* Most of this unsolicited mail winds up in the trash, 44 percent of it unopened, according to the Consumer Research Institute. The time you spend opening the rest consumes eight months of your life, time you could be doing aerobics.
- *Save money.* Junk mailers often seduce you to buy things you wouldn't have if you hadn't gotten the mailer. Most offers and products you want or want to know about are available online. So here's another way to bust clutter: Don't buy it.

Convinced? Here's how to stop your junk mail:

- *Log on* to www.dmaconsumers.org. This is the Direct Marketing Association Web site, where you can have your name removed. This will cost one dollar. Be sure to register all your aliases.
- *Remove* your name from credit card and insurance mailings by visiting www.optout prescreen.com.
- *If you still get* unwanted mailers, contact the companies directly and ask them to remove your name.
- *Support* the movement for federal junk mail legislation, a law that would allow people to opt out of all direct mail advertising (like the National Do Not Call Registry law, which curtails telemarketing), at www.newdream.org/junkmail.
- *Pay bills online* and you'll stop getting bills in the mail.

All that will be left in your mailbox is stuff you actually want. Don't you feel cleaner and lighter already?

For five minutes online and one dollar, I help the planet, plus I get a cleaner home, more time, and less trash. And maybe I'll also get better abs. Or maybe for that I need to say no to junk food. Uh, no.

Better filing and less mail are two ways to help reduce clutter and streamline a home office, which almost every home today has. However, organizing that office so it's not only neat but also functional is the key to making working from home work.

10

Organizing the Home Office:
A Second Chance for Order

At my house we have the added fun of having not just one but two adults who work from home. When Dan isn't traveling, he's home working. One big day he declared he was moving out. Me? I helped him pack.

Dan had promised that when we finished building out our basement, he would move his office out of the bonus room and into the new quarters. Some days that vision and a primal scream were all that got me through. I see his moving out as a second chance for both of us. He gets a fresh crack at setting up his home office, and I can reclaim the bonus room, which I'm renaming the game room, the salon, the study, the teen crash pad, *anything* but bonus room.

I never should have called the sixteen-by-sixteen room at the top of the stairs a "bonus room." The term implies a room where everyone can have his way. My family did just that. Dan declared the space his office and parked his desk, phone, and computer there, along with a few boxes that multiplied like mice on their honeymoon. The boxes claimed an entire wall, and threatened available floor space. This is the male version of middle-aged spread. That, however, did not deter my children from claiming the room as their upstairs TV lounge, homework station, caterpillar farm, boxing ring, and cheesepuff arsenal. For them, Dan's stacked boxes, and his eight-year-old pile of *Business Weeks*, doubled as a climbing wall. The room also became a default guest and game room. I put in a rollaway sofa and stuffed board games in the closet.

Eventually, the only way to find anything in there was with a metal detector and K-9 patrol. Because this room-slash-eyesore has no door, just an arch, there's no hiding it. When visitors touring the house get to the threshold, they run fresh out of politeness, until you feel compelled to say something like, "Oh, and here's where we keep the hostages."

"Will you move this downstairs for me?" Dan asks. He keeps handing me boxes he has supposedly gone through for me take to the basement. But I know him. This is a man who hoards gas station receipts and old airplane boarding passes.

"Sure thing." I trot straight out the front door and toss it in a Dumpster across the street. We continue like this, assembly-line fashion. Every so often I take a box to his new digs, because deep down I do have a shred of conscience.

I also recognize this as the second chance that it is, another chance for Dan to get an organized fresh start on creating a productive work space at home. So I contact a pro. On Dan's behalf, I ask Barry Izsak, president of the National Association of Professional Organizers, and owner of Arranging It All, in Austin, Texas, for some pointers. "The systems he puts in place now will have a big impact on his productivity," says Izsak.

"And our marriage!" I add. I'm all ears.

Once we'd moved the last box out, Dan looks longingly back at the upended bonus room. "What are we going to use this room for now?" he wonders.

"Don't worry." I push him out the door. "I've got plans."

Here are Barry Izsak's basic office organizing rules:

- ***Pick a desk layout that suits your work style.*** The parallel workstation has a desk with a credenza behind it. The L-shaped has a desk with a return for a computer. And the U-shaped layout has a desk in the center and two returns, one for the computer and a second work surface. Don't place your computer on top of your main desk.
- ***Keep office supplies in your desk to a minimum.*** Don't store all twenty-four pads of sticky notes in your desk. Have one or two there, and the rest in auxiliary storage. Likewise, put items you don't use often, like your hole punch, in a supply closet.
- ***Create a two-part filing system.*** One for active files, such as bills to pay and new business, and one for reference, or any information you may need later. Keep active files close by, either in a desk drawer or in a vertical stair-step file on your desk. Archive reference files elsewhere.
- ***Get machines off the desk.*** Move them to nonwork surfaces, like the top of a file cabinet.
- ***Go paperless.*** As much as possible, store information on your computer. Don't keep hard copies of material you can easily retrieve.
- ***Exercise cord control.*** Have holes cut into your desktops and shelves to run cords through. Put cord wraps on visible cords so the back of your desk doesn't look like a scene from *Snakes on a Plane*.
- ***Practice magazine management.*** If you want to save magazines that relate to your work, get decorative magazine holders. When the holder gets full, say after you accumulate a year of issues, toss the oldest issues.
- ***Start clean habits.*** Clear your desk after each workday. Sort and toss unnecessary papers at the end of each week. Pretty soon, you'll feel like Izsak, who says, "Being organized isn't an option; it's a necessity." Maybe now that will be true for Dan.

11

Clutter Busting:
The Price of Consumption

As I MENTIONED, the urge to purge for me often comes on the heels of the holidays. After the seasonal bounty, I always feel a little sick of the excess. Putting new stuff on top of old stuff makes me want to go live in a monastery for a month. I want to pare down not just my hips, but my closets and cupboards as well.

"It's the creep factor," says Jane Reifer of Clutter Control Organizing Services, in Fullerton, California. "All year books, clothes, and kitchen gadgets keep creeping into your home until it drives you crazy."

Dan calls this time of year white-tornado season, and tells me there are medications for this. He backs off, however, when he sees that single-minded look in my eye, and the Container Store mailer in my hand. Those pictures of closets all neatly cubed and cubbied, sectioned and streamlined, basketed and binned make me realize how desperately out of control my home has gotten.

"Who are these clean, orderly people, and where do they put the kids' sports gear and Halloween costumes?" I rant.

"She's just having a bad closet day," Dan explains to the kids and assures them it's temporary.

Confidentially, Reifer—who specializes in what she calls hopeless cases—tells me I'd be surprised how many homes are a "complete blizzard." Of course, we're on the phone, and she hasn't seen my house.

When I do reach the end of my closet pole, I roll up my sleeves, order my kids to their closets, and try to enlist my husband, who's suddenly remembered an urgent appointment at the driving range. We start clutter busting, and do like the pros suggest:

- *Make stacks.* Create piles for donate, repair, relocate, and toss. For items you feel ambivalent about, have a trial-separation pile. These items go in the attic or garage for three months, during which time you can reconcile, but in my experience, this only leads to permanent parting.
- *Practice ruthlessness.* Move with purpose through the linen closets and kitchen cupboards. When your energy starts to flag, remind yourself that this is the price of consumption and that what you donate helps others.
- *Seek to simplify.* Look hard at your stuff, and get rid of what used to be you but isn't anymore. If it's irrelevant to your life today, think of it as weight and lose it. The more streamlined your home is, the less congested your life feels.
- *Divide, then conquer.* Do only one closet, or part of a closet, at a time. If you find something that belongs in another room, put it in that area, but don't start organizing there, too. That's called zigzag organizing, and you'll never get done. Get rid of any clothing you don't wear or don't look great in. Why wear something you just look okay in when you have other choices that make you look terrific?
- *Consider a closet system.* Once you've figured out what's for keeps, a system can work wonders, but not miracles. You still have to maintain it. To outfit a basic eight-foot wall closet costs from $100 for the do-it-yourself coated-wire kits from Home Depot to $800 for a professionally installed system of laminated particle board. Both do the job, though *Consumer Reports* rates the wire-coated systems slightly lower on durability than their particle-board counterparts. When the girls were in grade school, I put a system in each of their closets. While it did help order the chaos, it didn't keep Marissa from using the shoe cubby as a secret candy stash. When Paige saw the shelf tower for her sweaters, she promptly moved all the sweaters to the floor and proclaimed it "a great Beanie Baby condo."
- *Ordain areas of clutter.* Allow yourself a messy drawer, one chair to toss clothes on, a corner of your office that gets out of hand. But that's all. Limit the havoc.

Sometimes imposing order is easier when you do it for someone else.

Love It or Lose It

"This just hit me so fast," my mom said over the phone. Her anxiety tremors were registering 8.0 on the Richter scale.

"Mom, we've been discussing this for a month." I was flying to California the next day to help my parents clean closets in the home where they have lived (and stored stuff) since 1964. Based on Mom's enthusiasm, you'd think I was coming to personally extract all her teeth.

"But I may not agree with you."

"We're not going to throw away anything you still want."

"I'm sentimental."

"We're simplifying your life, not erasing your past."

I hear a long train of steam exit her nostrils, a familiar sound I know means she's teetering between resistance and resignation.

My parents are in their eighties. Though they both, thank goodness, have their wits, they're frail. Mom's balance isn't great. Dad runs out of air. Something had to be done about the closets before an avalanche crushed all the spiders. Dad was all for it, but Mom prefers the status quo to just about everything.

"The problem with this house is I have no storage space," Mom says as we hit the first closet.

"You will when I'm done," I say. "What's in here?"

"Miscellaneous."

"And here?"

"More miscellaneous."

My goal is three closets in two days: their bedroom closet, the den closet, and the guest room closet. Mom has clothes in all three; some she hasn't worn in fifty years, and many are from days when she was thirty pounds heavier.

"Have you seen yourself?" I ask, holding up a top that would fit two of her. She has outfits with oversized shoulder pads from the 1980s when it was fashionable for women to look like armadillos, shoes with three-inch heels she can't walk in, and what's this—old maternity clothes?

"I'm all for medical miracles, Mom, but seriously?"

"I thought they'd make nice drapes."

We find bundles of Christmas cards saved by year going back to William the Conqueror.

"Out?" she guesses.

We put the cards in the toss pile, along with a reel-to-reel tape recorder that weighs as much as a sewing machine, a wooden recipe box stuffed with grocery coupons that expired in 1996, boxes inside boxes filled with bows from every present she's received since Watergate, and enough baskets to re-create the miracle of the loaves and fishes.

"They're good boxes," she says. "And I put cookies in the baskets to give people."

"But you don't need fifty." We agree to whittle the collection to five boxes and ten baskets.

Dad appears in the background, grins, points two thumbs up, then goes back to making himself scarce.

"Oh, look, a dead badger," I say, pulling something furry from a box.

"Wigs were in style once."

"Why get one laced with gray?"

"I wanted to look natural."

I don't mention that body odor is natural but you don't go out of your way to acquire it, and instead ask the key question: "Will you use it?"

"We sometimes pass it around at parties, and the men try it on."

I decide that's hilarious, and we keep the wig.

After two days, we fill several trash and recycle bins, and half the two-car garage for a thrift-store pickup. As Mom collapses in a chair with a bag of frozen peas over her eyes, Dad surveys the mound. "I've been trying to get rid of this stuff for forty years," he says. "How'd you do it?"

"I just gave back what you guys gave me: unequivocal love and an occasional kick in the behind."

Actually, pulling teeth might have been easier.

As I sorted through my parents' belongings, I applied organizing methods I've adopted over the years that really work:

- *When sorting, ask two questions:* Do I love it? Will I use it? If you don't answer yes to one, the item goes. The following rationales are not reasons for hanging on: But I only wore it once. It's still in good condition. It was expensive.
- *Put related items together.* Before you put stuff back that you're keeping, group like items. Then look at how much of each category you have. For instance, Mom had stashed wrapping stuff—boxes, gift bags, bows, ribbons, and baskets—all over the house. We gathered it, thinned it, then stored it together. No more miscellaneous.
- *Hang up some logic.* After we pared Mom's wardrobe by 25 percent, we put clothes she wears every day in her bedroom and her Sunday best in the den. The guest closet can now hold guests' clothes.
- *Ditch the boxes.* Mom stored a lot of items in the boxes they came in. But boxes hog room. Plus, you forget what's in them. If you see an item, you're more likely to use it. Labeled bins are fine for small like items, but when possible, lose the box.
- *Sort someone else's stuff.* If your storage areas need tough love, phone a friend and trade services. You help her sort, and she'll help you. The outside opinion helps, plus the job's more fun. If no one's available to recruit, consider hiring a professional organizer. They charge between $35 and $75 dollars an hour. "My clients are people who get traumatized by letting go," says Jane Reifer. "They're people who have seven egg beaters, or seventeen black T-shirts."
- *Now's the time.* Doing this now lets you, or a loved one, reclaim quality space, enjoy a better-functioning home, and share stories.

We've tackled time, paper, the office, clutter, and closets. The next domain is the kitchen, the most used room in the house. When you get this room under control, everyone in the house wins.

12

Your Kitchen Is Under Arrest

WHEN I WAS a kid, I used to play Barrel of Monkeys, a game where you stick your hand in a plastic barrel and pull out a string of as many linked plastic monkeys as possible. Until recently, this game sprang to mind every time I fished a utensil out of my kitchen drawer: The whisk's connected to the tongs, which are connected to the egg beater, a garlic press, and a charger from an old cell phone.

"How long are you going to put up with that?" Dan asks, watching me.

"Show me a woman with a tidy, well-organized kitchen drawer, and I will show you a woman who has too much time on her hands," I say as I shake loose a sea-serpent chain of utensils, sending a meat fork flying toward Dan.

"Hey!" he wails. "I was just saying . . . "

"I know what you're saying. And I'm saying if you want a woman who never has a chip in her nail polish, who shows up to dinner parties with homemade peanut brittle, and whose drawers are clean, you didn't marry one."

"All righty then." He hands me the meat fork and makes for the door. Deep down I know the truth. I'm out of control and need professional help. So once again I call Barry Izsak, president of the National Association of Professional Organizers (now there's a barrel-of-fun group). "People call me when they've reached a point of pain," he says. While my tipping point was the tangled drawer, for others it's a lost tax refund, or finding out you sent your Pap smear results to school in your kid's lunch money envelope.

Izsak and I got right down to business and discussed my drawer problem. He then sent me straight to the Container Store for drawer dividers. I went reluctantly. But when I realized I didn't have to spend the rest of my life rummaging for the potato peeler, I started to come around. I ran the numbers: An organized kitchen drawer could save on average thirty seconds a day, or three hours a year, time I could put to good use combating unwanted body hair. I was sold.

Once I entered the mother of all storage stores, I caught organizing fever. I bought dividers not only for my utensil drawer but also for my knife, junk, bathroom, and jewelry drawers. I returned home on a mission. I started emptying drawers all over the house. Never mind that it was dinnertime, as my family kept reminding me. Dinner could wait. I was changing my life.

I started with the utensil drawer, separating spatulas, peelers, and presses. Then I moved to knives, which had fought so long in their dividerless drawer that the blades were dull as tennis shoes. I wrestled open the junk drawer. "You can have a junk drawer," says Izsak, "just as long as it's organized." "Organized junk drawer" sounds like an oxymoron, but he's the expert. I sorted batteries, shoe polish, screwdrivers, my high school student ID, an extracted molar, extension cords, and fish gravel into three piles: weird stuff, weirder stuff, superweird stuff. When I moved to the jewelry drawer, both daughters had their hands out.

The process was cathartic and felt good the way a leg wax feels good. Afterward, I spent the night wandering among the drawers, opening and closing them, feeling deeply self-satisfied, like how you would feel if you had your oil changed, teeth cleaned, and a hundred viruses purged from your computer in the same day. And I learned this: You can have creditors after you, sky-high cholesterol, kids on drugs, and a marriage as combustible as a live grenade, but clean, orderly drawers will make you feel utterly in control.

Besides organizing drawers, here are other tips Izsak offers for taking control of your kitchen:

- ***Clear the deck.*** For a less cluttered look and more workspace, keep counters clear. Okay, you can have a coffee maker out if you use it daily, but put the toaster and blender in a cupboard. Appliances used twice a year—that bread machine—could go on a top pantry shelf or in the garage. And, seriously, that pasta maker?
- ***Place items with logic.*** Put items you use often next to where you use them. For instance, keep dishes and silverware in the cupboard and drawer between the dishwasher and the table. Pitchers can go on a top shelf, and party platters in a more remote area.
- ***Use your wall space.*** Put up open shelving or a baker's rack to store decorative cookware, folded dishtowels, and cookbooks.
- ***Don't fall for glass-front cabinets.*** Most of the stuff we put in cupboards just isn't that hot to look at.
- ***Keep it up.*** Maintenance is the key. The best system in the world won't work if you don't stick to it.

Having an organized kitchen isn't quite enough, however, to help you get meals on the table without feeling like you've just finished a triathlon. A kitchen coach changed my ways forever.

Coach Helps Reduce Kitchen Friction

"Faster meals" was all I needed to hear. After reading a column of mine on drawer organizing, a "kitchen coach" e-mailed and offered to help me rearrange my kitchen to make meals faster. What woman could pass that up?

"You mean I could actually serve dinner before everyone has given up, found a box of cereal, and gone to bed?"

"Absolutely," she assured. This, of course, assumes I have food in the house.

"Bring it on!" I said.

That is how I opened my kitchen to public humiliation.

Here's how dinner at my house usually happens. I get hungry. The kids get hungry. Somebody asks what's for dinner. Then everyone looks at me. I look around, too. When it's clear I'm the only hope, I dash to the store, come back huffing, turn on a lot of burners, run a few laps around the island wielding a wooden spoon, and eventually put dinner on the table.

"So what areas of your kitchen aren't working for you?" asked kitchen coach Mary Collette Rogers, author of *Take Control of Your Kitchen* (Frederick Fell Publishers).

"The cook."

"I mean, are you aware of any weaknesses?"

"The food."

She pushed up her shirtsleeves, and starts opening cupboards and drawers. My fingers find a hole in my sweater and start twisting.

"Your problem," she said right off, "is that your kitchen isn't set up for smooth meal making."

"That's all!" I was relieved. I always thought my problems were much deeper.

"Show me how you make coffee."

I got the carafe, walked to the sink for water, walked back to the coffee maker. Then I went to the pantry for the coffee, over to the cupboard for a cup, and back to the fridge for milk. Her eyes darted after me like a person watching a tennis match.

"Save your steps!" she cried. "Get your workout at the gym!" She went back to opening cupboards.

"Oh, your cookbooks are over the kitchen desk. That's good," she continued.

"You can refer to them when you sit down, plan meals, and make your grocery list."

I nod and twist at the growing hole in my sweater. Telling this woman—*who's actually written meal-planning software*—that I rarely plan meals, use cookbooks, or write grocery lists would just be too much disclosure at once.

"Your pot holders," she said, moving on. "They're next to the sink? Not next to the oven or stove? Is that convenient for you?"

I twist.

"And your baking things?"

"Baking things?"

"You bake?"

"Not unless I want to hurt someone."

"Not even muffins?"

"Last time I made muffins, my kids fed them to the birds, who wound up in the ER, where they reported me to wildlife endangerment."

She made a clucking sound. "You keep this old fish aquarium next to your toaster because? . . ."

"They're the same size?"

"I see the logic."

And so it goes.

Halfway through her inspection, she looked at me with concern (my eyes must have been twirling pinwheel style like a cartoon character's). "Are you okay, Marni?"

"Fine," I said, pushing my hand through the sweater hole.

❋

When Rogers was done looking the place over, she gave me her recommendations for faster meal prep. "Do this," she assured, "and you'll have dinner served in no time."

- *Work your prime real estate.* I knew about the kitchen triangle, the one between the stove, refrigerator, and sink, which experts say is the key to good kitchen design. What I didn't realize was that all the cupboards and drawers within this magic triangle should be stocked with the cooking stuff you use most. "There's no food in your triangle," she observed. "That's what my family says about the kitchen in general," I said. We emptied one cupboard that had corncob dishes, sushi servers, and other specialty dishes I don't use often, and moved in cooking essentials: seasonings, oils, and vinegar, so I could grab them from the stove.
- *Use the pantry correctly.* Those essential cooking items had been in the pantry, which I learned I was using all wrong. The pantry is for storing little-used appliances and backup food. The extra six cans of diced tomatoes, fine. But keep two cans in the

kitchen triangle. We moved the bread machine, electric knife, and pitchers into the pantry to free up more prime real estate. Next, organize the pantry so you don't buy mustard when you already have two jars. Put like with like—canned fruits and jellies in one place, condiments in another, cereals together, and so on. Put small items in front, large in back, so nothing gets buried. Be sure the whole household follows the system. As you get down to your last jar of a staple, like canned tomatoes, write it on the grocery list. Dedicate a section to complete dinners, so all dry ingredients for one meal are together on one shelf. Stock all the ingredients for several meals, like tuna casserole. This will buffer you against emergencies.

- *Create kitchen centers.* Think activities—making coffee, setting the table, baking—then organize around them. When she'd had her way, the coffee maker, cups, filters, coffee, bean grinder, sugar, and creamer were all in a space of four square feet. I could make coffee in my sleep, which I often do, without moving my feet. For the table-setting center, she recommended locating silverware, plates, and place mats together between the dishwasher and the table.
- *Practice efficiency.* Buy square or rectangular plastic storage containers. Round wastes space. Convert deep lower cupboard shelves into shelves that roll out. Sharpen or have your knives sharpened regularly. (A sharp knife can cut kitchen prep in half.) Put cutting boards by kitchen knives and hot pads by the stove.

Now I just need food and a cook.

Among the drawers in my kitchen that needed organized attention was one particularly scary drawer. In it were family photos that had accumulated over several years. It was stuffed, and these snapshots were just the tip of the iceberg. Many more lay beneath the kitchen, in the basement. There I have dumped willy-nilly into a giant coffin-sized plastic bin of photos that dated back to premarriage and children. Besides what's stuffed in the tub and in the kitchen drawer, I have more on my computer, and others lurking on digital memory sticks that I can't find. I haven't put a photo in an album since Marissa was born. Here was another area of home life in serious need of a grip.

Before you panic, don't worry, I didn't stick my photos into some cleverly stenciled, calligraphy-captioned memory book. I did resolve to scan all photos worth keeping onto my computer and file them by year and occasion. Here's how you, too, can tackle the memory monster.

13

Photo Management: Someone Manage These Memories — Please!

S<small>OMEDAY.</small>

That's what I said whenever I thought about organizing years of family photos. Someday, when home life is no longer hectic, when I'm on top of all the bills, when five nights' worth of dinners are in the freezer, when all the laundry is put away, when my hair doesn't need coloring, when I'm caught up with work, when friends don't need calling, dogs don't need grooming, kids don't need rides to practice, and I'm tired of playing computer solitaire, I'll get to it.

I'll crack open that enormous blue bin of family photos, and let the memories flow like tears at a wedding.

Someday.

That's what I'd been saying until I learned about the importance of scanning all my snapshots onto a DVD. The news that digitizing photos provides better protection and easier management shocked me out of my complacency like an electric cattle prod. I got the message: Putting your past into the present is the future.

Still, dealing with my photo coffin and marinating in all that nostalgia seemed like too much, so I called Mitch Goldstone, the owner of ScanMyPhotos.com, to see if I could get out of this. ScanMyPhotos converts analog pictures (that's Russian for snapshot) into digital for-mat. Turns out, scanning photos is on the same must-do list as wearing seat belts, flossing, and using sunscreen. You don't have to, but you'd better.

Years ago, I tried sticking photos in albums. Then kids came along, and the blender speed of daily life went from chop to liquefy. No picture from the day my second child was born ever made it into an album, prompting the kids to believe we were in some witness-protection program.

"Do we have a past?"

Until I committed to scanning, I couldn't stop feeling guilty about not creating adorable scrapbooks. Many far more competent women created these (some made one for each child!) while I was meeting a newspaper deadline or drinking, or both. You know, those amazing scrapbooks where each picture is artfully displayed and captioned in calligraphy, where Johnny is holding a starfish, and the picture is cut in a star shape and the frame around the picture is a star. Some paste in the actual starfish. It just makes me feel so inadequate.

I consoled myself by knowing that for the past several years, our family photos have been digital, and most made their way to the computer, although a memory stick or two is at large, probably propping the short leg of a table somewhere. But what about all those images that weren't on the computer, the ones languishing in that blue bin?

Smile. Click. Ouch.

The ouch hits when you finally do something about the thousands of Kodak moments occupying more than a cubic yard of your home's storage space. That explains why, when I decided to tackle this job, the photos covered my basement floor, forming a silver-halide sea of my family's life.

This is my fault, but I prefer to blame Goldstone. He got me into this mess.

Goldstone is on a self-induced mission to convert the world's analog photos to digital, which is better for preserving memories, so no one will ever forget how stupid your hair looked in the 1980s. "We need to protect old photos from fading away, getting damaged, or lost through divorce." Goldstone estimates 3.5 trillion analog photos need digitizing. Two trillion are in my basement.

"I know I have to do this," I confess, "but it's so overwhelming."

"Send me your box," he says.

"It's not a box, as in, say, a shoe box," I explain. "It's a bathtub-sized plastic vat, so stuffed with photos that you need two people, or Vin Diesel, to lift it."

"Nothing I haven't seen before."

"Can I throw away the ones where I look fat?"

"Please don't. People often throw away the shots they think they look funny in, but those are the best ones. Just send them all. It's easy."

It's not easy. It's mounds of work. But it is necessary. So I agree, partly because Goldstone's company will scan a thousand photos for $50 (5¢ each). I had no more excuses. (I upgraded to a service that cost $125, which included the box, to-and-from priority mail, and scanning for up to two thousand photos. That works out to about 6¢ apiece.)

Using the promise of manicures, I bribed Paige and Marissa to pitch in. We spent an entire evening sorting through photos, laughing till our ribs detached.

"Look how young Dad looks!"

"Right, then you guys came along," I said.

"Mom, it's illegal to wear pants that high."

We got through maybe a third of the photos, until the basement floor looked like one wall-to-wall glossy. We needed to spend a couple more evenings sorting, laughing, and, yes, *purging*. Because I don't care what Goldstone says, I threw away the ones that made me look fat.

Then I still had to sort, bundle photos by date and size, and put labeled index cards ("Grand Canyon 2001") on each bundle.

"This could take weeks, centuries!" I cried to Goldstone.

"We have a 24/7 live-support chat line to help you," he said.

I took full advantage.

Me: What can I do about the fact that my hair looked like the working end of a sink scrubber from 1994 to 1998?

Support line: Is there a technical question I can help you with?

Me: Do I really need to put photos in chronological order? I'm tempted to just bundle up random stacks and send them in.

Support line: Most customers organize their photos in advance so they don't have to afterward.

Me: Would you please talk to my husband about scenery shots? Whenever we take vacations, he snaps peopleless shots of mountains, rivers, golf courses, and palm trees. We can get any of his shots off Google Images for free, and they're better.

Support line: Memories are highly personal.

Hmph. Some help.

As I sorted, the past hit like storm waves. The kid you once burped is now asking for your car keys. The four-year-old playing dress up in your high heels and pearls now really is wearing your high heels and pearls. That handsome young man, with all that dark hair and promise in his eyes, is your husband.

The first year I tackled was 1992. I put birthdays, summer vacation, Halloween, and Christmas all in independent batches with index cards labeling the occasion and year. By 1998, the index card just said "Family 1998." By 2004 it said "Planet Earth, 3rd Millennium."

Me: I'm drowning.

Support line: Is there anything else I can help you with?

I sign off. What I really need is digital therapy.

The present is the best time to get a handle on your past. Here's what the pros say you need to know and do:

- *Convert memories that matter to digital.* For those who have just woken from a ten-year coma, digital is the best way to store memories. It's more permanent than analog, takes less storage space (3,000 images fit on one DVD), and makes photos easier to retrieve, manipulate, and copy.
- *Copy, copy, copy.* It's cheap insurance. Copy the digitized photos to your hard drive, then make a lot of backup discs. Put one in your safe-deposit box and send others to relatives, to keep discs safe from flood or fire.
- *Don't use rewritable disks* for long-term digital storage. And don't label them with sticky labels or tape. Mark them with a Sharpie pen, and store in a cool, dry place.
- *What if the service loses your photos?* Goldstone says his company has scanned tens of millions of photos and hasn't lost one yet. The company returns the originals with the DVD (custom-labeled with up to three thousand images per DVD saved as 300 dpi, jpeg photo files). Until it does, save your negatives and duplicates.
- *Get used to migration.* Not the bird variety. Every ten years or so you'll have to transfer your memories onto the next generation of storage. Memory sticks will likely be obsolete, so you'll have trapped images unless you move images forward with the times. Even DVDs will decompose. We need to vigilantly manage—love this term—"data rot." Converting old photos to digital formats is a good start. Meanwhile, store DVDs carefully, make a lot of backups, and roll forward with the next generation of technology.
- *Let go.* Once you have your DVD backed up, some people feel comfortable tossing negatives, duplicates, and, if they're really brave, the originals, leaving one less box of clutter. "We won't need snapshots in the future," said Goldstone. "Print shots will go the way of the pay phone, as everyone will share pictures electronically." But not everyone agrees. DVDs can corrupt. What if the designated family historian forgets to redo them in five or ten years? Someone may need to rescan the originals in a hundred years. My advice: Toss duplicates, negatives, bad photos, and envelopes. Save worthy originals with care, but digitize them, too.
- *Does this mean I don't have to make photo albums?* "Once photos are on a DVD, making albums is easy," says Goldstone. Easy. Right. For now I'm just happy my photos are organized, hogging up less space, and safer. As for those albums? Maybe someday.
- *Getting started is the hard part.* But once you have a photo-management system, maintaining memories really is easy.

PART * THREE

The Finer Things in Life

Give me the luxuries of life and I will
willingly do without the necessities.
—FRANK LLOYD WRIGHT

Five mantras I live by:

1. *The closer something is to your body, the better it should be.*
   This argues for fine sheets and cheap drapes.

2. *Surround yourself with quality, not clutter.*
   Buy it once, buy it right.

3. *Every room needs something living:*
   Flowers, a goldfish, a pet.

4. *Honor the acts of daily living.*
   If it's a habit, make it beautiful.

5. *Life should sparkle.*
   Every house needs bling.

14

Building a Better Bed

Mantra 1: The closer something is to your body, the better it should be. This argues for fine sheets and cheap drapes.

To borrow a line from Oprah, here's one thing I know for sure: Once you get past, say, age twenty-two, you should have a bed you love, a bed that at the end of each day feels like a well-earned reward—like a diploma, the end of the rainbow, a chocolate truffle all in one.

Before age twenty-two, don't bother. Between ages two and twelve, kids don't like going to bed. They devise ingenious ways to avoid it; they believe sleep is something forced upon them by weary parents bent on making them miss out on all the good stuff. From twelve to twenty-two, they appreciate sleep, but are so darned good at it they could comfortably slumber on a train track. After age twenty-two, people care about their beds.

Because the cost of good bed ingredients—mattresses, pillows, blankets, sheets—adds up, it pays to get this right the first time. I, for one, am sick of stuffing my linen closet with sheets that are too scratchy, that don't breathe, or that don't fit my mattress, or with pillows that are too hard or too lumpy. So I set out to invest in perfect bed ingredients, and to make no more mistakes.

First I called a few bed experts, including the folks behind Westin's Heavenly Bed, to find out how to make a fabulous, cushy, sumptuous bed.

The famed Heavenly Bed debuted in 1999 after researchers test-slept fifty different hotel beds (tough job), said Chris Roberson, Westin spokeswoman. "The mission was to build the best bed in the industry." Frankly, that wasn't much of a challenge.

Their findings (guests like white!) triggered the death of the dreaded hotel bedspread—a public service up there with the discovery of de-odorant. I mean, what's creepier? Just imagining what happens on a ho-tel bedspread makes me want to sleep in the bathtub. Fortunately, more hotels are now covering beds with cushy layers of freshly laundered whites. That right there makes travelers sleep better.

"Westin/Starwood deserves credit for defining what a hotel bed should be and getting other hotels to kick their beds up a notch," says Jennifer Marks, editor of *Home Textiles Today*. You can buy the entire Heavenly Bed package—mattress, bedding, and pillows—through Nordstrom for between $2,500 and $3,000, or you can just apply some of their comfort findings at home yourself, which will likely cost less. Plus, you get it your way. (I say we do that.)

❊

To build a dreamy bed, start at the bottom. Here's what it takes:

- *A mattress you love.* (See next section.) To select a mattress you love, lie on a bunch. Pillow-top mattresses are popular because they offer a cushy feel with support. (The Heavenly Bed package has a thirteen-inch pillow-top mattress.) Flip and deodorize your mattress every few months.
- *A great mattress pad.* If you can see through yours, spring for a new one. Mattress pads provide an important buffer between your mattress and fitted sheet. If your mat-tress isn't a pillow top, you can get mattress covers in soft foam, wool, or down. (Yum! See section below.) Even if you like a firm mattress, a layer to sink into feels good.
- *Great sheets.* (See section on sheets.) Feel or weave is as important as high thread count, and go for all cotton. Heavenly Bed sheets, though clean, white, and crisp, don't have high thread counts because they wouldn't withstand rigorous hotel wash-ings. At home, we can enjoy even finer sheets. Heavenly Beds use three sheets—a bottom fitted sheet, a top sheet, and then another top sheet over the down blanket. "Part of what makes the bed heavenly is all the layers," says Roberson.

- ***Übersoft covers.*** Go for natural-fiber blankets (not synthetic) and comforters that provide warmth and breathe. Expect to spend a bit, says Marks. "You won't get a great blanket for $29.99." The most luxurious blanket—but pricey—is all cashmere. A down comforter is also dreamy. Next best, cashmere blend, all cotton, or all wool. Stick your hand in the bag and feel the fabric.
- ***Perfectly plump pillows.*** If yours are more than five years old, are just a fraction of their former selves, or have become lumpy or stained, say adios. "People don't replace pillows often enough," says Marks, who explained that those brown spots aren't drool stains; they're bacteria growing on drool and sweat. Yuck. To test whether your pillow is shot, place it on a table, fold it in half, and rest a tennis shoe on top. If the pillow tosses the shoe off, it's still good. (This won't work on down.) Buy pillows based on your sleep style: Stomach sleepers prefer a soft pillow with little elevation, back sleepers a medium pillow with moderate elevation, and side sleepers a firmer pillow with higher elevation to fill the space between ear and shoulder. The Heavenly Bed plops five pillows (two down, two hypoallergenic, and one boudoir pillow) on each bed, so guests can use what they like. This is also a good tip for home guest rooms.
- ***A good look.*** Your bed should beckon. Part of the draw is visual. Pick a duvet cover you love and layer it with pillows. While most people still like an opulent-looking bed with fat comforters and fluffy pillows (me), others are trending toward a flatter, sleeker bed thanks to contemporary and Asian design influences. "It's less bed to put together in the morning," says Marks, "so it cuts the hassle factor."

If you're building a bed for two, differences of opinion can cause the wrong kind of sparks to fly in the bedroom, which is what happened to my friends Susan and Michael.

Mattress Matters—When Couples Disagree

"Do you have any mattresses without formaldehyde?" my friend Susan asked the unsuspecting salesman. She was in the mattress store with her husband, Michael, trying to prove a point.

"Formaldehyde?" the salesman repeated.

"You know the liquid those frogs you dissected in science class were soaking in?" Susan clarified.

Michael rolls his eyes.

"Of course our mattresses don't have formaldehyde," said the salesman.

"Wonderful," said Susan. "Then your corporate office won't mind providing me a letter confirming that no toxic chemicals went into your mattresses."

Michael sighs.

The salesman stutters.

Susan prompts him to call his headquarters.

Susan and Michael listen to the salesman's side of the conversation, which grows progressively quieter. He hangs up and says, "We have no chemical-free mattresses, but chemicals aren't a problem. That's all I can say."

They leave.

Michael says Susan is nuts. Susan says Michael is nuts.

Later that day, when I stopped by Susan and Michael's house to pick up a book, the bedroom sparks were still flying. As they shared the mattress store scene with me, I listened as if at a tennis match.

Susan, who's into yoga, organic food, and this daily green drink that tastes like cow cud, wants a mattress free of alleged toxins like formaldehyde, and made from cotton grown without pesticides. "I don't want to breathe in toxins all night," she argues.

Michael, who runs on logic and numbers, is adamant: "I'm not going to buy a mattress without first lying down on it." The mattress Susan wants is only available online and costs more than those available at local stores. "I need to know it's comfortable."

Hoo-boy. Like most marital arguments, including most of mine, this one wasn't just about their mattress but also about money, power, principles, sex, and who won the last argument. Fueling the fight was the fact that they also needed a mattress for the guest room—fast. Guests were coming in three days.

Seeing no easy resolution, I slipped like a coward out the nearest exit. Next day, I called to see how it shook out. Michael answered. "So how'd it go?" I asked.

"We hammered out a peace treaty," he said. For the guest room, they will buy a nonorganic mattress, one that he's tried and knows is comfortable, plus is cheaper and can arrive within two days. But they'll buy a "toxin-free" mattress for their room.

"You gave in?" I said.

"Nothing good comes of an angry woman in the bedroom."

"What if the mattress isn't comfortable?"

"Well, there's always the guest room," he said, "where I would have wound up anyway."

❋

Whether or not you go green in the bedroom, finding a mattress you and your partner are both comfortable with—and on—is important. No matter how beautiful the bed is, or how yummy the bedding, if the mattress keeps you tossing, you've missed the point. Here are some tips for buying a mattress, from Nancy Butler, spokesperson for the Better Sleep Council, in Alexandria, Virginia.

- *Lie down on the job.* Picking a mattress is subjective. Try several. You have to lie on the mattress long enough to feel where pressure points occur. Don't feel embarrassed about lying in the position you usually sleep in. Tell the salesperson to go away for a while, and spend ten to fifteen minutes lying on each mattress you're considering. If you sleep with a partner, do this as a couple. It's not true that harder mattresses are better.
- *Know the different core cushioning systems.* Foam and spring mattresses are most popular. Some mattresses have memory foam, which offers a slow rebound. A lot of people love this, while others feel as if they're sinking or stuck. Air mattresses offer adjustability, so one side of the bed can be firmer than the other, a feature many couples like. Folks with allergies often like Latex mattresses because of their natural rubber content.
- *The box is part of the package.* Manufacturers engineer mattresses to work with certain box springs. If you want to replicate the mattress feel you felt in the store, you need both parts. If you don't use a box spring and just want a mattress—popular among those who want a lower-profile bed—that's fine. Just know that the mattress will wear out faster without the foundation.
- *Look under the bed.* You could have a great mattress and the right box spring, and still not have the right feel because of what's holding up the system. Wood slats usually aren't strong enough. Have someone lie on the bed, then look under it. If the

❋ *continues*

continued

slats bow, build in a supporting leg from the center of each wood slat to the floor. Steel slats are stronger than wood ones.

- ***Don't hand it down.*** When replacing your old mattress, which you might consider every decade or so, don't hand it down to your kids or put it in the guest room. That's just rude. Old mattresses have an ick factor.
- ***Don't lose sleep.*** If having an organic mattress made of pesticide-free cotton and no synthetic chemicals is important to you or your partner, then get one.

Next up when building your perfect bed come sheets, which also are highly personal. Do you prefer crunchy or silky? Knowing what you like is step one.

Don't Get Shorted on Sheets

My husband sleeps around, literally. I actually don't mind because he gets paid for sleeping around, which is more than most men can say. One hundred days a year, Dan travels the country staying in hotels, where he allegedly gives talks and gets paid. I'm not sure about the talk part, but I'm sure about the hotel part, because I get the credit card bills, and I'm sure about the paid part because the money shows up in our checking account. Now, as the wife of a traveling husband who sleeps around, I have questions. Good, legitimate questions.

"How are the beds? Particularly the sheets? Are they scratchy, smooth, coarse, or fine? Is the thread count higher in a four-star hotel than in a three-star?" And the king—or queen—of all questions: "Is any bed better than ours?"

Dan's perceptive analysis: "I don't pay much attention."

How is it that the same man who can perceive the slightest fluctuation of interest rates simply by sticking his finger in the wind doesn't notice what he sleeps on? "But you're the perfect one-person focus group," I insist. "Not everyone gets to test-drive a hundred beds a year."

"Not everyone is the Princess and the Pea," he says.

"Are you insinuating that I'm fussy?" I start, but he's not listening.

He furrows his brow, as a thought surfaces: "I did stay at a lower-end hotel recently, and the sheets felt like sandpaper."

"Bravo!" I say. This is progress, even though an armadillo can tell the difference between Motel 6 sheets and ones at the Hyatt.

This is because I care deeply about sheets. Remember my mantra, the closer something is to your body (and what's closer than sheets?), the better it should be? I'm even more passionate about sheets since I recently learned about—and I hate to be the one to shock you—thread inflation. Apparently, we are in the midst of an epidemic of thread inflation! Some companies, knowing that consumers think higher thread counts equal better sheets, have *misrepresented* their thread counts. Gasp! There have been lawsuits. I haven't been this appalled since I heard that when Monica Lewinsky first met President I-never-had-sex-with-that-woman Clinton, she showed him her thong. I still have a hard time picturing that exchange. "An honor to meet you, Mr. President. Would you like to see my? . . ." Anyway, I don't know about you, but thread inflation is enough to make me toss and turn all night on my 300-thread-count (or maybe not?) Percale sheets. If you can't rely on thread count, what can you count on?

"As for which bed is best," Dan interrupts my silent rampage, "ours is. There's nothing better than being in your own bed," he says, being the highly perceptive man that he is.

❋

To avoid a sheet scam, I asked Norma Keyes, director of product standards for Cotton Incorporated, in Cary, North Carolina, how to rest assured that you're getting a great set:

- **Measure.** Before you shop, measure the dimensions, including depth, of your mattress; otherwise, you'll have to arm wrestle your fitted sheet onto the mattress only to have it pop off in the night and wrap around you like a sea serpent.
- **Know what you want.** The look, feel, and function of sheets depend on the fabric. All cotton is by far the most popular. Cotton blended with polyester won't wrinkle, but doesn't breathe as well as pure cotton and tends to pill. "They're a good choice for kids

❋ *continues*

continued

or college students," says Keyes. "For people creating a nest that's their heaven on earth, I'd recommend all cotton." Egyptian or Pima cotton is best. Those varieties typically offer a longer staple length. That's textile talk for smoother surface. Weave also matters. If you like a crisp, light sheet, you'll prefer Percale cotton. If you like a weightier silky sheet, go for Sateen. Cotton flannel sheets are nice in winter, but cling to pajamas.

- **Understand the numbers.** Thread count—the number of threads both up and across in one square inch of fabric—does affect quality, but higher is not always better. "I've felt 1,000-thread-count sheets that were stiff," says Keyes. Typically, sheets under 200 threads per inch feel coarse, whereas sheets over 300 feel softer. The confusion comes with two-ply cotton. Some sneaky companies twist two threads into one thread and still count that as two threads. They bill a sheet that really has a 200 thread count as having a 400 count, which just makes me want to crawl in bed with a pint of Häagen-Dazs. "Read the label. When you see two-ply, cut the thread count in half," says Keyes, "and always feel them first. You will get a wonderful sheet set if you find all cotton with a 400 to 600 thread count, made of single (or one-ply) yarn."
- **Appeal to the other senses.** When selecting color, you can't lose with white. I'm not a fan of patterned or colored sheets, unless they're pastel. Dark sheets seem suspect and dirty even when clean. To keep sheets smelling fresh, wash them often in hot water with pleasantly scented detergent. Wash new sheets before using them to rinse out sizing. Avoid fabric softener, which coats sheets (and towels) and makes them less absorbent. For a nice touch, spritz sheets with lavender, a scent that invites relaxation, or rose water. Sweet dreams.

So we know how to score the right mattress and the yummiest sheets, but we're still not done. Next comes the fluff, which is serious.

The Lowdown on Down

I trundle down the stairs buried beneath a boatload of every piece of down bedding I can wrap my arms around. I must look like the abominable snowman.

"Whoa!" Dan says and flattens himself against the wall.

"Look out! I can't see!" I holler as I head toward the yard.

"Are we sleeping outside now?"

"I'm airing our dirty laundry."

"Not again," he sighs.

This is what happens when you're a home columnist. One minute you're in your office peacefully writing the next week's column, in this case on the glories of down bedding. And the next minute you're catapulted out of your chair when your research reveals that you should wash down bedding twice a year, once at the minimum! Somehow, because my down fillers stay under wraps beneath duvet covers and pillow cases, I blissfully and ignorantly assumed they remained pristine.

I'm not going to confess how long it had been since I washed my down bedding, but, trust me, I was way behind. Outside, I strip the duvet cover from the down filler, and give both a good shake. "Dust mites, dead skin cells, stale odors, be gone!" Feathers fly. The birds at the feeder take one look and hightail it to the next town. I hang the down comforter over the deck railing to air out. Then I take two down pillows and put them in the washing machine like it said to in my online research. Moments later, feeling virtuous and back in charge of my life, I return to my column.

Although it's expensive, down is good stuff. That light fluffy foof found beneath the feathers of ducks and geese is the world's best insulator—not counting good parents, friends, and pets. Given a choice between down and anything else, choose down. I like it in jackets, furniture cushions, pillows, and especially in beds. It's warm. It's soft. It's cuddly. It's 100 percent natural. It lasts. It breathes and makes me feel pampered. I wish men came in down.

Rat-a-tat-tat-tat! What the . . . ? Machine-gun fire in the laundry room! I dash in and arrive too late. Our twenty-year-old washing machine had gotten so agitated while spinning those down pillows around—bam, bam, bam, bam, bam—it just, well, gave up the goose. (See Chapter 48 on buying a new washer and dryer.)

"Now what are you doing?" Dan asks, wondering at all the racket.

"The pillows did her in," I say, patting the newly deceased appliance, which now won't kick into any cycle.

"You broke the washer?"

I assume a guilty expression.

Told you down is expensive.

What's up with down?

- **Before you jump in bed with any chick,** know your down from your feathers. Down comes from ducks and geese. (Other fowl don't spend enough time in the water to have plumage that insulates.) The Federal Trade Commission says that to be called down, fill must have at least 75 percent down clusters; the rest can be down and feather fibers and small feathers. One down comforter provides the warmth of a dozen wool blankets, but because down draws moisture away from your skin, you don't over-heat. The color of down ranges from pure white to black speckled. Some people prefer all white for looks, but color doesn't affect the down's loft or warmth. If down feels or sounds crunchy, it has too many quill feathers.

- **Know your fill power.** The higher the fill power, the warmer you'll stay. Products with a higher fill power will also be loftier (fluffier). As a gauge, light comforters have a 600 fill power; warmer ones can exceed 800. Some people change comforters with the season.

- **Avoid allergies.** Properly processed, down is thoroughly washed and sanitized, so it should be free of 99 percent of natural allergens, say the folks at Downlite, a leading maker of down bedding based in Mason, Ohio. Tightly woven casings add another barrier of protection. But for the supersensitive, a down alternative, such as PrimaLoft, makes a good second choice.

- **Put it under wraps.** Anything down filled should have a casing made of tightly woven fabric, so feathers don't poke through. Finely woven cotton is ideal because it keeps tiny quills in, but still feels soft and gives. Adding duvet covers and pillowcases over casings adds style and keeps down clean longer and protected. But you still need to wash pillows occasionally.

- **Keep feathers in their place.** Down blankets and comforters should have boxes sewn through the garment (baffling), so the down doesn't shift. Some down pillows are dual wrapped so they better hold their shape.

- **Handle with care.** The folks at Downlite say the best way to clean down products is by machine washing with a small spoonful of Dawn dishwashing detergent. (Be sure your washer is up to it, or go to a Laundromat.) Don't dry clean, and don't use regular laundry detergent. Dry bedding on low heat. (High heat can scorch the casing.) Shake it during the dry cycle so it dries evenly and completely. Trapped moisture can create mildew. Between washings, hang down bedding outside on nice days to freshen it.

- **Know when down is dead.** Though down lasts longer than synthetic fillers, well-used down pillows do collapse over time. If they won't fluff, have no loft or crown left, or smell musty, it's time to let go.

❋

Wrap that package: One of the most luxurious gifts you can give yourself is a fabulously outfitted bed, one that you love. What goes into it matters, and so does what goes on it. Though you can buy ready-made comforters, pillow shams, and dust ruffles, if you have the energy, I'd go for a custom set—one that you design. The bed, after all, is the centerpiece of the bedroom. Do it well because looks matter.

- *Start with something certain.* Your inspiration might be a painting; a theme, such as birds or baseball; a fabric or wallpaper; or the color of a flower outside the window. Pick two or three colors that work together.
- *Gather swatches.* Build a file of possible bedcover fabrics, accent fabrics, and trims. Also collect photos of beds you find alluring.
- *Lay samples out in the room.* Building around your lead fabric, create a patchwork of possibilities, figuring what fabric will be the top of the coverlet, and which will be the reverse. Will the shams match or contrast? (You could do the shams in the same fabric as the top of the coverlet, and border them with the fabric used on the reverse side or vice versa.) What fabric will the bed skirt be? Next pull together fabric and trim for throw pillows. (See Chapter 18 for men's opinions of these.)
- *Combine patterns.* Once you've gathered fabrics in your color scheme, mix them up using these guidelines: Mix a large-scale pattern (big print), with a geometric (stripe, plaid, or dot), with a solid, and maybe a small print. Add interest by picking fabrics with varied textures. For a makeover of Marissa's room, she chose a color scheme of white, peony purple, and black. (I know, peony! See Chapter 40 for my reaction to that.) We pulled together a textured solid (white mattelaisse) for the main bedspread fabric and shams (removable and washable), a shiny small-patterned lavender silk blend for the dust ruffle, accents of a large floral cotton print in peony, and a black cotton polka dot for fun accent pillows.
- *Decide what goes where.* This is where I leave the room screaming. You have to make umpteen detail decisions or your stuff will look like ready-made—exactly what you're trying to avoid. Bed skirt gathered, flat, or pleated? Border or not? Square or oblong shams? Edge detail: ruffle, flange, knife edge, welt? (See Chapter 18 for tips on designing custom throw pillows.) Aaargh! After you've made up your mind, have a seamstress measure and tell you how much of each fabric you need—before you buy it.
- *Ask for all scraps.* I use them for additional throw pillows and accents, and for future projects and repairs.
- *Sleep like a queen.*

15

The Towel Trap

Mantra 2: Surround yourself with quality, not clutter. Buy it once, buy it right.

My five houseguests are due any minute. The guest rooms are ready except for towels. I head confidently to the linen closet. One of the few things I pride myself on is that I tie sets of sheets and towels in ribbons, precisely so I can easily retrieve full, coordinated packages when I want them.

I open the closet with pride. What's this?! The linen closet's been ransacked. Ribbons are untied. Once folded towels are in wads on shelves, frayed, faded, and aging badly.

Apparently, my ribbon system didn't prevent certain members of my family from having their way with these sets. These hoodlums have helped themselves to a pillowcase here, a face towel there. These items go in gym bags, on sleepovers, or into the Black Hole of Calcutta and never return. I try to patch together a few complete sets. When I do find a bath towel, face towel, and washcloth that were a family, no pieces match. Colors have taken detours. I can't give these towels to my friends.

Ding-dong. Aaach!

"I'm sorry about the towels," I say when I hand my friend, who has arrived with her husband and three children, a scrap pile of terry cloth not fit to wash the car.

"Sorry?"

"I had no idea such degeneration had occurred in my linen closet."

"Same thing happened to me," she said, reminding me of why I love girlfriends. "I got these lovely green towels for the whole house, but after a few washings they all turned different shades. I have to get new ones."

I tell her how my teenager turned her towels into a tie-dye project. (Heads-up, parents of teens: Benzyl peroxide, a common ingredient in acne medicines, bleaches colored fabrics.) Marissa used her towels to remove purple nail polish.

The towel talk made me feel better, not so alone. Then I started investigating. A towel expert who did not want to be outed divulged that stores push colored towels because they sell more. Color is a cheap, short-term design thrill for people seeking easy change. But like romance, dreams, and skin tone, color fades, so towels look tired; color trends change, so consumers keep buying new ones, ushering out mauve for persimmon.

After I learn about this conspiracy, I call my friend, who's now back to her home and its faded towels. "We're victims of the color trap!" I exclaim. "The only winners are towel companies!"

"So what's the answer?"

"White!"

I tick off the virtues: White doesn't fade, never goes out of date, and goes with everything. White towels are the stuff of fine hotels. They're likely more sanitary because you can bleach and scald them, which makes you wonder what colored towels are hiding. If you buy plain white towels, when the new puppy uses the hand towel as a teething toy, you can pull a piece from another set and it will match.

"So we need to throw in our towels," she says.

"And buy white," I say.

"The color of surrender."

"The color of smart."

❋

If I had to do it again (and that phrase could open half of this book's chapters), I would buy white and only white towels. And that's what I've started doing. The mantra "Buy it once, buy it right" means not clogging cupboards with towels that just keep looking worse. Here are more pointers to buying towels you love that will last:

- *Don't rely on towels to provide bathroom pizzazz.* People often buy colored towels to jazz up a bathroom, but towels shouldn't be the focal point any more than toilet paper should be. Add punch and drama with wall color, fixtures, art, mirror frames, and accessories. Let the towels be white.
- *Fabric is key to function.* Look for high-grade combed cotton. Avoid synthetics. Higher-grade cottons (Egyptian, Supima, Turkish) have a long staple, or fiber, so last longer and absorb more. Combed cotton has had the shorter threads removed, so towels don't pill or cover you with lint. Edges should be double turned and double stitched to prevent fraying.
- *Dense loops equal thirsty towels.* Most towels are terry, meaning they have loops. Look for tightly woven loops that stand up straight, like grass. You shouldn't see the base of the towel. Velour towels feel nice, but aren't as thirsty.
- *Don't be a sucker for softness.* Many people buy towels for how soft they feel in the store. Manufacturers know this and coat towels with sizing to achieve that silky feel. Sizing, however, repels water, so towels push water around on your skin. After several washings, sizing comes out—a good thing—but towels feel coarser, leaving you feeling deceived. Adding vinegar to the rinse cycle helps cut through sizing. *Never* add fabric softener.
- *Too much of a good thing.* Thick towels feel luxurious, but towels can be too thick. Thick towels get heavy, take longer to dry, and hog shelf space. Find a happy medium. My criteria: A towel shouldn't be so thick that you can't dry inside your ears.
- *Cover your bottom line.* When buying bath towels, open them for size. They run from twenty-seven by fifty inches to forty by seventy inches, and many sizes in between. If you're taller or larger than average, you may prefer a bath sheet. Select a size right for your body, erring toward generous. It should wrap you and cover the basics.
- *Resist adornment.* Though it's tempting to buy embellished, patterned towels, if you stick to plain, you can always mix sets and have pieces match. Or add your own adornment—tie pretty ribbons around the towels, which you can change with the season.
- *If you must display fancy towels,* go ahead. Just don't use them. I have trophy towels—spice colored, satin embellished—in my master bath, where Dan is under orders not to touch them.

16

Flowers for Every Occasion Including Every Day

Mantra 3: Every room needs some life: flowers, a goldfish, a pet.

"What are those for?" Dan asks as I walk in the kitchen with a bunch of tulips.

"For me."

"You bought flowers for no reason?"

"They're part of my new lifestyle."

"I'm glad you think we have money to burn."

"Honey, in case you haven't noticed, our way of life needs a makeover."

"What's wrong with our way of life?"

"Who are those for?" asks Paige, coming through on her way to the refrigerator.

"Can't a person just bring home flowers around here without a cross-examination?"

"They're for her lifestyle change," Dan says.

"If she's changing, I have some suggestions," Paige says, heading to the pantry.

"I've wanted a better lifestyle for years, and this year I'm going to make it happen."

"I hope that means better food around here," Paige says.

"I'm starting with fresh flowers, regularly, not just on special occasions, like—*ahem*—Valentine's Day." I look at Dan under arched brows.

"And better food?" Paige asks.

"Don't get her started," Dan warns.

"And less clutter. We're going to organize drawers, cabinets, files, and closets. I want systems so I can put my hands on anything I want instantly."

"You can put your hands on me," Dan says.

"Sick," Paige says.

"At the end of every day I want to climb into a sumptuous bed lightly scented with lavender. I want every garment in my closet stylish, clean, pressed, lint free, with buttons on, zippers working, and coordinating shoes polished. I want all our photos stored safely in digital, indexed albums, every lightbulb working in every room, and the dogs to behave civilly."

"You mean they can't get it on with the GE repairman?" says Paige.

"Sick," says Marissa, who's just walked in. She looks at me. "Why the flowers?"

"Don't get her started," Paige says.

"For heaven's sake," Dan says, "just get her a vase."

❋

Never mind what your family thinks. Just start buying flowers. It's a small lifestyle change that costs less per week than your coffee habit, or at least mine, and will give you much more in return. You don't need a constant feed of long-stem roses. Get some gerbera daisies, or daffodils. Who knows, you might even teach your family to appreciate one of the finer things in life. Here's how to pick them, arrange them, and treat them so they'll last, according to Bridget Behe, professor of horticulture at Michigan State University:

- *Buy right.* Pick flowers like produce. Look for fresh, not wilted, leaves. Select blossoms not yet open. At the flower shop, peek in the water. It should look drinkable, not murky.
- *To save money, buy loose stems.* These can cost half as much as the same flowers arranged. Plus you're not stuck with another cheap vase.
- *Transport with care.* Don't let flowers get too cold or hot on the trip home. In temperatures below forty degrees, cover blossoms; over seventy degrees, keep the car cool and get the flowers home and into water fast. One hour in eighty-degree heat can shorten vase life by two days.
- *Have the right gear.* DIY flower arrangers must have sharp flower clippers, tape, floral foam, and plastic trash liners (to line nonwaterproof containers).
- *Use floral preservative.* Made correctly, this extends flower life, and will double the life span of fresh flowers. Use a clean vase and follow directions exactly. Preservatives have a nutrient, that provides flowers an energy source, and a biocide that keeps stems from clogging, and smelly bacteria and fungi from forming. Ask the flower shop for extra packets to use when changing water.
- *Make the cut.* While holding stems underwater, trim an inch off each stem with a clean sharp knife or floral clippers. Immediately put stems in the solution-filled vase. Stems are like straws. If a flower is out of water too long, an air bubble will travel up the stem and get stuck at the top, causing the flower head to drop. For uniform arrangements, cut stems the same length.
- *Strip leaves* below the water line. Soaking leaves generate bacteria and fungi, which stink. Don't pluck leaves above the waterline; they help the flower breathe.
- *Matchmake vases to flowers.* Use containers from around the house: an old coffeepot, a crystal bowl, a pitcher, a jam jar, even a high-top sneaker (lined with a watertight plastic bag trimmed to fit. If it can hold water, it can hold flowers. Match vessel to flower type.
    - ○ Tall cylinder vases are perfect for line flowers, those that bloom all up the stem (gladiolas, delphinium).

❋ *continues*

continued

- ○ Trumpet, or V-shaped, vases work well with tall flowers that have important single blooms: roses, irises, lilies. The small bottom collects the stems, while the larger top lets flowers fan out.
- ○ Ginger jars are good for flowers with thin stems, because they offer neck support.
- ○ Bubble bowls, or low, wide-mouth vases, are perfect for flowers with big blooms: dahlias, peonies, lilies. Cut stems short so blossoms reach just over the edge.

- **Use foam like the pros.** Use a knife to cut floral foam to fit your container. Soak foam in water with floral preservative for thirty minutes. To keep flowers in their place, use rubber bands to bunch groups of flowers, then poke them in floral foam. Or run clear florist's tape or Scotch tape in a crisscross pattern over the vase top. Poke flowers in the squares where they'll stay put and be evenly distributed. For more arrangement ideas, go to www.flowerpossibilities.com.

- **Consider color.** When mixing flowers, combine colors like the pros: Use flowers in varying shades of one color (hot-pink gerbera and light-pink roses). Pair any one color with white (white stock with yellow daisies). Or accent a color in a multicolor flower (blue irises with yellow stripes plus yellow roses). The most sophisticated looks are all one color, and all one flower type.

- **Use greens as background, not filler.** Florists often stuff bouquets with greens to make them look bigger. It's a cheap trick. Greens should set off flowers, and are best around the edges.

- **Design with a look in mind.** For a rustic feel, vary colors and stem lengths in a natural container, like a basket or clay pot. For classic looks, pick one or two colors; go for symmetry and traditional containers, like glass or crystal. For a contemporary arrangement, go with one or three long stem flowers of one type in a sleek vase. Think one tiger lily in a tall black vase.

- **Place with care.** Keep arrangements away from sunny windows and air vents. Also, don't put them by the fruit bowl. Many fruits, particularly apples, emit ethylene as they ripen. This colorless, odorless gas also causes flowers to ripen, or age, faster. Flowers do better away from smokers, too.

- **Extend flower life.** Recut stems every few days to eliminate stem clogs. Add fresh water daily, or change the vase solution (adding more preservative). As flowers shrink, you may need to change containers and create new arrangements.

- **Questions?** Dr. Behe answers flower questions when you e-mail her at www.flowrmd.com.

- **If anyone asks** what the occasion is, tell them you are the occasion.

17

Is a Soap Dish
Too Much to Ask?

Mantra 4: Honor the acts of daily living. If it's a habit, make it beautiful.

"Would a soap dish be too much to ask?" Dan is in our master bath fishing a slippery bar of soap out of his sink. It lands there often because, lacking a soap dish, he has to park it on the sink ledge. "Or a drinking glass?" he adds. Now he's on a roll.

It's not often Dan asks for a home improvement, even a minor one, so I seize the opportunity.

"They're against the rule," I say.

"What rule?"

"The rule that says you shouldn't buy accessories for a room until you've finished the major decorating."

"What decorating?"

I sweep my arms around the bathroom: "We need drapes, wall coverings, and new mirrors in here before we get accessories."

"Look, all I want is a drinking cup and a soap dish. You're telling me I have to pay for drapes first?"

"That's the rule."

"Is that why every time I bring a kitchen glass in here, it disappears?"

"That's the other rule: If it doesn't go with the decor, it goes away."

"So we do without basics until you find just the right basics, which you can't find until we wallpaper?"

"Or paint. We could paint."

"Have you lost your reason?"

"No. I have a reason: Buying accessories before you decorate is like buying the shoes before the outfit, or eating dessert before your vegetables."

"Oh, like you've never bought a pair of shoes that didn't go with anything."

Dan 1. Marni 0.

The problem with my self-imposed accessory diet is that sometimes it takes years to decorate a room. At least at our house, just as we've put a little decorating money aside, someone needs braces, or brakes, or bail—and, well, there goes the budget again. Meanwhile, you don't enjoy the space. Because I don't like ugly stuff where I can see it, I'd kept the bathroom counters bare. It had that just-moved-in look—for two years. When I needed a tissue, I opened the cabinet and rummaged for the box. The lotion I used daily was also inconveniently beneath the sink. When rinsing my mouth after brushing my teeth, I inelegantly stuck my mouth under the faucet.

Dan was right. We shouldn't have to live like this.

Then I recalled another rule to live by. This pearl came from a leading interior designer I once interviewed. *Honor the acts of daily living,* she said. It took me a while to get what she meant, longer to put the advice into practice. What she meant was this: There's an art to interior design, but there's also an art to living. What a space looks like matters, but how you live in that space matters more. Designers often talk about designing with clients' needs in mind, but often that's just hooey, and people wind up with homes that don't accommodate daily life. Like the time I went along with a designer I'd hired (single male, no kids) and bought three white sofas while I was pregnant with my first child. When was the last time you looked at a home in a shelter magazine and saw the mail, the kids, and the dog? That's real life, and it's missing.

Persuaded by my own arguments, I trotted off to the local bed and bath store. I bought two drinking cups, two soap dishes, two lotion or soft-soap dispensers, and one tissue box cover. The accessories—a bronze ceramic collection with antique metal detailing—were a splurge, like dessert, but worth it. The day after I set them out, I drew my tissue and lotion from handsome dispensers that were easy to reach, and took my vitamins with water from my own lovely cup. I felt like a princess. If my new accessories don't look right when I finally do decorate the bath, I'll get new ones. By then I'll probably need a denture cup. And while buying accessories twice may seem wasteful, life is too short to drink water with your mouth under the faucet. I raise my new water glass to Dan's, and we toast.

"To breaking the rules," I say.

"To reason," he says.

❀

You don't have to work with a top designer to have a home that honors the acts of daily living. Start by noticing what you do every day, then design around those acts:

- *Newspapers.* Rather than let the daily newspaper clutter the kitchen table, put it in a large attractive basket where it's easy to reach and read.
- *Mail.* Instead of letting the mail pile up and become unsightly, put it in a beautiful porcelain bowl. (Yes, you still have to periodically purge.) Our builder built in mail slots over the kitchen desk area, so every member of the family can find his or her mail. (See Chapter 9 on stopping junk mail.)
- *Keys.* Set out a lovely silver tray to receive your keys every time you come in the door. I hang mine in the kitchen on an antique iron hook.
- *Big idea.* The design rule we can all try to live by is this: Quality of life trumps any design rule any day. Now pass the dessert.

Another grace note in a well-appointed house is the addition of throw pillows. They soften rough edges, add appeal and spark to a room, and, when strategically placed, can even hide a stain. But don't expect the man you live with—or your dogs—to appreciate them.

18

Pillow Talk

*I*T'S ONLY A matter of days before those working on the human genome project find the male anti–throw pillow gene. What else could explain men's universal dislike of these essential home accessories?

Here's an example: At a neighborhood Super Bowl party, the neighbors were taking their seats around the big screen. Dan and another guy stood staring at the sofa, which was artfully decorated with coordinating throw pillows. Without any discussion, both men started taking the pillows off the sofa and setting them on the floor.

"What are you doing?" I said, horrified.

"What?" Dan said in a defensive play. "There was nowhere to sit."

The other guy ran interference, adding, "They were in the way."

The hostess shrugged and said, "My husband does the same thing."

That's what I mean. Guys don't get that throw pillows complete sofas and beds the way jewelry and handbags complete outfits. To them, throw pillows are just one more thing women put between them and getting in bed.

And they really, really don't get *custom* throw pillows. Talk about a luxury item. To guys, custom throw pillows rank up there on the necessity list with pink sandals. One day Dan overheard me on the phone discussing some pillows I was having made. After I hung up, he squawked, "Forty dollars each?"

I nodded. I didn't tell him that was just to sew them, and that fabric, filler, and fringe were extra, because I didn't have time to drive him to the stroke center.

Even my dogs, both male, have a thing against throw pillows. Every day, as I'm settled into my office working, hunched over my computer like Snoopy at his typewriter, Oliver nudges Theo. He gives a signal, a tail swish, an ear twitch. They tip-paw into the living room, where I have two couches (conveniently, one for each dog) facing each other. Each sofa has seven pillows. Each dog takes a sofa. They start at one end, then take off, rooting and tunneling between cushions and couch, shoving the pillows aside like a snow thrower.

"Knock it off!" I yell when I hear the scuffling.

They stop for a moment of respectful silence, which is more than my kids do, then continue scuffling, until every pillow is on the floor. The first dog to get all pillows down wins. Satisfied, they then go to the green chair in the family room, and kick off its pillow, then continue around the house clearing pillows from beds and chairs, as if doing a community service.

Back home after the Super Bowl party, Dan saw the dogs at their pillow game. "Atta boys," he said proudly. "Tackle 'em."

Throw pillows. They're a chick thing.

❀

You can get fun ready-made pillows off the shelf. But for those who want a custom touch at home (me!), and who care about the finer details of creating throw pillows, here's what to consider:

- *Fabric:* Throw pillows are your chance to add a spike to your room, by way of an unexpected color or print, or to integrate other fabrics in the room. (That's why you want to save scraps left from making bedspreads, drapes, or upholstered furniture.) Put print pillows on solid-color sofas, and solids on print sofas. One pillow made of two fabrics in the room plus a coordinating trim makes the difference between a custom pillow and one you buy off the shelf.

❀ *continues*

continued

- **Edging:** Certain edge details go with certain design styles. Pick the one most at home at your place:
    - ○ **Knife edge:** Two sides meet in a simple seam. This unadorned look goes well in a contemporary setting. But anywhere else it can look unimaginative.
    - ○ **Welt:** A line of piping around the edge, a welt can be in the same fabric (self welt) or a different one (contrasting welt), thin or thick. This tailored look goes well in traditional homes.
    - ○ **Gathered:** The look of ruffles, whether in fabric or lace, or layers of both, is popular in the Deep South, and in English or French country-style homes.
    - ○ **Flange:** An ungathered ruffle, this edging is a flat border that frames the pillow. You can make it of the main fabric, an accent fabric, or a layer of each. Flanged pillows go well in tailored settings, classic and transitional homes, and give a smart but relaxed look.
- **Forms:** Buy pillow forms two inches bigger than their covers: A twenty-inch square pillow takes a twenty-two-inch form. Think outside the box and consider shapes other than square, such as round, rolled, or rectangular. Save forms shaped like balls or hearts for the boudoir.
- **Fill:** Pure down is my first choice. It's the most luxurious and comfortable, but it needs plumping. Down blends are still soft but more practical, and synthetic fillers have come a long way since the days of no-give Dacron and are hypoallergenic.
- **Number:** If your room is formal and symmetrical, use an even number of matching pillows. Most rooms, however, particularly casual, modern, or eclectic interiors, invite odd arrangements.
- **Care:** To plump a flattened-out pillow, use karate. Punch each side in toward the center, then land a karate chop down the crest of the top. Practice on your mate if he still doesn't get it.

The nice thing about pillows in a household of careless hoodlums is that you can't break a pillow. Other beautiful home furnishings, however, can be crashing disappointments. Your choice: Either forgo all things fragile, or, if you can't resist a few precious objects (and I'm in that camp), display them at your own risk—and with care.

19

Something's Got to Give,
Just Please Not the Waterford

Mantra 5: Life should sparkle. Every house needs bling.

I swore I wasn't going to be one of those parents who let their kids dictate their home decor. I'd seen enough living rooms furnished by PlaySkool. Sure, I'd gate off the stairs, lock up the drain cleaner, and plug plastic covers into outlets. But no Lego centerpieces, no changing tables in the kitchen, no sheets covering the sofa, and no glass tables shrink-wrapped in quilt padding. Mine would be an adult house. We were here first. The kids would have to adapt.

So when our little blessings came along, I left the gorgeous, hand-blown, one-of-a-kind glass bowl on the living room table, where it looked perfect. I loved how the colors in this glass art dazzled by day and danced in the light by night. When Paige became a toddler, she liked the bowl, too. Despite our little talks about how certain pretty things were just to look at, one day, like Eve in Eden, she picked up the glass bowl in her two precious hands, and raised it about eight inches. As I dove forward for an interception, she panicked, pulled her hands apart, and the bowl crashed on the table, shattering like Humpty Dumpty.

This is when mothers lock themselves in their closets, muffle their screams in a stack of sweaters, then, after swallowing four Valium, emerge to say calmly, "It's okay, honey. Mommy shouldn't have had a fancy glass bowl on the table."

I then did what any stubborn, impractical woman living in La-La Land would do: I bought another bowl similar to the lost bowl, and set it on the same table. Paige steered clear. Her fast-growing younger sister, however, didn't get the avoid-the-bowl memo. Marissa was too busy being a fairy princess, donning fairy princess jammies and a plastic silver tiara, and waving her 79¢ magic wand. The wand's business end had a large pink plastic crystal, which she'd tap around the house transforming stuff. She tapped the dog. Poof! He became her white horse. Her stuffed animals—Alacazam!—became her coachmen. And for a carriage—Ping!—she tapped my hand-blown, one-of-a-kind crystal bowl, which, of course, shattered like all fairy tales ultimately do. The 79¢ wand, incidentally, remained unscathed.

Realism replaced La-La Land. I cooled it on the glass art and placed a basket of boring but indestructible silk flowers on the table. Maybe when the kids are out of college and I have disposable income again, I'll get another glass bowl I love. And that really does seem like a fairy-tale ending.

❋

Sandy Sardella, owner of Pismo Glass, which sells high-end glass art around the world, insists that kids, pets, and fragile art can coexist. Here are the keys:

- *Consider preparation and placement.* "You have to teach kids to appreciate and respect art, even small kids," she says. But if you have an active house—and that includes one with agile and tail-wagging pets—niches, high shelves, and glass cabinets can help display breakable art while keeping it out of harm's way.
- *Use museum wax* to secure nice pieces to furniture, even on pieces high up. A pea-sized ball will affix most pieces, and won't damage furniture.
- *Don't be intimidated.* "Glass art is sturdier than you think," says Sardella. She's heard stories where parents have come home and found out their kids have used the Dale Chihuly bowl for guacamole. "I'm not recommending that, but the bowl survives." The kids, however, may not.

20

Marriage, Like China, Can Be Tough to Get Right the First Time

MARRIAGE AND FINE tableware go together. I mean, what single person has fancy dishes? The moment you get engaged, which I did the first time at the illegal age of twenty-two, everyone makes a fuss and hustles you down to the nearest department store to "register." There a gray-haired lady with glasses on a cord squires you through the selection process. You're to pick the china, crystal, and silverware you will love till death do you part, though your taste is as developmentally advanced as a pollywog.

My first attempt at marriage ended after four years. Afterward, I wound up with enough humility to make Donald Trump seem grounded, a great macaroni and cheese recipe, and the wedding china—twelve five-piece place settings. Now I know some women look sentimentally at their china and, with dewy eyes, gush about all the family meals it has seen them through. I have no such warm feelings. First off, I long ago outgrew the pattern—silver rimmed with a band of pink and baby-blue roses. Second, I harbor no romantic notions about handing the set down to my daughters. I can think of no circumstance when saying "and here's some china I can't stand that came from my failed first marriage to a man you never met" would ever sound meaningful.

Because husband two came to the table with no fine china and no feelings about china, and because buying new china felt like an unnecessary extravagance, we used the same china, holiday after holiday, for almost twenty years.

Then that changed.

My fine china breakthrough came while on vacation with three girlfriends. I did something no woman could do with kids and a husband around. My friends and I shopped for china. For hours. We played a fantasy game of "If I Had to Do It Over," and picked what china we would get today, now that we know better. We really had no intention of buying. Honest . . .

My new china is solid ivory with a beaded rim. It has square plates, a country-French flair, and is distinctive but not limiting. It can be fancy or casual, and is microwave and dishwasher safe. I love it.

While I admire people who get love and china right the first time, for me it took two tries each. But, fortunately, some things improve with age. Judgment is one. Taste another.

Cheers to a Better Wineglass

Like many women, I often struggle to find the perfect birthday, Valentine's Day, or Christmas gift for Dan, a simple man, well, materially anyway. (Beyond that he's more complicated than a French Bordeaux.) He doesn't care about clothes. He drives a ten-year-old car. He has probably paid to see a movie in a theater five times in the twenty years I've known him. (He waits till he can rent them.) And his answer to almost every gift idea I float by him is, "Don't waste the money."

"How about a new pair of slippers, honey, since I can see the bottom of your feet coming through yours?"

"Don't waste the money."

So recently when I asked him what he wanted for Christmas, I was shocked to get an answer.

"I'd like some nice wineglasses."

"Perfect!" I was off like Secretariat. In my mind I was already at Cost Plus, where they sell glasses in boxes of twelve. I was thinking I

❋

According to Robin Long, spokeswoman for Replacements, Ltd., of North Carolina, the largest supplier of old and new china, the merchandising in home stores and magazines has expanded our visions of how creative tables can look. "Examples no longer come just from Grandma's table." But that doesn't make choosing china easier. When choosing or rechoosing, here are some pointers Long says to consider:

- *Know your terms.* China refers to all types of dishware, from fine to casual. Fine or formal china is typically bone (which has actual bone ash in it—don't ask) or porcelain. These dishes are thinner and translucent, but stronger, and thus more expensive. Everyday china is heavier and more porous, typically earthenware or stoneware. Many think fine china is more fragile, so use it less. In fact, because they've been fired more, porcelain and bone china are more durable and chip resistant than casual dishes.
- *Note the trend.* Women today don't feel they must have both everyday dishes and fine china for special occasions. Many choose one versatile pattern. China manufacturers have responded by offering crossover patterns: dishware made of fine porcelain, but designed with more casual shapes and decorations.
- *Go simple.* If you want china for the long haul, select a plain or traditional pattern: solid white or ivory, either plain or with a gold, silver, or cobalt blue band, or a simple edge detail. Change the mood of your table with linens, placemats, flowers, and accents. "Almost every dishware manufacturer has a solid program, because they recognize that customers want flexibility," says Long.
- *Avoid bold patterns.* Because dishware follows fashion trends, manufacturers come out with lines in the color du jour. Recently, majestic colors were big, so we saw dishware in royal purple. Don't fall for it. Also picture how food will look on the plate. Many purists believe food looks less appetizing on a busily patterned or strongly colored background.
- *Mix it up.* Another trend is to buy one mainstay pattern, then have a set of holiday or festive accent pieces. "You don't have to get twelve place settings of Spode Christmas Tree," says Long. "If you have plain china, add holiday salad plates and a couple serving pieces to transform the table." At Thanksgiving, for instance, mix in a few pieces or a serving platter of Johnson Brothers' His Majesty.
- *Fill the gaps.* If you've inherited a pattern you love that's incomplete, fill in what's missing. Companies like Replacements can help if your pattern is discontinued or pieces are hard to find.
- *Stuck?* If you can't afford the cost or cupboard space for new china, consider selling your old dishes on eBay or to Replacements (if they're buying your pattern). You'll clear your cupboards and can apply the proceeds toward something you just may love till death do you part.

might even find some in a fun color to jazz up the table. Dan wouldn't care about the color. We could use them over the holidays.

Just as I was mentally wrapping this plan up, he said, "And don't get some cheap discount pack in something colorful. Get some nice ones."

"Oh, you want wine *snob* glasses."

"Yeah, wine snob glasses."

I obviously needed to do some research. There are few areas of consumerism I know little about, but he'd hit one. The first thing I learned was that every wineglass I have ever purchased (and what are the odds of this?)—from the cobalt blue ones made in Mexico to my fine Waterford stemware—has been all wrong.

❋

What you spend on stemware isn't the issue. You can get a decent glass for under ten dollars, or you can pay as much as seventy dollars a glass. But whatever you spend, said the wine pros I consulted, wineglasses should meet this criteria:

- *Make them clear.* A wineglass must be clear glass, the thinner the better. Colored glass looks festive, and cut crystal sparkles. But both detract from seeing the actual color of the wine.
- *No fat lips.* The top edge of the glass should be fine, and not have a rolled lip, as if it's just had a collagen injection. A bulge on the rim keeps the wine from flowing out of the glass smoothly. Worse, it screams: cheap glass!
- *Get a grip.* You want stems. These keep you from pawing the bowl, which messes with the temperature and gets fingerprints all over, making the wine harder to see clearly. (Ladies, here's an etiquette tip: When drinking, isolate your lipstick print to one spot on the glass; don't goo up the whole rim. It's classier.)
- *Bottom heavy is good.* Contrary to the ideal female figure, the ideal glass base should be larger than its top. Champagne glasses are the exception. For these you want a narrow, tapered flute, so bubbles last longer. Though some companies make many glass shapes to suit the character of different wines, for most of us, three shapes should do: One for reds, bigger bowl; one for whites, smaller bowl; and narrow flutes for champagne.

- ***Room for slosh and schnoz.*** The glass should be large enough to hold an ample pour when the glass is one-third full. This lets you swirl the glass vigorously without splashing wine on your shirt, and also lets you stick your schnoz inside to get a full whiff.

- ***Wash once, rinse twice.*** Some wine purists believe in washing glasses with only water. Soap can leave a residue that will affect the taste, they argue. Some compromise and wash only the outside of the glass with soap, not the inside. Personally, I'm a fan of soap and water. Wash glasses (by hand if they're expensive) with a mild detergent, and rinse super well. You don't want that first aroma to carry overtones of berry and lemon-scented Joy. Hand dry without twisting.

- ***Right side up.*** When storing glasses, don't set them upside down, which can chip the all-precious rim and trap odors.

- ***What's in a name?*** Any search of quality wineglasses will lead to Riedel (rhymes with needle), the Chateau Laffite Rothschild of the wineglass world, or to Spiegelau, a company Riedel bought several years ago. Both companies offer affordable stemware for as low as $7 a glass. The Riedel Vinum line, available at Bed Bath & Beyond and Williams & Sonoma, runs for $20 to $75 a glass. Riedel's top Sommelier line costs $60 to $100 a stem. Any quality difference would be lost on me. I just know that if I bought a $70 wineglass and broke it, I'd curse louder than if I broke a $7 glass.

PART * FOUR

Six Secrets of Great Design

The way to have a beautifully decorated home while staying married to a cheap mate is to learn the key rules designers play by, and do the designing yourself. Of course, you're welcome to hire a wonderful interior designer and hand him or her a checkbook attached to a very well-funded account, but if you don't have such a checkbook, or if doing so would land you in divorce court, I have another way. Follow these six principles of great design. You'll have fun and save a bundle.

Design Secret #1:
Manage the Snowball
Effect of Decorating

Design Secret #1: It's not any one item that makes a room; it's how all the items work together.

One of the most overwhelming parts of interior design is the domino effect. Picking a sofa or carpet isn't necessarily so hard. But worrying about whether the sofa will go with the carpet, or with the drapes, or with the wall color, and trying to manage the whole picture can just make you want to drink a bottle of Tylenol.

When my kids were little, we used to read a book called *If You Give a Mouse a Cookie*, by Laura Joffe Numeroff. In it, a demanding rodent wants a cookie, then a glass of milk to go with it, then he wants a straw for the milk, and a mirror to see if he has a milk mustache, and so it goes, until this two-ounce dictator has driven one indulgent boy to exhaustion.

This is exactly like decorating. One decision detonates another until you unravel like a cheap rug. I confronted my own mouse-and-cookie problem every day while facing my bathroom mirror. No, I wasn't fretting about my waistline. I wasn't even peering into my soul to reflect upon guilt or failure, though I could have gone any one of those places. This reflection was more superficial, and literally about the mirror. It was the wrong shape, had the wrong frame, and was just as wrong as O. J. Simpson. I needed a new one.

But like the mouse getting his cookie, if I got a new mirror, I'd need something else. I'd need two, one for over Dan's sink, too. But before I hung them, I'd want to paint the wall, or maybe wallpaper. But that would mean picking a wall color, which would mean choosing drape fabric. The drape fabric would need to work in the adjoining master bedroom, because master suites must share unifying window treatments it says on page three of the U.S. Constitution. The drape fabric would also need to coordinate with the bedspread, which I planned to change to I wasn't sure what. And, back to the bathroom, I'd really like to install a great ceiling light fixture, but then I'd have to choose the metal finish, which should go with the mirror frame, which must go with the cabinet hardware. And if I changed the knobs, would I also need new faucets?

This is why so many rooms never change.

Decorating decisions can spiral. So often when I consider redecorating a space, I soon feel like a cheap umbrella in a tsunami—underequipped and overwhelmed. When I finally grew sick of facing the mirror and in it my cowardice, I bit the cookie and hired a tile guy to use the same tumbled marble I'd used on the bathroom floor and counters to craft frames for new mirrors over each sink. (For more mirror frame ideas, see Chapter 35.) A glass company custom cut mirrors to mount inside the marble-tiled frames. Whew! Next I found some antique copper–colored wallpaper that looked like faux finish on plaster. It warmed up the room, added character, and is neutral enough that it didn't limit my fabric options. Drapes came next. Someday I'll tackle new bedding, as soon as I gather more courage.

❋

Next time your decorating decisions start to snowball, here's how to get control:

- *Watch that first step.* The first decorating decision you make in a room is often the hardest because it sets the tone, and has a ripple effect on every subsequent design decision. In home design, fools often rush in. Don't make a move until you have a plan in place for the room. Take your time, think of the future impact, and choose well. Choosing should get easier as you go—unless you do something impulsive, like buy a red leopard-print carpet and then get stuck.
- *Think layers.* Start from the walls and floors, and move in. First, choose flooring, wall color, and tiles in colors you can build on. Next layer in window treatments, furniture, and accessories.
- *Divide and conquer.* True, to achieve great design, everything needs to work together. But don't let that overwhelm you. Once you have a plan for the space, break the process down into all the steps you'll need to make. Write a list, then tackle one task at a time, keeping in mind the big picture as you go.
- *Spend wisely.* The more expensive something is and the longer you plan to keep it, the more neutral and timeless it should be. Be more trendy and personal with less expensive touches that are easy to change. In a bathroom or kitchen, for instance, pick tile and cabinets you (or the next home owner) won't tire of. Add pizzazz with fun soap dishes, artwork, and rugs.
- *Think of it as an outfit.* Dressing a room is like dressing yourself. Start with good basics. Be sure the wardrobe staples are well constructed, classic, and tailored. Then accessorize with the scarf, the shoes, the jewelry. Or the vase, the drape, and the perfect mirror.

Design Secret #2: Apply Magic Measurements

Design Secret #2: The biggest mistake amateurs make when designing a room is they get the scale wrong. Proportions — how big, how small, how high — are choices that matter even more than color, fabric, and finish.

Once you're aware of the importance of scale, you'll understand—and notice more often—why some spaces just don't come together. How big should a rug be? How low should a chandelier hang? Now you'll know.

"Come over and tell me what you think of this dining room rug." My neighbor is on the phone asking me to do what neighbors so often do. Stick their feet in their mouths.

"Sure," I say, and hustle over, glad to take part in someone else's home decorating angst. I know how tricky finding the right area rug can be. I've lugged home dozens, dragged the rolled-up contenders in like dead sea mammals, only to take them all back to the store.

"I don't have to keep it," she says, letting me in the front door. "But my husband liked the price." That's code between wives. Translation: "It would be next to impossible to find another decent rug this cheap."

I tread carefully. I'd already created trouble between this neighbor and her husband once before. He asked for my honest opinion about the shade of brown they were painting their house's exterior. He said he was feeling ambivalent about it. Because the job was in process, as in maybe not too late to change, I really was honest, and said (will I ever live this down?), "Well, it is a little rose." The poor man didn't sleep for three nights. He would lie in the dark and moan, "Rose," like it was some other woman. Occasionally, he threw out my name, too, leaving my friend to wonder at the roots of his insomnia. I had some serious straightening out to do.

And now she was giving me a shot at redemption!

I look at the rug, which is under her dining room table.

"Do you think it works?" She looks at me with the eagerness of a labrador.

"Well," I stammer, stuck again between the twin evils of honesty and kindness. The color was great, but the rug was too small. Someone once broke this harsh news to me: When a rug doesn't extend far enough from under a table, chairs get hung up as people scoot in and out. When seated, guests feel off balance when front legs teeter higher than the back legs. But how do I say this?

"I like the color," I say.

"I've been searching for that rusty red," she says.

Then I blurt, "Does the rug come larger?"

She shakes her head. Because I'm already in deep, I gingerly point out the problem. It's one of those problems you may never realize if no one points it out—like wearing a gold necklace with silver earrings. Once you know, you can't go back.

Sensing disappointment, I beat an exit to her kitchen. As I note the rug under her kitchen table, she says, "Oh, that's going."

"It is?! Put your new rug here."

Suddenly the two of us turn into Amazon women; we lift dining and kitchen tables with Superwoman strength. We put the new rug under the kitchen table.

"Perfect," I say, and mean it.

"It was the right rug all along," she says.

"Just in the wrong place." We get that giddy, pop-the-champagne feeling. Then her husband comes in.

"I thought that rug was for the dining room," he says.

"It works better here," my friend explains.

"Great, now we have to buy two rugs?"

I gulp. "I think that's my cue to leave."

A little design knowledge can be hard on friendships. But when you know that certain proven dimensions make home interiors look and function better, it's hard to keep mum. So you don't have to guess, or get this wrong, here are some magical measurements:

- *Area rugs* beneath dining tables should extend at least three, even four, feet from the table edge on all sides. Leave twelve to eighteen inches between the rug and the walls. In seating areas, don't float the rug. Try to have at least the front legs of the furniture on the rug.
- *Chairs,* when pushed against the table, should have a minimum of three feet clearance between chair and wall. Four feet is better. A person sitting will need to pull the chair out two feet; you want another two feet for someone to pass behind.
- *Chandeliers* should hang thirty to thirty-two inches above a table in a room with eight-foot ceilings. Add two inches for every foot of ceiling height, so thirty-four to thirty-six inches from a ten-foot ceiling. But don't exceed forty inches.
- *A light fixture* needs to be in proportion with the room. To find the best size for your space, add the length of two adjoining walls in feet. Divide that number in half to get average wall length. (A twelve-by-sixteen-foot room has an average wall length of fourteen feet.) Double that number to get the ideal size in inches of the fixture for this room. Here, the ideal fixture would be twenty-eight inches wide.
- *Art* should hang eight to ten inches above the furniture it's over, whether a table or headboard. Shorten the distance to four to six inches for larger pieces. Most people hang art too high. The eye-level rule only works on art that's hanging free on an open wall. Otherwise, art should work in context with what it's next to.
- *Kitchen counters* should be thirty-six inches off finished floors. Bathroom counters, particularly in kids' rooms, can be lower.

23

Design Secret #3:
Throw the Weight Around

Design Secret #3: Decorating is a balancing act. Something heavy, whether an armoire or a big painting, needs something of equal visual weight across the room.

When DIY decorators don't know that rooms crave balance, they often create rooms that feel lopsided. Solution: Keep basic balance rules in mind when arranging furnishings.

Dan walks in the family room and sees me, arms outstretched, tilting to one side like an airplane banking a turn.

"What are you doing?"

"Fixing the wall," I say, leaning deeper left.

His eyebrows furrow into a concerned line. "How does holding your arms out fix the wall?"

I imagine how this must look, my arms like a human seesaw, Calista Flockhart on one side, Kirstie Alley on the other.

"The wall's off balance. The side with the big screen is too heavy. Ka-thunk."

He looks at the wall and tilts his head. "So you're saying you have a weight issue?"

"You think I have a weight issue?"

"No. That's not . . . oh, never mind."

"See, the wall's out of proportion."

Paige walks in. "Is Mom practicing her sobriety test?"

"We're dealing with her weight issue," Dan says.

"Not again."

"I don't have a weight issue! It's the wall's."

"Why does this only happen in my family?" she sighs.

"See, the right side needs more weight."

"So sit over there," she says.

"*Visual* weight!" I holler.

Here's what we faced: In our family room, the builder centered the fireplace on one wall. We added floor-to-ceiling stone around the fireplace, which covered the center third of the wall. Fine. To the right of the fireplace was a window surrounded by drywall. To the left, the builder had put in a dry-walled cavern large enough to park a Ford Fiesta to hold a big screen, which, naturally, Dan wasted no time getting. To help minimize it, I had a cabinetmaker surround it with a wooden built-in, which included cabinets to hold DVDs and hi-fi components. So the left third of the wall had handsome dark wood covering. The center third was stone covered. But the right third, with its window floating in light-colored drywall, made a flimsy neighbor. It needed substance.

I mulled over my options. Darker paint? Perhaps. Heavy drapery? Maybe. Then I hit on the solution. To give the right side weight and symmetry, I would cover it in wood veneers to match the built-in. I called the cabinetmaker and said he needed to fix my weight problem. There was a long pause. Once the wood veneer was in, I added a valance over the window, to break up the hard surfaces, and set a small table in front of the window. To everyone's great relief, well, okay, maybe just mine, the seesaw evened out.

When I first heard the concept of visual weight, I wanted to lie on the roof and lap straight gin out of the rain gutters. But eventually, I grasped the notion. Here's what I learned, and what you should know about adding weight where you need to.

- *The concept:* Successful design incorporates proper scale, proportion, and balance. Balance in a room literally means when you walk in you don't feel as if the room's weight is on one side; rather it's well distributed. Walls should feel that way, too.
- *Two types of balance:* Balance can be symmetrical or asymmetrical. Symmetrical balance is usually more formal and means both sides of a room match. Think of two sofas facing each other. Asymmetrical balance is more informal, as when a sofa faces two chairs. But both carry the same weight.
- *Visual weight isn't actual weight:* In the world of design a large dark tapestry can "weigh" as much as a tome-filled bookcase. The more visual weight something has, the more it engages your eye.
- *Adding visual weight:* When a room or wall feels off balance, try one of these ways to add weight in the light spots.
    - ○ *Paint* the wall darker. Dark colors weigh more visually than light colors.
    - ○ *Cover* the wall with texture, such as drapery, tapestry, stone, brick, or wood.
    - ○ *Hang* a large striking piece of art, which can carry the same visual weight as a chest of drawers.
    - ○ *Try* a sculpture or tree. Items with irregular edges hold the eye more (so are visually heavier) than objects with straight lines.
    - ○ *Repeat* what you're working to offset: If you have a table and lamp on one side of a bed or sofa, put a table and lamp on the other side. (Hint: If you have matching tables, have matching lamps. If your tables don't match, the lamps shouldn't match, either.)
    - ○ *Add* a piece of furniture.

24

Design Secret #4:
Practice the Virtue of Restraint

Design Secret #4: Too much of a good thing is just that, too much. However, a series of timid, same choices is boring.

The best home interiors employ a lot of consistency—tightly controlled color schemes, matching hardware, moldings, and wood finishes—punctuated by strategic and occasional novelty.

I'm standing inside my local Great Indoors store looking as if I just got hit by a taser gun. I'm mildly aware of customers making a wide circle around the dumbstruck woman in the towel bar aisle. They don't know that this is how I look when making even the simplest home design choice, in this case picking new towel bars. I'm staring blankly at a wall of them.

The pressure is on because at this moment, my wallpaper man, Tom Johnson, is hanging wallpaper in my master bath. Though I've had the paper six months, and have known for a week he was coming, I'd put this errand off until it had the urgency of a grade-school fire drill.

Once upon a time consumers had two towel bar choices: chrome or polished brass. Now we have to ferret through oil-rubbed bronze, pearl or polished nickel, satin chrome, weathered black iron, and assorted combinations (nickel with brass, chrome with gold, and so forth). Once you pick your finish, you face umpteen design styles: beaded, braided, twisted, round edged, square edged, filigreed. I steady myself on my shopping cart, and feel a twitch start in my left eyelid.

Tom could reinstall the old bars, but if I wanted to change them later, the holes for the new hardware might not line up, and the walls would look as if I roomed with a woodpecker. Besides, I was acutely aware that two events were converging that were as rare as a total solar eclipse in my backyard: One, the original towel bars and TP holders were off the walls, and, two, a willing man was in my bathroom with tools and know-how. Carpe diem!

As I perused the overwhelming selection at the home store, the antique bronze finish turned my head. The new wallpaper had a metallic bronze background. I put two bronze towel bars, a TP holder, and a robe hook in my cart. As I rolled toward the checkout, a thought nagged: All the other fixtures in that bathroom, the faucets and knobs, were brushed nickel. A small, knowing voice whispered, "Restraint."

"Restraint?" I answered. "This is my chance for change! Surely I don't have to stay married to brushed nickel?"

"Restraint," the voice whispered louder.

"Restraint means skipping dessert, observing curfew, wearing a helmet, obeying copy editors, applying muted makeup, and dressing in gray. Where's the fun in that?"

"Restraint takes discipline," the voice said.

"Mixing metals feels fun, like playing hooky, eating chocolate lava cake for breakfast, staying out all night, wearing red, driving fast in a convertible, splurging on the latest trendy fashion."

"Too much novelty is a sign of a weak character coupled with bad taste and a lack of dependability," the voice said.

"Like a marriage between Pamela Anderson and Kid Rock?"

"Sort of."

I turned the cart around, put the antique bronze hardware back, and reached for an updated set in brushed nickel. It felt right and safe, like wearing a seat belt.

To people who thrive on the thrill of novelty, using restraint in home design can feel stifling. For reinforcement, I ran all this by Gary Gibson, a top Los Angeles designer, whose tasteful interiors exude restraint. He had these rules for those of us who have trouble resisting temptation:

- **Decorating is like dressing.** You have to edit yourself, says Gibson. You can have a beautiful necklace, stunning earrings, and a great bracelet, but together they look junky. Pick one great piece and put the rest back.
- **Go crazy in little spots.** If you're feeling adventuresome, express yourself on a small scale. Say you like a duck-head door handle. If you must have this handle, put it on the door to the library, but don't put it everywhere. "One is cute," says Gibson. "Twenty-five all over the house look stupid."
- **Accessorize, don't excessorize.** Use restraint when setting out accessories. Fewer well-selected accessories look smart; a bunch looks excessive. And a few large accessories look better than a lot of small ones. A good rule: Don't set out any accessory smaller than a cantaloupe.
- **Consider the point of view.** I told Gibson that I'd recently helped my neighbor pick drapery panels for her living, family, and dining rooms. She had a dozen contenders of ready-made panels in different fabrics. We quickly picked which ones would look best in each room. Then I reconsidered. Her open floor plan lets you see into all three rooms at once. While each fabric made a nice statement in one room, together they made a visual racket. We chose a fourth plainer fabric that looked great in all three rooms. That was the right move, he confirmed.
- **Exercise color control.** Varying shades of one neutral (beige, brown, taupe, sage) will always look classic and timeless. Such neutrals are a particularly good choice for permanent or large objects: flooring, sofas, and walls. If you're feeling adventuresome, express yourself in an orange lampshade that's easy to change.
- **Sometimes the best choice is right in front of you.** The latest look is tempting, but you're usually better off matching what you have. When doing a room addition, for instance, make door handles and moldings match those throughout the house. That will make the addition flow.

25

Design Secret #5:
Look to the French

Design Secret #5: Every day is all there is. Use the good stuff.

You may not always agree with their politics, but Europeans, particularly the French, are superior to Americans when it comes to culture. They've had a lot longer to get it right.

Because Dan travels more than a hundred days a year, one thing we do have—while money is usually in short supply—is miles. So when Dan said we could fly anywhere for vacation, as long as our accommodations weren't too expensive, I had us going to France before he could retract the offer. We rented a small 300-year-old house in a medieval village for the four of us for only $114 a day. Contrary to what my family would tell you, the house had a lot going for it. When I first walked in, I liked it so much I jumped up and down, until I remembered the floor's age.

I was even more delighted when I learned that the owner, Madame Galewska, was an interior designer with an international clientele. She had decorated the home, actually the top two floors of a trilevel building, beautifully: walls upholstered in colorful suede, antiques, leather-bound books, a spiral staircase, a modern kitchen, and sumptuous drapes.

Okay, so the place also had a few not-so-enthralling features that the Web site didn't note: It was on a busy street, had a truly crazy man who yelled incessantly living on one side and a barking dog on the other. The ground floor tenant's sour cooking smells wafted through old floorboards every afternoon, and the plumbing was, well, French.

Dan blamed me. Mme. Galewska blamed her agent, who blamed the Web site's translator. That's France for you. Problème? Blame the translation.

I didn't notice the nuisances, because the small pleasures more than compensated. Pure lace-trimmed linen lined the shelves. We ate on Limoge china with real sterling because that's all that was in the house. (American rentals feature Wal-Mart plates and silverware lifted from the local diner.) Real orchids bloomed in the bathroom, and original charcoal drawings hung on the walls.

Whatever minor irritations existed dissolved even more as I got to know the stylish Mme. Galewska. One late afternoon I invited myself over to her place nearby.

"Don't be forever," Dan called as I hustled out. He knew how long I could be, and the dinner hour was approaching.

Two hours later I returned to a hungry, hostile family. "Okay," I said, holding my hands up. "So I got involved in our conversation, but I've learned the secret of life!"

"The secret of life is food," Paige said. "Can we go to dinner now?"

Over dinner, I told my less-than-riveted family about my conversation with Mme. G. We sat in her parlor drinking Côte du Rhone from fine crystal glasses, talking about French design and what Americans get wrong. This may be as good as life gets.

❈

The worldly Mme. Galewska shared with me the following French secrets regarding home design and the art of living. Secrets Americans should be let in on. Maybe you'll care more than my family:

- *On color:* American homes are too beige and white. A bathroom floor, a laundry room counter, your sheets should be white. Put color everywhere else. Many people paint everything beige because they don't want to make a mistake. Beige is a mistake.
- *On synthetics:* Many new homes feel like plastic cartons, with their fake floors and Formica. Use real wood, real stone.
- *On art:* Buy what you love, particularly originals from unknown artists. That will give your home personality. It doesn't matter if the artist isn't famous, only that you love the work.
- *On home size:* Americans have these big, sterile homes. They work very hard, and their goal is to sell the house and move to a bigger plastic home. That's not living.
- *On accessories:* Everything you need to furnish your home, you can find at garage and estate sales, flea markets, and the Salvation Army. You need time and a good eye.
- *On crystal and china:* Americans put their crystal and china in glass cabinets and never use them. The French use these things daily because small things matter. Life and fine things are for us to share. The pleasure is for now, not tomorrow.

26

Design Secret #6: Put Home Improvement in Its Place

Design Secret #6: If it's not within your means, you'll never enjoy it.

Though the first five design tips come from the world of design, this last one comes from the field of psychology. It involves keeping design in its place.

Whether your household budget, or the larger economy, puts a crimp in your decorating plans, you're not alone. I have an endless list of home projects I'd love to do but can't afford.

I want new light fixtures, bookcases in the family room, more landscaping, and a furnished basement. Not only don't I have the money for these home improvements but I can also no longer justify these by arguing that they will increase our home's value, which has flattened. The whole situation just chafes like a cheap bra.

But I'm not going to let some pesky old household budget or a tight economy ruin my fun. Just because I have to stop spending on improving doesn't mean I have to stop improving. In the face of budget restraints, I do three things: Figure out cheap ways to do my home improvements anyway (see Part Five). Wait. Rethink them until I decide they really aren't worth it.

To reinforce this nonspending perspective, I called Sally Palaian, a Detroit-based psychologist and author of *Spent: Break the Buying Obsession and Discover Your True Worth* (Hazeldon). Admittedly, I was a little nervous calling. Talking to psychologists always makes me feel as if my neuroses are neon. Plus, I worried she'd be able to size up my true worth over the phone. Gulp! However, on behalf of all of us, I asked her how we might rethink home improvement spending.

"The upside to down times is that they force us to slow down and really think about what we want and how much that's worth to us," she said.

"But even when I think slower, I still want to fix up my house," I said.

"Having a nice home is important. People put a lot of emphasis on their homes because they're looking for attachment and connection, and believe home is where that happens."

"If home isn't where that happens, don't they have other issues?" I ask. (I always wanted to be a psychologist.)

"Not everyone values a nice home in the same way."

"No kidding! Husbands, for instance, see it way differently from wives."

"What matters is that before you spend, you get clear about what's important to you, so you can align your money with your values. If you value a nice home, then look at how that fits into the household budget, and adjust."

"I can just picture the announcement: 'All right, kids, no more clothes, music lessons, or orthodontia. We're redecorating the master.'"

"Again," she said, "it's all about priorities."

To help us adjust, Sally Palaian offers these ways we can view home improvements and save:

- *Learn to love what you have.* If we can do a better job of connecting to what we already have, she says, we're not likely to search out other things.
- *Know what makes us want new stuff.* We're less attached to our belongings and buy more than folks of earlier generations because we've had a long run with easy

❋ *continues*

continued

money and easy access to cheap stuff. Plus, the media constantly stir in us the desire for the latest trend. "We don't want Grandma's linens; we want the newest style and color of linens from Target." An awareness of what drives us to buy can help us temper that impulse.

- ***Question your motives.*** When moved to improve, first ask why, so you improve for the right reasons. Rethink your project if you're doing it to impress others, a trap for those who try to have a sense of self through possessions. Also, if you think the improvement will fix something in your life, you'll be disappointed. "A new kitchen won't fix your marriage," she said. "It's just a kitchen." However, if you love to cook, and want a studio in which to express your passion, then go for it. Taking on a project is healthy if you have the money, vision, and desire to express yourself on the canvas of your home.
- ***Seek less expensive alternatives.*** For instance, instead of buying all new cabinetry, maybe refacing or painting your cabinets and changing the hardware will give you the updated look you want. Hunt down sales and cheaper labor—as in maybe yourself. (See next section for ten cheap design tricks.) Palaian and her husband and two other couples swap home improvements. The couples take turns meeting at one couple's home, where they do a home improvement project followed by a potluck. Past projects have included laying press-down wood floors, painting, and tearing out landscaping. The labor is fun and free.
- ***Measure success.*** We've all made purchases that left us feeling empty. But think about the times you got it right and why. I appreciate my remodeled mudroom every day. I lived in my house four years before I dialed in exactly what I wanted and nudged my husband to do it. "You hit the target," said Palaian. "You lived in the space, thought about what you wanted and why, achieved it economically, and now have a sustained good feeling." For those who care about living well, that is the most important secret of great home design.

Between Dan's money-saving ways, the economy's ups and downs, and a desperate desire to have the home of my dreams before I'm in a rest home, I have become the Queen of Cheap. The next section reveals my favorite cheap tricks.

PART FIVE

Desperate Times Call for Desperate Decorating: Ten Cheap Design Tricks

Whether the housing market is up or down, finding inexpensive ways to get million-dollar looks on a shoestring budget is always a worthy pursuit. Here's my philosophy on no-budget decorating along with my favorite cheap design tricks to glam up your home without giving your spouse heart failure.

No-Budget Decorating

W HEN ECONOMIST TYPES say people aren't spending, I want to tell them they're not spending because people like my husband are ordering those who share their bank accounts, "Stop spending!" Specifically, Dan has issued a decorating freeze. "Don't get one more thing for this house unless it's free." This is hard on people like me who battle remodeling addiction. Still, I obediently put all my credit cards in a Ziploc bag, and stuck the baggie in the freezer.

"What's this?" Paige asked, moving the bag aside to get to the ice cream.

"My spending freeze."

Later, when Dan catches me looking online at a settee, he says, "I thought we weren't spending money on the house."

"I'm not *buying*. I'm *browsing*," I say, pointing up a distinction every woman knows, but few men get.

"Isn't that like going to a football game blindfolded?" he asks.

"Not at all," I explain. "See, there are times in life when you just look. This prepares you for the times when you power shop."

He shakes his head, and mutters something about tempting fate.

I know that "just browsing" is most men's idea of torture. In fact, many men, like Dan, go to great lengths to avoid the mall. Case in point: "Dan, honey, I can see your socks through the soles of your shoes."

"No! Not the mall!" He darts for the duct tape, slathers some on the soles of his shoes, and insists they'll be good for another fifty miles.

While some might take Dan's no-decorating edict to literally mean "no decorating," to me it means "get creative." Desperate times call for desperate decorating. Desperation breeds resourcefulness. For instance, I look at that old dresser collecting dust in the garage, and think, "Hmm, maybe with a coat of paint and some new knobs . . . "

Lean times offer good opportunities to plan future improvements, even if they're months away, and to explore options, compare pricing, bargain hunt, and gather funds by winning the lotto, robbing a bank, or selling a kidney. So when purse strings do loosen a bit we can buy at a good price with certainty and not overpay on an impulse.

❇

Besides window-shopping and salvaging what you have, here are a few more ways to advance your decorating cause when your budget is zero:

- *Spring clean.* It gets your frustrations out and makes your home look, feel, and function better for nothing.
- *Build your wish list.* For each space, write down what you'd like to buy for or do to the room to make it your dream space. Be thorough and idealistic. (You can cut back later.) List items you have, items you need, and labor required. Dreaming is free.
- *Work on your vision bag.* I have a large leather tote that holds a design file folder for each room in my house and the yard. Each folder contains inspiring photos that inform the area's design direction; samples of paints, fabrics, trim, stone, tile, carpet, or flooring; sketches for built-ins, photos of fixtures, window treatments, and furniture; floor plans with measurements; names of contractors and suppliers; and estimates. On the inside cover of the file folder, I write or staple a to-do list with budget numbers. This keeps me focused and prevents aimless spending.
- *Make a budget.* Figure out what your wish list will cost, then look for ways to save. Can you do some of the labor yourself, or barter for a job? Ask what you must have and make cuts until your dream list matches your budget.
- *Set priorities.* While you wait for the spending freeze to thaw, decide what's most important.
  - *First,* do necessary home repairs to ensure your home's soundness. Don't neglect home maintenance. A sinkhole in the driveway, a leaky roof, a broken air conditioner will negatively affect your home's value. These problems will get

called out in a home inspection, and buyers will likely want you to fix them. Also many maintenance issues just get worse, and more expensive, if you postpone them.

○ **Second,** do improvements that add to your home's base value. Separate home improvement into two categories: stuff that will stay with the house when you move (landscaping, window treatments, built-in bookcases) and stuff that won't (area rugs, furniture, art, freestanding bookcases). The first will add to the home's base value, or should if you do them well. But if your home is losing value in a soft market, you may want to do more improvements in the second category. In other words, if you can't take it with you, think twice.

○ **Third,** acquire decorative items, starting with furnishings for the most public rooms and ending with the most private.

○ **Finally,** ditch all the aforementioned criteria if you find exactly what you want at a fire-sale price—like the settee I just found at a local antique fair, which was the perfect size and style and an amazing price.

Talk is cheap. And that's okay. Ideas are often free, too, or cost a lot less than their execution. What you want to avoid, both in home design and in life, is making a big change without a lot of thought. Decorating without a plan is a very good way to waste money. That's why Cheap Trick #1 is plan. Window-shop, look at decor magazines and home design TV shows, and, if necessary, pay a pro for some good design direction before you take off.

28

Cheap Trick #1:
Find Some Direction

*K*NOW WHERE YOU'RE *heading to avoid expensive mistakes.*

Start with a Plan

When faced with decorating a room from scratch, what I need most is a running start. But I'm often stymied at the starting line. I can either wing it myself or hire a pro. In the first case, the results usually land someplace between timid and terrible. But I can't afford a professional for every room. Plus, interior designers are bad for my marriage. Mention "interior designer," and my husband becomes like Steve Martin in *Father of the Bride*. He hyperventilates and seizes the bank accounts.

So when a designer I've known for years asked me to test-drive an affordable online design service he was launching, www.designerat home.com, I perked up. You pick a room you want to decorate, answer a short online questionnaire about the room's purpose and your preferences, and send in room measurements, photos, and $299. Two weeks later, you get a design scheme, like paint-by-numbers for your room. You take the job from there.

A little voice inside said: *Things too good to be true usually are, especially virtual things.*

Good designers usually charge $100 to $150 an hour. A design scheme for a room, including furniture layout, colors, and fabrics, can cost from $1,000 to $2,500—just for the plan. Designers also get a 30 percent cut of all furniture and fabrics purchased. That's great for those who can afford it, but I can't. So I agreed to give Designer at Home a try.

Although many rooms in my house could use a makeover, I pick the upstairs bonus room because it looks the most vandalized. You'll recall this was Dan's former office before he relocated to the basement. The sixteen-by-seventeen-foot room sits near my teens' bedrooms. Done right, it could be the perfect place for them to hang out in pajamas, watch television, kick back with friends, and avoid doing their home-work. At present, it's a refuge for unclaimed furniture and tacky ribbons from their horse shows and gymnastic meets. So I gathered my what-have-I-got-to-lose attitude, and sent in photos and measurements.

Two weeks later, a smart-looking package arrived containing two design boards: One had the furniture layout; the other had numbered fabric samples and photos of suggested furniture. I loved it, but needed to consult the real clients: my family.

"What about my horse ribbons?" Paige asked.

"In the plan," I said, and showed her a drawing the service included for a more attractive ribbon display.

She stuck her thumb up.

Marissa took one look at the three cubed stools to be covered in marigold, copper, and lime suede and said, "Swee-eet!"

I was off and running.

❋

You don't have to get professional help, but don't start decorating or redeco-rating a room without a plan. Here are some options.

- *Design it yourself.* Have some courage, or work with a friend who does. If you have an eye, why not? Look for inspiration in magazines, design books, from hotels or B&Bs you've stayed in, or TV makeover shows. Just make sure you factor in everything—backgrounds (wall treatment and flooring), a scaled floor plan, furnishings, and

❋ *continues*

continued

accessories (rugs, artwork, lamps), so you're not disappointed and your rooms come together.

- **Try an online service.** This is a great compromise between doing it yourself and hiring a pro. Other services may be available, but this one proved a good value; at www.designerathome.com you get a high-level design that would normally cost a lot more. (The company offers multiroom discounts.) Though I worried the company might recommend pricey furniture, the suggestions I received were from modestly priced suppliers. Plus, the service allowed me access to fabrics available only to the trade, at close to trade prices. (This is huge.) The plan incorporated some items I already had. As I had said, I wanted to keep the carpet and wood blinds, and, if possible, the pine armoire. The downside of this service is that the headaches involved in ordering and installing all these items became all mine. (That's partly why you pay designers big bucks.) Although I would rather have headaches than markups, not everyone wants the hassle.
- **In-store designers.** Many home furnishing stores have designers that will help you. I'm leery of them. While they may have a design credential (and not all do), their job is to sell you their store's merchandise. They're not interested in looking at other suppliers, and so not only are your options limited, but you also can't "shop" for deals.
- **Hire a pro.** When I've been really stuck, I have paid a designer by the hour to come over, talk through ideas, and give me a color scheme and a rough plan. I make it clear up front that I will do all the execution myself. (Not all designers will work on that basis, so ask.) That design direction can cost several hundred dollars, but for important projects, like living rooms and kitchens, that's money well spent. Then I can take my time finding deals and not paying a markup.
- **Bottom line.** I can make a room look good, but not great. That's where spending a little on professional advice and creative ideas can save a lot.

29

Cheap Trick #2:
Color Your Walls

SOME PEOPLE IN *the design world (namely, those who sell paint) will tell you that changing a room's wall color is the easiest way to make a big difference. Wrong. Painting may be a cheap way to transform a space, but it's not easy. Painting itself is tricky, and picking the right color is one of the hardest design decisions you can make. However, the time and care you spend getting the shell of your room a shade that enhances and enlivens, as opposed to a color that completely misfires, is worth the effort. Here's why choosing is hard, and how you find that perfect color.*

Find Your Neutral

"I'll just paint the walls white," my friend says, looking over a rental house she wants to freshen up.

"Which white?" I ask. I learned long ago that "just" and "white" don't belong in the same sentence.

"What do you mean *which white?*"

"Do you want a bluish white, grayish, or tannish, or do you want white with a hint of peach, taupe, sage, or cerulean?"

"Just basic white. How hard is that?"

How hard is that? I want to tell her it's überhard, harder than finding the area of the universe, the perfect black dress, legal tax evasion strategies. Finding the perfect white is harder than marriage, which,

like white, looks easy to the uninitiated, when it's in fact a complicated amalgam and a foundation for all that follows.

Last time I wanted to refresh a room with a coat of white paint, I
wound up with a five-inch stack of paint chips, and intestinal problems. The choice involved six trips to the paint store, eight quarts of
test paint and a pint of Pepto-Bismol, four false starts, and three calls
to my mother.

"Why are you making this so hard?" I remember Dan asking. "It's
just white."

"What do you mean *just white*? It's our neutral! The background for
everything! This is how God felt when choosing the sky and earth."

"Could you be overthinking this?"

"Thank you, Mr. Black-and-White, but everything hinges on the
subtle hue in this undertone, my future carpet, sofa, dishes, wardrobe,
lipstick, car, even my mood."

"Working with whites is tricky," agrees color maven Leatrice Eiseman, author of *More Alive with Color* (Capital Books) and executive
director of the Pantone Color Institute. If it were so simple, why
would Ralph Lauren Home offer sixty shades of interior paint colors in
its "Perfect Whites" collection? Eiseman notes that well-done homes
usually have a great neutral wall color, often a shade of white, ivory,
taupe, beige, gray, or khaki. The right background color doesn't shout
but gives a home a sure hand and pulls it together. The wrong color
makes everything in the place argue. The neutral is good for transi-
tional spaces, like entries and hallways, and rooms that open onto one
another. But it shouldn't prevent you from adding punch colors in specific rooms, like bedrooms, powder rooms, and offices. However, even
these punch colors need to get along with your neutral.

*Once you've figured out your neutral, add some punchy color in other
rooms. This choice is tricky, too: Where a soft color whispers "wrong," bold
colors shout. Choose with caution, and beware of marketing color ploys.*

✳

To simplify the process of finding the right neutral, I asked Eiseman to share the most common white color crimes, and her best advice.

- *Pick a color you look good in.* Depending on your personal coloring, Eiseman says, you will feel more at home in a shade of white you wear well. People with platinum hair, blue eyes, and fair skin, or, conversely, blue-black hair and very dark eyes, look best in a pure white. Those who have warm brown or reddish hair, warmer skin tones, and brown or amber eyes look great in creamy-warm white. People who aren't clearly one or the other do well in off-white; that is, a white that's not creamy but has a dollop of some other color in it. Don't pick a white with undertones that don't suit you, then build on it.
- *Go with what you have.* If you have a sofa or carpet you plan to keep, pick paint with an undertone that goes with those. Changing paint is cheaper than replacing the carpet or sofa.
- *When determining an undertone,* hold the color next to pure white, and the undertone—often taupe, ivory, peach, gray, or sand—will jump out. In real estate, the mantra is "location, location, location"; in selecting a color, the key is "context, context, context," says Eiseman. "The color isn't as important as what it's next to." When in doubt, choose a "dirty" white, "a white with a teeny bit of muddiness."
- *Don't put two whites next to each other that don't have the same undertone.* Dark and light shades that have the same undertone work well together, but if the carpet has a mushroom undertone and the walls are stark bluish white, both will suffer. If you're stuck with two mismatched whites, you can make them work. For instance, if your kitchen has all white appliances and cream tile, pull the two fields together by getting a window treatment or wallpaper that has both cream and white in the mix. Then add an accent color like Chinese red or ocean blue.
- *Balance warm and cool colors.* Every room should have one predominant color scheme that's warm or cool. Then you should deliberately pull color in from the other side. For instance, in a room that has deep gold and burgundy furnishings, pale gold walls look nice, and green plants will add a cool balance. Similarly, if you have pale blue walls and a light blue sofa, add peach pillows to warm the palette.
- *Don't chop up a small house with different wall colors.* If you can see into several rooms from one vantage point, paint all the walls the same neutral. It will make the home flow and feel larger. However, painting a room that is set off a different color can add a nice element of surprise.

What Color Are the Emperor's Clothes?

Quick! What color is surreal? Or real? What color is nature, or nurture? And optimism? If you don't know, paint companies will be happy to tell you, because those were the *in* colors for 2009.

Or so they wanted you to think.

Sometime after paint companies started calling rust "robust" and light blue "limerick," they started cooking up color stories for every new year to rev paint sales. Here's how it works: Once a year paint marketing teams sit locked in a room hooked to IVs of caffeine. Their task is to come up with language that is at once edgy and vapid, then bridge that to a message that prompts consumers to buy paint. Consider past themes: organic comfort, modern tranquillity, and reactive. If these color descriptions leave you wondering, that's the point.

One prominent paint company's color theme for 2009 was "Surreal/ Real." The concept aimed to "convey two divergent yet equally compelling directions of home décor," said the company's press release. "The four Surreal/Real color palettes let consumers choose—fantastical or rational—creating a unique and personalized color story for each and every home."

Uh, could you clarify that?

"Picture someone standing with her two feet planted on the ground and her head in the clouds—living, in a sense, between earth and sky. That's what today's experience is all about—the duality and the dynamism."

Right. Got it. And what does this have to do with color?

Another paint manufacturer's description of its upcoming color trends was also clear as squid ink. For the same year, they proclaimed their trend colors "draw on inspiration from both nature and nurture. Key drivers for this year's color choices include aspirations that create a comfortable and tranquil home environment, coupled with a return to authentic and sustainable materials."

Huh? What color is authentic and sustainable? Anyone? And how is this to help me decide what color to paint my kitchen?

And, finally, a third leading paint company boldly declared the color of optimism: It's yellow. But not any yellow, St. Elmo's Fire yellow. The company's marketing rationale: "We're headed for transition, and this zesty citron yellow conveys a sense of optimism about what lies ahead."

Whew! I feel better about my stock portfolio already.

Now, I don't mean to sound snarky. I'm a color junky. I could spend all day flipping through a Pantone color book. I enjoy watching colors cycle in and out of vogue, and appreciate paint's ability to transform a room. But does anyone else think that paint companies might be trying a little too hard? I expect to be confused when someone explains the human genome project. But why make choosing color more complicated than Proust?

❋

I ran this color confusion by Sonu Mathew, interior designer and senior manager of color and design for Benjamin Moore. With a few broad brushstrokes, she offered some insights into the world of color marketing. Here's how we can make sense of the nonsense, and choose well for our own homes:

- **Know the game.** Then get in it. Paint manufacturers, as well as makers of other interior design products, car manufacturers, and those in the fashion industry, all look to color forecasters to see where color trends might head. The forecasting groups plant seeds for color trends two years ahead. Manufacturers then interpret the forecasts for their products and customers.
- **Isn't that manipulative?** Sort of. Sure, paint companies are trying to sell paint. One way to do that is to make certain colors seem hot and others feel dated. But we benefit, too. Consumers want to change up the color around them because the renewal feels uplifting.
- **Start with what you love.** Though it's nice to find a color that expresses your personal style and is also current, if you don't love a color, it doesn't matter what the forecasts say. Her advice: Find something in your home—a piece of art, a handpainted heirloom chest, a quilt—to draw color inspiration from. That passion will last longer than any trend.

❋ *continues*

continued

- ***If you do use a color that a paint company is promoting,*** don't worry that it will soon be passé, assures Mathew. Color evolves. The yellow that's in today will change only slightly in tone over the next few years.
- ***Combinations count.*** Color depends on context. Color pairing matters as much as individual color. Golden yellow with chestnut brown can look out, while citrus yellow with graphite gray can look in.
- ***Pick your palette.*** Consider these three main palettes when deciding the mood you want: Monochromatic schemes use similar shades of the same color, and are the most restful. Contrasting schemes place light next to dark and add energy to a space. (Think bumblebee.) Analogous color schemes incorporate two colors next to each other on the color wheel, like blues and purples, and are the most comfortable to live with.
- ***You decide what's in style.*** "We're just here to spark ideas," says Mathew. "How you create your environment is still in your control." Meanwhile, if the paint companies have gotten you thinking about color, they've done their job.

Okay, so we've mastered soft and bold colors. We've graduated from Beginning to Intermediate Paint Color class. Ready for triple-black difficulty? Faux finish. You can master this. And it's fun. I swear.

Conquering the Fear of Faux

"You want to see my what?" I ask the artist, not sure I'd heard right.

"Your closet."

"What does my closet have to do with my dining room?"

"It tells me what colors you're comfortable in."

Jade Wieland, decorative artist and owner of the Stencil & Faux Shoppe, in Denver, has come by to talk about jazzing up my dining room walls. As we head upstairs, all I can think is: What will Dan say when he hears about this? He's never let me forget about the dog psychologist I hired years ago, or the crystal I hung in the kitchen to attract more chi. Now I have a wall artist in my closet.

"Just what I expected," Jade says, spinning around my walk-in.

"How so?"

"Look here." She grabs a handful of sleeves. "Every color you wear is in your home: khaki, brown, black, cream, and punches of warm red."

Okay, so that's eerie.

Actually, Jade had won me over two days before when I visited her studio. There I stood surrounded by sample boards of wall treatments she'd invented. On some, raised plaster created three-dimensional relief. On others, matte and sheen painted patterns alternated to create a tone-on-tone wallpaper effect. Some samples had the pattern recessed into Venetian plaster, like embossing. My prior notions of faux finishing suddenly seemed like finger painting compared to the Sistine Chapel.

She pointed out a fleur-de-lis wall stencil. "Here we just let the background color show through three layers of topcoat."

Just! In home design and life, I'm suspicious of any sentence with the word *just*. Like in yoga class: Now, just lift your ankle over your head and rest it gently on the back of your neck.

"Do you realize," I say, "how hard this is for the rest of us? Picking a background color alone can take three weeks. Then you have to pick a pattern and two or three topcoat colors. Talk about glazed over."

"It's fun," she says.

Fun, like a traffic ticket. Fortunately, decorative wall artists like Jade are at home among decisions that would pull the rest of us under like a riptide.

Day One

Jade arrives in her van and unloads stacks of stencils, cases of paint, and buckets of supplies. As we collaborate in the dining room, really three bland walls surrounding a big table, she sets her stencil stacks on the table and says, "Pick."

Anyone who still thinks that stencils come only in cliché patterns of cows and grape clusters needs to take another look. I'm overwhelmed with choice, but eventually find my opinion. I rule out anything that has urns, too Grecian. I want nothing too formal (not my house), or that looks like a coat of arms (too conceited), or too literal (no silhouettes of tulips or violins), or that has vegetation you wouldn't find growing nearby, so no palm fronds because I live in Colorado. I settle on a fleur-de-lis motif, and an all-over botanical pattern. She approves. I'm mentally exhausted, and we're just starting.

Next we have to decide application and colors. My gray matter feels like pretzel dough. Should this pattern go over or under the chair rail? How far apart? Two-tone, three-tone, which tone? I steady myself on the edge of the table and resist the urge to open a can of paint and sniff deeply. We agree to paint the wall below the chair rail deep toffee, and apply the botanical pattern over that. Above the rail we'll run the fleur-de-lis stencil. We'll coat the walls in metallic-tinged glaze, and put a medallion stencil on the ceiling. Whew!

After Jade leaves, my friend and fellow decorating addict Susan arrives to help paint. My family rolls in and sees the commotion for what it is: a design invasion that means Mom's not making dinner. Dan runs out and brings home Chinese food. As Susan rolls, I brush. We drink wine and talk into the wee hours, dissecting the marriages of everyone we know. Life is good.

Day Two

Jade arrives and announces with confidence, "You're going to do everything!" Gulp. We map walls to determine where stencils go. This requires division and almost does me in. We start painting the motif above the chair rail. I fall so in love with the process, I forget time, and any obligations I have or ever had. All that matters is where to put this dab of metallic green. Susan comes over and paints an accent wall. We yak about what a headache teenagers are. The neglected dogs forage in the trash for the leftover Chinese food. Life just gets better.

Day Three

I'm wearing the same clothes for the third day running—one of Dan's frayed dress shirts over old exercise leggings. We move south of the chair rail. We paint the all-over stencil pattern, incorporating desert sand, raw sienna, and burnt umber. Jade teaches me how to blend colors this side of making mud. We consume coffee by the pot. That night, as Susan and I paint, we start talking about our families, but since I can't remember if I have one, we talk about where we'd love to travel. Life is perfect.

Day Four

A warrant is out for my arrest. My family has charged me with negligence. They allege that in the past four days there have been no cooked meals, no homework editing, no chauffeur services, and the house has gone to heck. They're right. Tarps and old newspapers cover the floor. An obstacle course of paint jars, rollers, brushes, and Power Bar wrappers clutters every surface. Furniture lies in disarray. Lamps burn without shades.

I'm having a blast.

Day Five

After five ten-hour days together, Jade is wishing she weren't stuck with me. We're closer than Siamese twins, have shared every grab-and-go meal, played ceiling Twister—one person paints, the other holds the stencil—atop a ten-foot ladder, and have become so familiar we've stopped apologizing for letting a bad word slip when a stencil doesn't behave. I'm having a dinner party in two days, and we still need metallic glaze over every surface. Though I've been holding back, I finally blurt, "Will we finish in time for my party?"

She looks down at the tray full of faux paints in her hand, which she surely wants to press over my mouth.

Day Seven

Twelve guests are due that evening for a sit-down dinner. My dining room is a shambles. Furniture's shoved out. Drapes are down. An extension ladder is up, and Jade and I are putting a coat of caramel glaze on the walls and ceiling. We're at the faux finish line, and I'm in a tizz.

Meanwhile, my family—as payback for the neglect—is finding perverse joy in the corner I've painted myself into.

"Look at this place!" I say.

"Watch out," Paige warns Dan and Marissa. "Mom's in one of her states."

"Can't any of you offer a shred of sympathy?" I beg.

The dogs whine on cue.

"At home with Marni Jameson," scoffs Paige, rubbing in the obvious burn that, because I'm a home design columnist, all my home projects should go swimmingly.

I flash back to advice I've dished in past columns: "When hosting a dinner party, do all the preparation you can, including setting the table, the night before." Ha, ha, ha.

I grab a faux brush and set to work. Jade instructs me to relax and apply glaze in loose Zen-like circles. As I work, I start doing mental math: If we finish painting in thirty minutes, then I'll need one hour to rehang drapes and put furniture back, another hour to set the table, prepare the centerpiece, stage the house, and ice the champagne. That leaves two hours to prepare food, take a shower, do my nails, change outfits three times, and . . . I'm hyperventilating. Jade sees I'm rubbing my paintbrush so vigorously in one place I'm wearing a hole in the drywall. "I'll take it from here, Marni," she says, relieving me of my brush.

I disappear into the kitchen and try to forget the state of my dining room. An hour later, Jade comes in and takes my hand. "Close your eyes," she says, and leads me to the room. "Now open."

I scream, a good scream, a having-your-raffle-number-called scream. The long days spent painting, fretting, stenciling, scarfing fast food off newspaper, plastering, ignoring my family, and faux finishing have converged—beautifully.

As guests arrive, I take their coats, hand them a glass of champagne, and wait for them to notice the dining room. They don't. They head to the kitchen toward the hors d'oeuvres. I've accepted that no one will notice. But, as we gather around the table, one astute guest observes, "I love your walls. Did you change them?"

I resist the urge to kiss her, and instead wave my hand dismissively. "Oh, you mean the paint job? We did that a while ago." Other guests look the room over and comment favorably on the faux stenciled ceiling and faux-finished walls. I continue to feign nonchalance, but pride blossoms inside me like a firework. Dan shakes his head. I raise my glass: "Cheers, everyone. May all your house dreams come true."

❊

Picking a decorative wall treatment is paralyzing for several reasons: First, faux finishing can look awful, way worse than plain paint. (Those cheesy sponge jobs!) Second, picking several colors and a pattern at once is downright daunting. Finally, hiring a faux finisher is expensive. But with the right guidance, the results can be fabulous. If you learn how, it will cost you only time and materials. Here, says Jade Wieland, are some ways you can take the fear out of faux:

- *Know where to apply it.* Decorative techniques such as stenciling, faux, relief, and plaster adornments can enliven walls, ceilings, and floors, and add artistic value. Most people embellish dining rooms and powder rooms first. Other popular areas include over doorways or arches, around ceiling edges where crown molding would go, around light fixtures, and above chair rails.
- *Fit your design style.* Faux finishing works in any home. Just be sure the technique suits the architecture: A mottled antique application works in Old World homes, and linear or geometric treatments go well in contemporary spaces. Don't forget ceilings.
- *Consider all the elements.* Pattern and color are the obvious tools in the faux art box, but texture and sheen also matter. Using the same overall color but varying the sheen (matte with shiny) and texture (trowel techniques) can create some wonderfully sophisticated looks.
- *Mix it up.* Faux color washes can go on walls alone or over decorative effects, like stencils or plaster details.
- *These aren't your grandmother's stencils.* When many people think of stenciling, they picture rows of ducks or vines of ivy. If you look beyond the local craft store, and seek professional artists or higher-end vendors, you will find upscale, unusual patterns.

❊ *continues*

continued

- **Pick pattern first.** When selecting a patterned wall design, pick pattern before color. Most people pick the color first, but that's backward. Can't decide on a color? Look in your closet.
- **Practice your technique.** Success depends as much on what you put on the walls as how. Start with a good base coat of paint. Then choose either a colored glaze, a scumble (another color-wash product), or a metallic sheen. Buy professional grade products, available through faux-finish stores. Better products have more open time (the time you can smear the paint around before it sets), making application easier. If mixing your own glaze or scumble, use one part paint to four to six parts finish, or get a premixed product. Test combinations on small boards, then on an inconspicuous part of the wall to be sure chemistry works.
- **Play with tools.** Depending on the texture you want, you can apply finish with rags, cheesecloth, linen, feather dusters, sponges, chamois, paper towels, or other household items. At my house, Jade applied glaze with a brush called a Neon Leon, a round, soft brush, the size of a hamburger bun, with two-inch bristles. She rolled on the premixed glaze with a four-inch roller in a loose zigzag pattern, then brushed over it, rubbing in circles to create a mottled effect.
- **Hire or learn from a pro.** Before you start slapping up a faux finish, consider hiring a pro, or at least learning from one. Paint stores often promise that anyone can apply faux finishes easily. True, but nothing screams amateur louder than a bad faux job.
- **To find a decorative artist near you,** contact the International Decorative Artisans League at www.decorativeartisans.org. Go to the member gallery, and search by state. Only members who have proper training in the field and who are in good standing can belong.
- **Warning:** Once you faux one room, neighboring rooms can look drab by comparison. After my dining room had its makeover, my entryway looked bleak.

30

Cheap Trick #3:
Become a Glue-Gun Decorator

As a favor *to society, I don't own a sewing machine. To compensate,
however, I am a glue-gun sharpshooter. Armed with a glue gun, I turn into a
domestic superhero. I can make drapes, stick trim on pillows and lampshades,
attach fringe to upholstered chairs and table skirts, reattach peeling wallpaper,
add glam to ceilings and picture frames, doll up plain window shades, cement
centerpieces to windy outdoor tables, create dried flower arrangements, make
napkin rings out of fabric-covered cardboard, and upholster walls. Beyond
home decor, I can also use a glue gun to put a bow on my sandals or the dog's
head, fix a hem, and possibly attach false eyelashes, though I've never tried.*

Make No-Sew Drapes

After I gave my dining room walls a faux-finish face-lift, my adjoining
entryway suffered by comparison. The entry's plain walls and un-
adorned doorway didn't look so bad before, when the dining room was
plain, too. They went together in that ordinary, nothing-done way.
But now that the dining room looked better, the entry looked worse.
The contrast reminded me of those Las Vegas cocktail waitresses with
the sixty-five-year-old faces and the twenty-five-year-old hair. Yikes!

Once again, one of my decorating projects detonated another.

I couldn't leave my entry like this. It needed warmth, texture, and
something to balance the visual weight of the dining room. Now!

Whatever the design solution, it needed to be fast and cheap. Some mailers I'd received from fabric stores having big sales got me scheming. If I could score some great on-sale fabric, I could make no-sew drape panels to hang on either side of the double front door. That would add texture, drama, color, and visual weight—and quick. Problem solved!

I ran the idea by Dan.

"Can't you take a break from decorating?" he asked.

I didn't bother to explain why that was irrelevant. Instead, I said, "But the entryway looks so bare now."

"It looks fine. It's always looked fine."

"It's cold and needs drapes!"

"It's a door, not a window."

"Drapes aren't just for windows, silly. And I can make them with my glue gun."

"You're going to glue gun the entryway drapes?"

"It will be cheaper than buying custom or ready-made drapes. You watch."

"It sounds tacky."

"Desperate times call for desperate decorating."

"Why do we need drapes at all?"

And another irrelevant male question went unanswered.

I'd made glue-gun drapes before for our guest room out of toile-printed cotton sheets. For the entry, I wanted statelier fabrics, tapestry and silk. Though the stakes were higher, my budget was lower than ever. I hit the fabric store sales. Right off I scored three yards of a discontinued embroidered silk remnant marked down from $57 a yard to $14 at Calico Corners. That wouldn't be enough for two panels, but I'd use it somehow as an accent. I found my lead fabric, a paisley tapestry, at half price at Jo-Ann's. Trim and drape hardware were also 50 percent off.

Because the pecan drape hardware looked too ordinary, I faux painted the wood rods and brackets with bronze and black acrylic paint. (See next chapter for more ways to customize your home's hardware.) While those dried, I fired up the glue gun, rolled out the tapestry

If you, too, want to create Depression-era drapes, all you need is fabric, some trim, a glue gun, and some courage. Keep these pointers in mind:

- *Be cheap.* Paying full price for fabric is against my religion. Wait for the sales. If you shop sales, making your own drapes will be cheaper than off-the-shelf drapes or hiring a seamstress. Here's what mine cost:

Main fabric (7 yards at $19 per yard)	$133*
Accent fabric (3-yard remnant)	$ 42
Cord trim	$ 44
Rods and brackets	$ 95
New 60-watt glue gun	$ 20
Total	$334

  *Of course, less fancy fabric would be even cheaper.

- *Make it custom.* Think of ways to customize off-the-shelf home decor products. For instance, the rods and brackets I found on sale came in pecan and black. I bought the pecan, and, using a small brush, gave the wood an Old World metallic finish by swirling on a blend of espresso metallic and black acrylic paint (available in two-ounce bottles for a couple dollars apiece from craft supply stores), while letting some of the original wood color show through.
- *Follow the rule of three.* An interior designer I respect taught me that great drapes have three elements—main fabric, accent fabric, and trim. Mixing materials not only lets you pull in a variety of colors from your home but also ensures no one else will have your drapes.

fabric, and cut panels a foot longer than my finished length. I turned the selvaged sides in one inch, ironed them and hot glued the edges down. I turned the top down six inches and glued in a rod sleeve. Once the panels were up, I glued cord trim down the inner drape edge, then chalked where I wanted the hem right at the floor line. I pulled up the ironing board, and, with the panels still hanging, pressed in the hem and sealed it with hot glue. For the crowning touch, I cut the silk remnant in half lengthwise, and fashioned a swag over the twelve-foot rod, which I mounted over the front doors. Ta-da!

Pleased with myself, I dragged Dan over. "What do you think?" I asked, waving my hand at the drapes like Carol Merrill used to on *Let's Make a Deal.*

"They're nice, I guess," he said. "But I'm still not sure why we needed them," a statement that further proves why the world needs women, particularly resourceful women.

Quick curtains and drapes aren't the only wonders you can work with a glue gun, which really is my favorite decorating toy. Here are more sticky ways to add custom touches to your home for not much money.

With a Glue Gun, You, Too, Can Be a Domestic Superhero

The gun is on the table. It's hot and smoldering. People in my house are anxious, but know better than to stand between me and my glue gun. I pull the trigger and shoot. At the moment my target is a peanut butter and jelly sandwich for Marissa. I guess, if your mother ever starts to make you a peanut butter and jelly sandwich and plugs in a glue gun, you have reason to be nervous.

The gun-sandwich incident started when Marissa mentioned she was invited to a Halloween costume party. The prize for best costume was an iPod Nano.

"Holy smokes!" I said. "When I was a kid, the best-costume prize was a bag of candy corn."

She rolled her eyes to let me know that was before the dinosaurs, then said, "I think I'll be a witch."

"Witches don't win costume contests," I said, getting, okay, a little competitive. "People who win costume contests come as a peanut butter and jelly sandwich."

"That's what I'll be!" she exclaimed.

Suddenly, the witch costume sounded pretty good, but thanks to me and my fat mouth, the black cat was out of the trick-or-treat bag.

I have a long way to go to become Glue Gun Queen. That title goes to Marian McEvoy, author of *Glue Gun Décor* (Harry N. Abrams

Books). I once spent a day with McEvoy, for a story I was writing. At the time she was the editor of *Elle Décor*, and before that of *House Beautiful*. We spent part of the day at her chic New York City apartment, which she'd decorated in red, black, and white. The really memorable part was that she'd covered every wall with a solid crust of white seashells. She'd glue gunned the shells on herself. As we talked, we'd occasionally hear a small clack, like the sinking sound your earring makes when it hits the drain, only these were shells plinking on her wood floor.

"That's why I have a glue gun going in every room at all times," she said, as if that were the most normal thing in the world. Now I understand.

Costume-party day, I zoom to the craft store for two thirty-inch square slices of foam, grape-purple and peanut-brown tissue, tan felt (for crust), and ribbon to tie the sandwich sign around Marissa's neck. Back home, I aim and shoot. My daughter, now a brown belt in glue gun, assists.

"Is this going to hold?" she asks.

"Honey, what do you think holds this house together?"

She tries on the sandwich.

"Hot dang!" I say, reveling in the instant satisfaction glue guns can bring.

Suddenly, Marissa gets a horrified look: "You're not going to write about this, are you?"

I give a crafty smile. "Not if you give me the iPod."

She won the contest. She kept the iPod.

So here's the story.

Beyond making no-sew costumes, here are some more home decorating glue-gun ideas and tips from Marian McEvoy:

- *Add imagination.* Use a glue gun to embellish walls, ceilings, furniture, frames, window coverings, lampshades, pillows, upholstery, flowerpots, and more with fabric, trim, appliqués, shells, and leaves.
- *Be tailored, not tacky.* Glue-gunned stuff can look cheesy. To avoid looking like a glue-gun amateur, think, plan, cut precisely, and glue with care.
- *Use cool tools with hot glue.* Get a glue gun that lets you change nozzles, glue flow, and temperature. Use professional stainless scissors, sharp manicure scissors, and razor blades to make clean cuts. McEvoy swears by Aleene's Stop Fraying to finish fabric edges. A soft toothbrush and tweezers can whisk away the inevitable spiderweb strands and excess glue.
- *Rough beats slick.* The best materials to glue onto are a little porous or rough. Mirrors and metal don't work well. Thick fabrics (velvet) work better than thin (sheer). Surfaces have to be clean.
- *Find steals.* Rummage through fabric store remnant bins, eBay, flea markets, and garage sales for unique ribbons, trim, and crewel fabrics. Turn to nature for pebbles, feathers, shells, pine cones, seeds, and leaves.
- *Wash and wear.* For clothes, curtains, or bedding, use washable glue sticks for fabric, available at most well-stocked craft stores.
- *Strike while it's hot.* Work in small sections because glue hardens in a few seconds. If glue dries too fast or lands where it shouldn't, let it cool completely, then peel it off.
- *Still think it's tacky?* Check out the images at www.chriskendall.net. Look under "Portfolio," then "Glue Gun Décor."

31

Cheap Trick #4:
Bring on the Bling

Hot glue won't work for every surface. For instance, it doesn't hold well on slick surfaces, like mirrors or ceramic tiles, or on areas that get a lot of heat or steam (light fixtures and bathrooms). Sometimes it won't defy gravity, so may not work for tacking decor on ceilings. For those situations, I like Liquid Nails. It's stronger, more permanent, and, like its makers say, you have to take the house apart before you break the bond. Use with care, and have fun.

Ceiling Jewelry

"What is she doing?" Dan pulls me aside in the kitchen and sounds panicked.

"Shhh! She'll hear you," I scold, then, to explain why the lanky ponytailed woman is atop a ladder in our dining room, whisper, "She's embellishing."

"She's gluing cheap jewelry on our ceiling."

"It will look good. You'll see."

The ceiling jewelry was my friend Susan's idea. I wanted to punch up the faux stencil I'd painted on my dining room ceiling around the light fixture. Though the stencil was a big improvement over the nothing there before, it needed oomph. Susan agreed and called over fine artist Liza Whitaker.

"Is she a gypsy?" Dan asks.

"No, she's an artist."

Liza had resurrected an underwhelming hanging light fixture in one of Susan's bathrooms. Talk about needing oomph. Until Liza worked her magic, the fixture looked like someone pinned a brooch to the ceiling. She painted a gem-encrusted design around where the fixture attached. The design echoes the fixture's lines; the fake gems glimmer when the light turns on, and the fixture looks twice as large.

I try selling this concept to Dan. No luck. Like a lot of guys, Dan doesn't get the power of bling. He's a wedding band and a wristwatch kind of guy, and would never wear neck chains or earrings, for which I'm grateful. But I love bling for me, and for my home.

Before Liza started embellishing, she, Susan, and I huddled in my recently faux-finished dining room, staring at the newly stenciled ceiling like umpires gauging rain clouds, and agreed. The ceiling stencil needed more mass, more texture, more dimension, more hubba hubba. Liza and I spent the next thirty minutes rummaging through a box of faux jewels, brass baubles, and polished glass stones, as if fishing for the best jelly beans. We laid our favorites on the table in patterns, then moved them around like chess pieces. Then she set to work affixing gems and stones along strategic points of the stencil using Clear Liquid Nails.

Every time I checked on her I squealed. And Dan groaned.

"We can get them off, right?" Dan asked. I didn't have the heart to tell him no.

My daughters cycled through, and I slipped them each a five to tell their dad how awesome they thought the ceiling was looking. Meanwhile, I kept trying to bring him along. "Just like the perfect necklace or earrings can make an outfit, house jewelry can make a room. Every room needs some bling."

Liza climbs down from her ladder. "Well?" she asks, looking at us.

"I love it," I say, rising up and down on my toes.

Because Dan has missed his cue, I elbow him hard. "Oh," he gasps. "Nice! It looks nice." I assure her we love it and help her pack up. The sun goes down. The light goes on. And the ceiling looks like fairies live there.

"See!" I say. "It's like the room has a tiara."

"That's just how I saw it," Dan says, then, after a pause, confesses, "I guess it is pretty cool."

A basic interior design principle says every room should have something shiny and something dull—a suede pillow and a bejeweled picture frame, a velvet chair and a crystal vase. Done well, adding house bling is an inexpensive, fun way to add whimsy and sparkle. Here are some ways Liza Whitaker suggests using Liquid Nails to add bling to your home:

Where

- *Put polished stones,* shells, or faux gems around ceiling fixtures or wall sconces.
- *Border* a plain mirror or fireplace. Consider first painting a border around the mirror or fireplace with metallic paint, then stick on embellishments.
- *Glam up* a boring glass light fixture, or a tile or stone backsplash. Instead of tearing out a boring backsplash, try sticking faux gems, stones, or one-by-one-inch square tiles to it. Hot glue works on lamp shades, but to add gems or sparkly trim to glass pendant lamps use Clear Liquid Nails, because hot glue will get soft and melt.

How

- *Before sticking,* lay your pattern out on a table or large piece of newspaper to create your mosaic.
- *Test your pattern* by tacking it up temporarily with hot glue. Once you're sure, peel off the glue and reapply pieces with Clear Liquid Nails or Clear Small Projects Adhesive. Be sure you like it, because then it's permanent.
- *Good to know.* If you use Clear Liquid Nails, or Clear Small Projects Adhesive, neither heat from lightbulbs nor steam from showers will affect it. Just be sure to let it dry overnight before turning on the light or the water.
- *To embellish a flat surface,* select stones, crystals, or beads with one flat side.
- *Find embellishments* at bead stores, craft supply stores, and even flea markets, where you can score old jewelry to disassemble.
- *Caution:* Just as with costume jewelry, when adding house jewelry consider the style of the room, color, scale, and context. Don't overdo. There's a fine design line between charming and cheap.

32

Cheap Trick #5:
Customize Hardware

*T*HIS CHEAP CHANGE *is truly easy, fast, and so basic it's often over-looked. It's your home's hardware, which is really a home's jewelry. Door handles, knobs, drapery rods, faucets—anything with a metal finish—add bling to your home. Changing them, or just painting them, can take a space from boring to brilliant.*

Hob-Knobbing with the Knob Snob

Don't blame me if after reading this, you, too, become a knob snob. Before I discovered the world of knob options, I was fine with my cabinet knobs. Like good men, they worked when I needed them to, and didn't call attention to themselves. Then I spent a day with Knob Queen Andrea Ridout, and suddenly my knobs really bugged me.

Andrea hosts a home improvement radio show and wrote *If I Had a Hammer* (HarperCollins), a terrific book of 100 DIY home improvement projects. She also used to own a hardware store and a hardware company that made reproduction antique hardware. She knows her knobs. After being phone friends for a couple years, Andrea and I met in person when I went to Dallas on business. While most women in this situation would go to tea, we, being home improvement nerds, went knob shopping.

Until then, I was aware in only the dimmest way, the way one is aware of music in the grocery store, of the blandness of my cabinet knobs, which all look like brushed-nickel mushroom caps.

"I thought all my cabinet knobs had to match," I said, worried that intentionally making some different might be a huge design gaffe.

"Girlfriend, you are in a knob rut," Andrea said.

She was right. I'd been knoblivious. Why should the knobs in my mudroom be the same as in my master bath, and the ones in my office match those in my kitchen? I'd been living with my head stuck in a cabinet, and was on the verge of discovering a whole world beyond the mushroom-cap knob.

Andrea took me to Elliot's Hardware, a charming, old-fashioned, pre-big-box-era hardware store that acquired Andrea's old store ten years earlier. The knob section is epic.

Happier than a duck in rain, I picked out new knobs for my office (glass half spheres covered with antique silver lattice), and for my daughters' bathrooms (frosted-glass confections in ballet-slipper pink perched on brushed-nickel stems). Each of these rooms needed only four knobs. At around $80 apiece, or $32 per room, I got a lot of wham. Eventually, I'll get around to the master bath, but I can handle only so much excitement at once.

EYE CANDY FOR CABINETS

If you're looking for a little affordable change that brings a big result, updating your home's hardware could be just the fix you need. Here's what Andrea Ridout says to consider:

- *Knobs or nothing?* Before you invest, first ask whether you need knobs at all. A lot of great-looking cabinets have sleek faces and open without handles.
- *Have a motive.* Beyond the fun of adding eye candy to your cabinets, changing knobs can help you further refine your home's design style. If the same builder constructed

❁ *continues*

continued

all the homes in your neighborhood, every home around probably has the same knobs. Changing yours will make your home more custom. Plus, different knobs can make a traditional cabinet look contemporary or rustic. Knobs can also play up a room's purpose; imagine teddy-bear knobs in a nursery or film-reel knobs in a theater room.

- *Find your knob style.* See examples of contemporary, traditional, vintage, antique, whimsical, or themed knobs at www.eknobsandpulls.com.
- *Don't get carried away.* Having matching knobs throughout your house isn't wrong; many purists advocate that. But too much consistency can get boring. Conversely, you don't want a different knob on every door. Find the balance between monotony and novelty. As a rule, keep all knobs the same in one room, and in rooms that look onto each other. If you can see your mudroom from your kitchen, keep knobs the same. But if you can't see other rooms with cabinets from, say, your master bathroom, change the knobs.
- *Match the finish.* Though you don't have to stick with matched sets, faucets, towel bars, toilet paper holders, door handles, and knobs should share the same metal finish.
- *Check the protrusion.* How far knobs stick out matters, especially in small spaces where it's easy to catch a belt loop or whack your hipbone.
- *Make installation easy.* If replacing existing knobs, be sure the screw width and length of the new knob match the old one, so swapping is simple. I swapped the knobs in my office and the girls' baths myself in fewer than five minutes per room. But then I was motivated.
- *Save the original knobs,* in case the next homeowner has knob-rut issues.

33

Cheap Trick #6:
Fake It

RAQUEL WELCH, *who should know, once said sexiness is 50 percent what you've got and 50 percent what people think you've got. I think about that quote not only when buying Spanx but also when designing my home. Not the sexiness part, but the reality-versus-illusion part. How much needs to be authentic? What can be strictly a facade? A lot of home design materials now on the market are made to look like more expensive alternatives. Some are worth it.*

The Virtues of Fraud

The stone veneer in our basement bar area gives the rocky impression that the room was built back in the 1700s, when walls and arches truly were built of solid stone. In fact, these walls are fake stone cemented to plywood, a facade no deeper than a stage set, or the moral fiber of a Ferrari owner.

Years ago, I wouldn't have settled for such fraud. I was a purist. Remember the days of DINKs? Double Income No Kids? Well, that was Dan and me. Now we're Double Kids No Income, and I can't afford to be a house snob. Plus, in prior homes, I paid a lot for real stuff only to later regret not buying the good imitation.

For instance, in our first home, a 1936 California bungalow, which we rebuilt, the architect specified redwood siding. We could have bought

Masonite—a wood look-alike—for much less. Back then the cost difference was $14,000: The price for real wood was $21,000 versus $7,000 for
the imitation, which never needs painting. I insisted on the real stuff.
Although I briefly enjoyed knowing our house wasn't a pretender, in the
end—as Dan still reminds me—we didn't get any more money when we
sold the house because we sprang for the higher quality stuff. Ouch! My
purist phase ended.

In our next home, the builder installed a plain living room fireplace of white precast plaster. Eventually, we felt the fireplace needed
more character. Our choices were to tear it out and replace it, which
would be messy and expensive; live with it; or have it faux finished.
Faux finishing is when a painter so thoroughly transforms a plain surface that onlookers gasp, slap their foreheads, and immediately repent
all former drug use. I had just met an artist who could paint a car to
look like a block of Swiss cheese. We gave him a square of Emperador
marble, dark brown with ivory veins. He replicated it perfectly onto
the fireplace. A real marble fireplace would have cost $12,000. The
paint job cost $2,000.

Since trading purism for pragmatism, fakery doesn't bug me anymore. Here's my rationale: I'm never going to live in an authentic re-
stored seventeenth-century European chateau, with genuine stone
walls, solid marble fireplaces, structurally necessary exposed beams,
and an easy commute to fine department stores and good schools. So
I'd better pretend. I figure if faking it is good enough for Ms. Welch,
it's good enough for me.

Faking It in the Bedroom

When my cousin called from Chicago to tell me that he and his family
were planning a road trip, and that my Colorado house was on the
route, I did some math, and realized I was short one bed. My cousin is
a firefighter; his wife is a cardiac-care nurse. They make fabulous
houseguests because we often need both around here. They have three
children, ages two, four, and six, and an au pair. I started playing

Places to fake it: Here are some of the other areas in home design where I've given up authenticity, saved a bundle while still getting the look I wanted, and happily become a fake:

- *Fireplace logs.* I used to insist on real wood, but now I'm a gas-log girl. I do miss the smell and crackle of real wood, but I don't miss playing Cinderella when cleaning the ashes. Plus, gas logs burn cleaner so are better for the environment.
- *Wood beams.* Some purists will say don't put a beam in a house unless it's structural. Anything else is an affectation. Phooey. I side with many designers who put fake beams in ceilings to cast a rustic or Old World spell. Many of these unnecessary beams masquerade as solid timbers, but are in fact hollow boxes clad with wood veneers.
- *Water features.* Years ago I turned my nose up at yards that featured man-made creeks and falls. "Those people should move to a theme park," I'd smirk. If it didn't spring from nature, I wanted no part of it. Well, today, I have a man-made water feature in my backyard. I love to sit on the deck, listen to the water burble over the rocks, and see the goldfish. Artifice? Who cares?
- *Flowers.* When I was growing up, Mom kept a sorry plastic African violet plant in our entryway. That put me off fake foliage for years. But, like me, artificial flowers have come a long way. And while nothing beats fresh flowers, today my home has several convincing silk plants and flower arrangements, which don't die, don't leave water rings, and ask only that I dust them now and then.
- *Leather and suede.* When a designer first showed me a fabric that looked exactly like suede, but wasn't, then squirted it with household cleaner to remove a food stain, I was sold. Now I have three large faux-suede pillows in my family room, and I no longer yell, "Bomb threat!" if one of my kids sits on them with a bowl of ice cream.

Who's Sleeping Where: My cousin and his wife would get the guest room. The kids could bunk in the bonus room. But the au pair?

A new bed wasn't in our budget. Still, my standards wouldn't let me just park a mattress set on the floor. I recalled an inventive headboard I'd seen on a magazine cover, a simple wood frame with fabric stretched over it. I hunted down some fun fabric and set to work. Meanwhile, I came up with more ways to fake a bed in the bedroom. Next time you think you can't afford a bed, consider these DIY headboard options.

TEN CHEAP BED TRICKS

Decide what size bed you want. Outline how wide and tall you want the headboard. It should extend about two inches on either side of the mattress. Then get creative.

1. Mount an antique door sideways.
2. Let a decorative folding screen or a bookcase be a bed's backdrop.
3. Install a fireplace mantel around the head of a twin bed. Paint the wall inside the mantel a strong accent color.
4. Get a large, stretched painting canvas. Make your own graphic with acrylic paints. Try a geometric, striped, or stenciled design.
5. Get a set of sixteen- or twenty-inch square blank stretched canvases and create a grid. Hang three squares across, or a block of six or nine stacked, edges touching, like a Rubix cube. Paint each canvas a different color.
6. Outline the headboard space with crown molding. Fill the inner space with a painted accent color, wallpaper, or fabric glued to the wall.
7. Mount a drapery rod where the wall meets the ceiling. Make the rod slightly wider than the mattress, then add finials and hang a fabulous floor-length fabric panel.
8. Make an upholstered headboard. Cut plywood (not particle board) the shape you want your headboard. Cut a piece of two-inch foam the same shape and glue it on. Wrap it with batting. Cover the surface tautly in fabric. (Choose an easy-to-clean fabric that will stand up to hair products and skin cream.) Use a staple gun to attach the fabric to the back. Mount to the wall with sturdy brackets.
9. Put an architectural ledge two-thirds up the wall. Run wallpaper from the edges of the ledge to the baseboard.
10. Create a framed fabric headboard. I bought four lengths of two-inch-by-one-inch poplar. (Be sure the wood is straight.) I had Dan build a rectangular frame, mitering the corners to create true right angles. Then I stretched upholstery-weight fabric over the frame and fastened it to the back with hot glue and a staple gun. For pizzazz, I stuck antique nail heads around the edge. Cost: $45 (wood, $13; fabric, $30; nail heads, $2). Building time: under two hours.

34

Cheap Trick #7:
Change the Backsplash

*T*HE FIRST SPACES *many people look to update are kitchens and baths. These rooms are also the most expensive to redo. If you're clever, however, you may give those rooms a fabulous face-lift by only changing the backsplash. Done well, a backsplash can be the defining accent in a kitchen or bath. If you have a boring backsplash, cutting in replacement tiles every foot or so can transform the room. Or consider changing the whole thing. Unlike flooring or counters, backsplashes are easy, and relatively affordable, to do over.*

Backsplashes for the Vertically Challenged

As I toured my friend Karen's newly purchased home, I felt I knew the home's previous owner by her kitchen design decisions: Huge pantry—she brought casseroles to neighbors in crisis and well-stocked coolers to soccer sidelines. A counter surrounded with barstools—a family woman, she doled out hearty portions of food and advice. A generic kitchen backsplash that screamed "missed opportunity" in the final stages of designing her kitchen, she caved like a half-baked cake.

Of note, the woman had put in a new kitchen before selling her house. The appliances still had the plastic on them, which delighted Karen. The antique-white cabinets and black granite counters were also new. But apparently when this woman faced her backsplash choice, she got Whatever Syndrome, a common affliction among remodelers. The vertical challenge proved too much, and she just said, "Whatever," then ran her countertop material up the wall four inches. I get that. Designing a new kitchen can feel like water-board torture.

"What faucets would you like?"

"Whatever."

"And for your backsplash?"

"Whatever."

All those decisions: floor plan, cabinetry, color schemes, fixtures, doors versus drawers, appliances, flooring, wall treatments, lighting overhead and under cabinet, counters. So when the deceptively minor backsplash decision comes up, you hit the default button: "Whatever! Just put what's on the counter up the wall."

❃

"**B**ecause it's a vertical surface, like cabinets, backsplashes are an important visual," says Cooper Smith, spokesperson for Dal-Tile in Dallas. Here's how he suggests you design one that rocks:

- *When designing,* pick decorative tiles early, when—not after—you select your counter material and cabinets; otherwise, your backsplash choices get limited.
- *When choosing accents,* don't just focus on color. Pick tiles that fit the style of your home. Contemporary choices include glass, stainless, copper, pewter, cement, and slab stone. Traditional choices include tumbled stone, colored or textured tiles, tile murals, and rustic iron. Certain porcelain, ceramic, and metallic tiles can be either. The trend is toward mixed materials.
- *Don't wait* to order decorative tiles. If you've designed your kitchen around an accent tile, buy the quantity you need right away and store it, before the tile gets discontinued or back-ordered. Standard tiles will likely be available, but specialty ones come and go.
- *Go big.* The minimum backsplash is four inches. If you can afford to run the backsplash up twelve inches, or to the bottom of upper cabinets, do so.
- *Don't worry* about your tile choice looking dated. "Tile trends move at glacial speed," says Smith.
- *Have courage.* Don't be so afraid of making a statement that you don't make any statement. Safe beats ugly. But a good custom choice trumps both.

"I'll redo that," Karen said, pointing to her new home's backsplash. I was glad to hear that. So many people have unimaginative backsplashes that are the same material as the counter. And that's too bad.

Even sadder is to see new construction torn up and replaced for lack of creative courage. But Karen knew what she had to do.

35

Cheap Trick #8:
Frame That Reflection

MOST HOMES COME *with cheap, frameless production mirrors in their bathrooms. A framed hanging mirror looks much better. However, if you have a flat production mirror, rather than yank it down, put a frame around it. It's brilliantly simple, as you'll see.*

Mirror, Mirror on the Wall — You Need a Makeover

As a home design columnist, I'm a magnet for weird stuff from PR people: the clear toilet that doubles as a fish tank, the weed-whacker-slash-golf-club that lets you pretend you're golfing while you hack crabgrass. But occasionally, I hear about something useful, like the DIY mirror framing kit. This kit could have prevented my four-year mirror drama.

Years ago an interior designer drew my attention to the utter lack of imagination reflected in plain, frameless mirrors, the kind slapped up in most production homes. Until then, I'd never really looked at my plain mirrors, just in them. So when building my current home, I haughtily told the builder he could keep his cheap mirrors. I would find my own fabulously artistic, custom-framed mirrors, thank you.

What is it they say about pride going before a face-plant?

We moved in, and not one of our home's four-and-a-half baths had a mirror.

"How am I supposed to fix my hair?" Paige whined.

"Or fix my princess crown?" Marissa fretted.

"Or shave?" Dan asked.

"Some religious orders don't allow mirrors at all," I pointed out. "Use this as a time for spiritual reflection. The wait will be worth it."

"Great, she wants us to be monks," Paige said.

"You and your standards," Dan huffed.

"Look, if a home is a mirror of the woman within, then the home's mirrors are the mirror of that mirror," I explained.

"You're way overthinking this," Dan said.

I soon found two hanging mirrors, with white painted wood frames, perfect for the girls' bathrooms, and for adjusting princess crowns. I also found two handsome antiqued wood-framed mirrors for the powder room and guest bath. But the space above the his-and-her sinks in the master bath stayed vacant. For months, Dan shaved and I applied makeup using Braille. When I finally bought two mirrors from a catalog, I soon saw they were as wrong as snow in July. The scale, frame, and shape didn't work.

"How could you shop for three months, then get it wrong?" Dan asked, a legitimate question.

Meanwhile, out in Raleigh, North Carolina, Lisa Hunting faced her own mirror crisis. She had just redone her master bath with a spa tub and custom shower, but sensed something missing. Her mirror—a large frameless ice pond—lacked pizzazz. Yanking it down seemed like an invitation to the guillotine. So she invented a frame that sticks to frameless mirrors and makes them look like hanging mirrors, and launched a company, MirrorMate. I love this woman.

Fast-forward four years. I finally got my master mirrors right. A tile mason crafted two frames over the sinks using scraps from the tumbled marble and granite already on my floors. A mirror company cut mirrors to inset. Looking back, I should have let the builder hang his flat mirrors, and ordered a size that would allow for framing space. Ah, hindsight.

But now, thanks to my mistakes, you can bypass that learning curve and make over your mirror in a weekend.

Whether you're shaving, plucking eyebrows, or seeing how big your butt is, your mirror is likely your bathroom's focal point. It should look great. Here are some inexpensive ways to enhance yours.

- *If you're building or remodeling,* don't default and just put in a plain, indistinct mirror. Either hunt down a fabulous framed mirror or install the production glass, leaving room for a border.
- *If you already have plate mirrors,* work with them. (Many people don't want to pull them off the wall because they're heavy and can be dangerous. MirrorMate offers more than thirty-five styles of frames in various finishes. Pick one, send measurements, and get a custom frame kit: precut molding, wood glue, corner wedges, and placement guides. Installation takes about twenty minutes. Costs range from $109 to $198 for an average mirror. Because frames stick right to the mirror, they work on mirrors that butt up against backsplashes, walls, and ceilings (www.mirrormate.com). Where was this company when I needed it?
- *Consider your decor.* Choose a border that coordinates with your cabinets, tile, or the room's motif. Have some fun: A bathroom with a seaside theme could incorporate layers of glued-on seashells and starfish. (See Chapter 31 on house bling.)
- *Build your own.* If you're handy, surround the mirror with wood molding. Your local lumber store will have many unfinished styles for a couple dollars a foot. For a professional look—and to cover clips and desilvering—overmount molding on the mirror. To fill the gap between the molding and the wall, find moldings that have a rabbet edge—a recess cut out. The rabbet should be as thick as the mirror, so molding covers the mirror's edge. Stain, varnish, or paint molding before mounting. Finish the underside, too, because the mirror will reflect it. Cut molding to fit the mirror, mitering corners. Attach using adhesive recommended for bonding wood on glass, such as epoxy.
- *Set in stone.* Framing the mirror with the same tile or stone you have in your bathroom can look great. Play with tile shapes to add interest, and consider adding accent tiles. Tile to the mirror's edge—not on it. Fill gaps with grout.
- *Do a height check.* Sometimes adding a frame above a backsplash raises the reflective surface too high. Look in it and see where the reflection hits you. Don't hang a mirror too high or make the border too thick. A mirror should frame you like a portrait, from the waist up.

36

Cheap Trick #9:
Make Something from Nothing

I AM A LOT *more impressed with decorating ingenuity than I am with conspicuous spending. That's a good thing, since a tight budget has caused me to look more to my cupboards and less to the stores for decor solutions. Now it's become a game.*

Use-What-You-Have Decorating

"What are you doing?" Paige asks when she finds me fiddling with a dark wood platter, a scrap of burlap, and some lemons.

"Making art from everyday stuff," I say.

"Can't you just buy decorations already made?"

"I'm trying to be one of those resourceful, creative people who turn ordinary objects into art."

"Mom, I thought you always said to go with your strengths."

"You know those homes," I say. "You walk in and admire some arrangement. Then the owner says, 'Oh, that!' and flips her hand as if shooing a fly. 'I just melted down an old beehive I found in the yard, added some hand-painted eggshells, and framed it with a worn-out bicycle tire.' It's so impressive."

"This isn't going to be like the butterfly jar, is it?" she asks, wincing.

Okay, so once, in a chic boutique, I saw this gorgeous jar containing two dried butterflies artfully perched on a willow branch. I tried to re-create this at home using a mayonnaise jar and a couple of expired butterflies I found on the grill of my car. It looked like roadkill.

"What's going on in here?" Dan asks.

"Mom's making something out of nothing," Paige says.

"Oh, she's the world champion," he says.

"Very funny," I say.

"Or how about the time you put the driftwood on the hearth?" she recalls, and the laughter begins.

"That looked artsy!"

"Is that the wood I threw in the fire and you got all upset?" Dan asks.

"Do I need to put a sign out: 'This is art, not firewood'? What do you people have against creativity?" I continue with the lemons and burlap, but I've lost focus.

Despite the lack of family support, I'm determined to imitate those irritating people I admire, the ones who make beautiful home accessories from everyday objects. I'm not giving up.

❋

For pointers, I turned to designer types across the country and asked them to submit their favorite ideas for creating home decor using stuff most of us have lying around, like husbands. I edited out any suggestions that were too difficult or too trashy. (Take beer bottles and decoupage them with your favorite gift wrap. Seriously?) Here are the ones that passed my criteria: easy, free, and original.

- *From the yard.* Use an interesting branch as a curtain rod, or hammer some nails into it and use it as a hat rack.

  Jennifer Schweikert, Burke, Virginia

- *From the bar.* Fill martini or other stemmed glasses one-third full of acrylic craft beads. Set votive or tea-light candles inside. Group an odd number of glasses on a table or buffet.

  Natalie Stemp, Washington, D.C.

- *From the pantry.* Create a kitchen tablescape by using ingredients from that evening's meal. On Italian night, get a large white platter, and set dried pasta, a fresh bell pepper, a few heads of garlic, a can of tomatoes, and a stand-up cheese grater on it.

  Diane Agricola, Cincinnati

- *From the garage.* Prop an old wooden ladder against the wall and use it to hang newspapers and magazines, or dishtowels.

  Kara Butterfield, Boston

- *From the game closet.* Create fitting art for your game room or den by hanging game boards (Monopoly, Checkers, Scrabble) to the walls. Use museum putty so they're easy to take down after game night.

  Diana Hudson Kresnye, Cleveland

- *From the crystal cabinet.* Get a crystal or ceramic cake stand, or a flat mirror. Put three pillar candles of varied heights on the stand. Surround the candles with seasonal decor—seashells, fall leaves, pine cones.

  Susan Matthews, Philadelphia

- *From here and there.* This is something I've done over the years to create seasonal centerpieces. Start by gathering three items:
  1. *Fabric.* Use a scrap, about a square yard, of material you have left from some interior project—drapes, bedding, pillows—or that old bridesmaid dress (yikes!). Think seasonal. I like humble fabrics, burlap or loose-weave linen in summer, cotton toile in spring, corduroy in fall, and velvet in winter. The scrap does not need finished edges, because you tuck them in. Scrunch up the fabric so it looks billowy, like it's tossed on, but, of course, it isn't. Don't smooth it out like a tablecloth.
  2. *Container.* Find a large wooden, glass, metallic, or ceramic bowl or platter. I prefer simple, so no hand-cut crystal or painted china. Set it on the scrunched fabric.
  3. *Seasonal accent.* Organic choices from the outdoors are my first choice. Fruit is perfect. Pears, apples, or citrus look great set artfully in your container. Here's how to turn groceries into a still life: Take the tacky little stickers off the produce. Arrange only one kind of fruit in odd numbers. Stack them a little. Vegetables, such as heads of ruffled cabbage or eggplant, can also look marvelous. Flowers, pine cones, or squash will also do, so long as the accent fits the season.

❋ *continues*

continued

Here are some seasonal combinations I like:

- *Summer:* Burlap, a distressed dark wood platter, and lemons.
- *Spring:* Lavender silk, a glass trifle bowl filled with water, and floating gerbera daisies.
- *Fall:* A paisley-printed cotton in harvest colors, a cream ceramic platter, and gourds.
- *Winter:* Burgundy velvet, a large silver bowl, and glass holiday ornaments in a single color.

The result is tactile, colorful, sensual, and easy.

37

Cheap Trick #10:
Screen It

*L*IVING BEAUTIFULLY WITH *others sometimes means resorting to camouflage or other screening tactics. Here's one of my favorite inexpensive ways to hide a mess and make a space serve double duty.*

Screens Play Dramatic Roles in Homes

Folding screens bring out the drama queen in me. This started when I was a kid. My mother, who was a school nurse, used to bring a large folding screen home from work, where she used it as a bulletin board to post health information. But I had other designs on it. When not telling kids how to brush and floss, the folding screen was mine. This was before video games, when kids had to invent their fun.

I would set up the folding screen in the living room, duck behind it, and deck myself with an odd assortment of wardrobe accessories, which usually included fishnets and a magic wand made of aluminum foil. Sometimes I would dramatically throw a scarf over the screen's top, or flail a stiletto out to the side. Then I'd emerge and perform some ditty for my awaiting audience, usually only my puzzled dog.

I still love folding screens for their powers of transformation. Only now I love how they transform rooms. As home accessories, folding screens are to decor what scarves are to fashion. Both can mask a mess (an ugly air conditioner, the laundry pile, bad hair, a saggy neck) while adding flair.

These versatile home actors add drama without hogging floor space. They can make a large room serve two purposes, living room on one side, dining area on the other. In a small space, they can stand flush against a wall and add color and dimension, while breaking up a dull expanse. I have one in my bedroom, which I snagged for $50 at an estate sale; it adds architectural interest, softens a corner, and creates a backdrop for a chair, tea table, and a tall plant.

When painted like a mural, screens can double as a freestanding painting. More strategically, they can hide a stash of toys, a storage area, a dead body, or a stain on the wall. They can create a dressing area, conceal the kitty litter, serve as a headboard, or partition off a home office.

And, of course, screens can serve as a backstage for dramatically prone children.

An often overlooked home accessory, folding screens are fun, flexible, functional, and affordable. Because they will make a statement, consider this advice when picking one out:

- *Function:* Ask what you want your screen to do. Add a decorative touch, hide toys, serve as storage, or carve out a guest room or office niche? If it's to hide stuff, be sure you can't see under or through it. If it's to block an ugly view out a window, a translucent one will do that and still let light through.
- *Size:* Measure the area you want the divider to cover, then get one at least 20 percent longer to allow for folding. You can often purchase the same style screen as a two-, three-, or four-panel divider.
- *Style:* Match your screen style to your room decor. Think of a whimsical painted mural on a playroom divider, or handsome leather covering a screen in the library. Among the many materials and styles available are wood, fabric upholstered, mirrored, Asian inspired, antique, craftsman, retro, and contemporary. Cheap trick: Get a plain one and cover it yourself.
- *Safety:* You can purchase folding screens online, but it's nice to see them first in person. Some aren't stable. You want them to pass the topple test: Nudge it. If it falls over, it could create a hazard for children and pets.
- *Make your own:* You'll need a few narrow-panel hollow-core doors, or shutter-style doors, attached with hinges. Paint as desired, and experiment with fun finishes or stencils. Here are two sites that offer inspiration and instruction: www.doityourself.com (search under "folding screen") and www.marthastewart.com (search under "stenciled lace-print folding screen").

PART * SIX

Specialty Spaces and Making Your Home Stretch

If you've ever stood in the middle of your house ready to scream, "Something's got to give!" this next section's for you. Houses do not come one size fits all. Most dynamic households need to stretch to accommodate a family's dynamic life. One day you're preparing a nursery, and the next you're childproofing the cabinets. One day you're hosting the football team, another you're starting a home-based business. Then someone needs space for an art studio or a gym—and Grandma moves in. Here's how to put elastic in your home to make room for work, pets, hobbies, exercise, guests, a growing family, and even for your soul.

38

Homes and Jeans,
They're All About Fit

Somehow I've poured myself into jeans so tight I can't cross my legs. This wasn't my idea. Paige and the saleslady in the Lucky Jeans store told me to buy jeans a size too small.

"You have to buy them too small if you want them to fit," says the saleslady. I don't tell her that sounds absurd because my daughter already thinks I'm a nerd, and is mortified enough that she and I are shopping in the same store.

"Are you sure?" I say, looking around the store for the hidden camera. "I don't want to look like one of those women who think they're a size they're not."

"She's right," Paige insists. "They'll give you a better butt."

I take that to mean they will hoist my rear end off the back of my knees, and buy them on the spot. The saleslady gives me the bag and a knowing smile. "It's all about the fit," she says.

As the pressure forces more blood to my brain, I realize what is true for jeans holds true for houses: A great house is also *all about the fit.*

With both houses and jeans, you don't just want enough room, but room in the right places. You may have enough bedrooms, but not enough storage; enough room in the waist, not enough in the derrière. When the surprise baby comes, or your divorced sister moves in with her St. Bernard, or the adult child you sent off to college comes home like a boomerang, or your mate starts snoring so loudly the shingles rattle, your home must give like good jeans.

Home stretching is Karl Champley's specialty. As host of DIY Network's *Wasted Spaces*, Champley is an expert at expanding homes without actually making their footprint bigger. "As people's lives start to snowball, they think their only alternatives are to move to a bigger house or add on," he says, "but many homes are filled with spaces to exploit."

As for getting those jeans to fit, apply petroleum jelly, hoist them on with a hydraulic pulley, do 100 deep-knee bends, and say no to the donuts.

❈

If you're busting at the seams, here are some novel ways Karl Champley suggests to find more space at home, and create better fit.

- *Explore the attic.* If your attic has a pitched roof, create storage space by installing a plywood floor and a pull-down ladder. (Don't store photos, wine, VHS tapes, or non-glass collectibles here unless the attic is insulated.) To turn the attic into living space, add insulation, drywall, and dormer windows. Lay carpet or other flooring on the plywood. (Peel-and-stick floor tiles have come a long way; stick them right on the plywood.) Install built-in cabinetry where ceilings slope low to turn angled walls into useful space. "For an investment of between $6,000 and $20,000, you can add a bedroom, game room, or office, and $60,000 to the value of your home," says Champley.
- *Drop the floor.* One of Champley's favorite projects is the underground wine room. Cut a trapdoor, about three by four feet, in the subfloor, remove a section of floor joist, and excavate a cavernous space, large enough for a ladder and cellar. (One stair system he's used activates the underground stairs as you pull open the trapdoor.) Trim the opening with low-profile molding, and the floor door with flat or recessed hardware. Add heavy-duty hinges. Run electrical for lighting under the subfloor. To keep the subterranean space dry, install a sump pump, French drains, a fan, or all three. Clad walls with treated pine, add some wine racks, and you're done. This space could also serve as a darkroom, or a place to store parents who get out of control at their kids' soccer games.

- **Exploit the kitchen.** Take advantage of every square inch, even the toe kick. The unused space beneath your cabinets usually occupies the first four to five inches above the floor, and is four inches deep. If the toe kick isn't under a sink or appliance, its faceplate probably covers open space. Build in thin drawers here to make ideal storage for platters, cutting boards, cookie trays, and place mats.
- **Create a niche.** Sink storage into the wall. Most interior walls have four to eight inches you can bust into. (Don't cut into exterior walls because they need to stay insulated.) Inset shelving, cabinets, or medicine chests as far into the wall as possible. A twelve-inch cabinet sunk six inches into the wall takes up half the floor space. If you have a two-story house and haven't finished the empty space under the stairs, you're missing a chance to create storage for sports gear or holiday decor. For easier access, put the door on the wide side rather than the narrow end.
- **Hide the guest bed.** No room for guests? Get a pull-down Murphy bed. Then build rolling bookcases to put in front of it. By day you have a book-lined study. When an overnight guest arrives, slide the bookcases apart, and pull down the bed.

Offices are standard in most homes today. Whether you use yours to pay bills, or as a control center for your growing empire, working from home doesn't always work. But here's how you can increase the odds that it will.

39

So You Want to
Work from Home—Ha!

*T*HE DAY IS young when Marissa breaks through my home office
door as if a live crocodile is on her tail and declares, "Mom! I just
found out my class is going on a rock-climbing trip, and I don't have
anything to wear!"

I recognize the thinly veiled ploy to go shopping, and say, "Last I
looked, rock climbers weren't the most fashion-forward group."

"Mom, seriously!"

"Uh, I'm trying to work here."

"You don't love me."

It's spring break. The kids are loose from school. And I'm the
world's dullest mother. Unlike every other school family, we're not jet-
ting off to Mexico, or visiting a theme park a day, because two members of this family have to work. The one trying to work from home
also has kid duty. I make my children cheese omelets, then look them
in the eyes and hold up two fingers: "Two hours," I say, "in my office,
no interruptions. If you interrupt me for even one minute, add fifteen
minutes. Clear?"

They groan.

My kids call my home office hours child abuse. Karin Abarbanel
calls them boundaries. Abarbanel is coauthor of *Birthing the Elephant*
(Ten Speed Press), a woman's guide to launching a business. Accord-

174

ing to Abarbanel, 2.5 million women start businesses each year, about two-thirds from home. Meanwhile, millions more in search of "balance" (what a joke!) have fled bona fide offices to be virtual employees at home. Men, too, are looking for ways to spend less time at the office and do more work at home.

But the women I'm familiar with, they're power multitaskers: "You bet, Mr. Dimwiddie, I'll have that report right off," one says, while putting dinner in the microwave with her feet. "Absolutely, I'll fax that proposal over in thirty minutes," another says, while applying ice to a child's chin. I'm not saying men can't do this, but show me one who can complete an Excel spreadsheet while nursing a baby.

Of course, working from home has pluses—you get the best parking spot, bad-hair days don't affect your work performance, and you can defrost chicken without giving your family salmonella—but some perceived advantages are overrated:

Fantasy: Your time will be your own.

Reality: "You may get flexible time, but you don't get more time," says Abarbanel. My first home office was in California, where, according to the rest of the country, everyone sleeps in. Someone from New York would call at 9 A.M. his time, start talking at eighty miles an hour, and wonder why I couldn't keep up.

Fantasy: You can wear more casual attire.

Reality: This happens by default because you work until 4 A.M. before crashing. The phone starts ringing at 6 A.M. Three conversations later, you hang up, and head for the coffee. A messenger comes to the door, and next thing it's 8:30. Your employees are arriving. You're still in your robe, haven't brushed your teeth, and yesterday's mascara is smudged down your face. This would never happen in a real office.

Fantasy: You have zero commute time.

Reality: True, but when you emerge from the room next door and holler to your mate, "Honey! I'm home!" the way they do in the movies, it's pretty anticlimactic. Even the dogs look at you funny.

❋

Here's what home entrepreneur expert Karin Abarbanel has to say about making working from home work better:

- *Create a dedicated space.* Don't share your work space with unrelated tasks and keep it from family traffic. This will help you—and those you live with—take your work seriously. A separate structure, like a converted guesthouse or pool house, is ideal. A dedicated room is next best. If you don't have a whole room to devote, set up a folding partition to section off your work area. Don't carve out a place in your kitchen, unless you're in the baking business.
- *Don't fall victim to image anxiety.* Design the space so you enjoy it, without over-spending on decor for appearance's sake. One entrepreneur Abarbanel interviewed, who now runs a multimillion-dollar firm, said when she worked from home, she didn't worry about what clients thought about her office. She used the local coffee shop as her conference room. Decorate slowly, as you can afford to: Once you close a big deal, reward yourself with a new office chair.
- *Even better, barter.* Trade services for office upgrades. If you're a Web site designer, build a site for a carpenter in exchange for shelving. My neighbor, a graphic designer, created promotional ads for a painter, who faux finished her office in exchange.
- *Beware of the blur between work and home life.* Domestic details—calling the plumber, picking up dry cleaning, running a gym bag to school—can devour work time. To stay focused on your paying work, establish office hours and don't let house-hold or family matters intrude. Get a separate phone line, and let personal calls go to voice mail. Once you get out of lockstep with the corporate culture, which makes you get down to business, you'll need to find your internal driver. If you don't have one, stay at the office.

(For ways to organize and set up your home office, see Chapter 10.)

Finding that sweet spot between barring kids from the house and letting them run the asylum takes a special blend of stamina, heart, and standards. While I want my home to accommodate their mess, bad taste, and general havoc attractively, when my daughter coaxed me into codecorating her bedroom, we both were tested.

40

Decorating with Kids:
You Want to Paint Your
Walls What?

"PURPLE," SAID MARISSA, when I asked what color she wanted to redo her room.

"Like a pale lavender, or a midnight plum?" I asked hopefully.

"No, bright purple." She showed me a wallpaper she'd found in a catalog. The color was so bright I had to feel my eyebrows to be sure they were still on.

"Oh, I see, something subtle." Sigh.

Marissa, who was on the cusp of becoming a teenager, first spotted the gaudy bright purple and white wallpaper in a catalog. The catalog called the color peony; I called it streetwalker.

At first, I did the mature thing. I hid the catalog. She found the wallpaper online. Then I tried stalling: "I'm not doing a thing to your room until you get rid of half your stuff." I figured that would buy time since she'd need a team of archaeologists.

The next weekend was eerily quiet. Come Sunday, I asked Dan, "Have you seen Marissa?"

"Who?"

We dashed to her room and found a mountain of trash bags outside her door. I noticed Marissa burrowing like a mole under her desk, strewing papers in her wake. I looked around: The closet, under the sink, her dresser top were clutter free and clean.

"Wow! You really want that wallpaper," I said.

"Why don't you?"

"It's just so purple." I felt myself squint.

"I'll love it forever, Mom."

I wanted to veto her plan, but thought of Randy Pausch, the Carnegie Mellon professor who died of cancer but left the world with his last lecture, which became a book full of good, life-affirming advice. "If your kids want to paint their rooms," he said, "as a favor to me, let them do it. Don't worry about resale value." Pausch decorated his boyhood room with quadratic equations.

But Marissa doesn't want to paint the periodic table of elements on her wall. She wants hot-purple print wallpaper. Worse, she wants a purple bedspread and matching stool—in crushed velvet. The only place I ever felt crushed velvet belonged was inside an electric guitar case. How can someone who shares my DNA think crushed purple velvet looks good? The more I say, "Ugh," the more she likes it. The only thing we agree on is that her room needs a redo. The bedspread has worn out, and she's outgrown the small French florals and doll shelves. She's moved on to posters of gymnasts at Cirque du Soleil, which she hopes to be in one day. (We'll have the career talk later.)

"I get that wanting to redo your room is a healthy developmental step," I say.

"Oh, please, not the development talk."

"I mean, kids need to find their individuality."

"And your point is?"

"Can't you separate more tastefully?"

"I like my taste."

"Maybe choose a color scheme that actually goes with the rest of the house?"

"Mom," she says bluntly, "I don't want my bedroom to look anything like the rest of the house."

Then I recalled a decorating experience I'd had a few years back, which helped me bridge her wishes with mine, and find a creative compromise.

I had volunteered to help get several fabulous homes ready for a home tour, a fund-raiser where nosy women buy tickets to peek in homes, and break that commandment about coveting. Because no truly lived-in home is design-tour perfect (isn't that a relief to know?), we hired designers to lightly redecorate, and make the houses into showplaces. My job was design liaison, in charge of stroking the homeowner's large but fragile ego while telling her that the designer thought her accessories looked like they came from the Salvation Army's dumpster.

At one home, the designer and I walked into the master sitting area and found a red velvet sofa shaped like a gigantic stiletto.

"Oh, no," I gasped.

"Don't panic," he said. "I can make anything work."

He got a black-and-white zebra-hide rug, painted the walls graphite gray, added a crystal chandelier and some framed red-and-black prints of dancing girls, and, amazingly, the stiletto sofa worked. "Context is everything," he said.

His words became my mantra.

"All right," I said to Marissa. "We'll do it your way."

The hug I got was worth any future visual discomfort.

With that peony wallpaper swatch in hand, we hit every fabric store within fifty miles looking for something palatable to go with it. Ten stores later, we realize: Surprise! Streetwalker peony isn't a popular color. Furthermore, few fabrics can live alongside the loud wallpaper.

I can make anything work.

"Wait!" a seasoned saleswoman said and rustled off to the back room. She returned with a book of mattelaisse fabric samples, those solid-color cottons stitched like quilts. She flipped open to one sample: streetwalker peony!

"Score!" Marissa shouted.

"Whew!" We agreed to pair this with white mattelaisse for her bedding. Compromise number two: The classic quilted mattelaisse fabric offset the tartiness of the peony wallpaper the way a strand of pearls can make a too-tight top look less sleazy. Context!

We papered one wall and painted the others pale lilac. We covered the bed in white mattelaisse with matching shams edged in street-walker peony, which we also used for two valances over the windows. We made the bed skirt of lavender silk, and draped a round table with black polka-dot cotton. Marissa added the finishing touch that was all her: a cylinder-shaped crushed-velvet stool, in streetwalker peony. And guess what? It all works. (See section on custom bedding in Chapter 14 to get more specifics.)

❊

I discussed the issue of Marissa's room redo with Angela Lamson, a licensed marriage and family therapist, in Greenville, North Carolina. "This isn't about the room, of course," she said, sounding very therapistlike. "When kids feel the urge to change up their room, there's a big reorganization process going on inside them."

"Does that mean parents have to undergo some remodeling, too?"

"I'm afraid so."

Here's what else Lamson says parents should keep in mind when kids say: I want my space my way.

- **Set rules.** While kids should have a big say in how their rooms look, they also need—and want—guidelines. One rule: No destruction. (They can't spray paint graffiti on the bathroom tile.) The room needs to be safe, and that means clean.
- **Get over yourself** and the fact that your child's room may spoil the visual flow of your house. It's more important that the room be a place your child can bring friends and say, "This is me in 3D," not, "This is what my mom thinks I should be."
- **Budget according to taste.** An adolescent can't foresee his taste changing in a couple years, while you know (or at least hope) it will. Thus, don't pay a lot for their more, uh, eccentric decorating choices. For instance, I agreed to the wallpaper—for one wall, not four. And she agreed to a well-made white quilted duvet cover (classic) instead of the purple velvet one. But she can adorn it with her (cheap to change) pur-

ple crushed-velvet pillows. She got her crushed-peony-velvet stool for her vanity, but I left the room's beige carpeting, because it was in good condition, went with the rest of the house, and would have been too expensive to change.

- *Get a second opinion.* If your child won't agree with your decorating judgment—no, neon orange isn't a good wall color choice—ask a design expert at a home improvement or design store to render an opinion. Slip him or her a five.
- *Focus on the upside.* No matter how hideous the look, redecorating a bedroom is a great way for a child to experience the reward of having a vision and realizing it. And isn't that what you want for his or her life?

Oh, but if children's messes were only confined to their rooms . . .

41

When School Projects Hit Home

O<small>N THE WAY</small> home from school, Marissa says the two words parents dread: *School Project*. My mood sinks because I know the next few nights will be a flurry of trips to the hobby store, a housewide scavenger hunt, hot glue guns, and meals eaten while standing because the kitchen table is in use.

Children learn best in three dimensions, the research shows.

But has anyone studied the impact of this 3D learning on parents? Or homes? I personally have never encountered a school project that didn't enter the house like a pipe bomb.

"I need to make Poseidon's house," she continues, "by Friday."

"What's his house like?" I ask, to get a grip on the hassle factor.

"I don't know, but he lived underwater and was the god of horses and fire."

"Oh, you picked one of the easy gods," I say, thinking, *Here we go again.*

I know houses are supposed to support—not suppress—the activities of those who live within. But I can't face another week of glitter glue and macaroni. I flash back on my patient mother, who endured my brother (I was pristine!) who lived at home while attending architecture school. The kitchen table often housed a model under construction, so we passed the ketchup over the east wing of the Williamsburg Courthouse.

In recent years, between my two daughters, we've made a California mission of painted Styrofoam, a firefly (black nylons over coat hanger wings, and a miniflashlight tail), a Hopi Indian maiden from a bottle of dish soap, a model of Quaoar (newly discovered planet beyond Pluto), an imaginary island (painted salt dough on plywood), and an archaeological "midden" (clear liter pop bottle layered with five distinct strata—think coffee grounds, flour, pudding, and messier—concealing artifacts from sequential stages of the student's life from pacifier to soccer pin). We've made African rain sticks (good-bye leopard-print scarf), a diorama of Jacques Cousteau with real fish, a habitat of the snowy owl (the owl a wad of dog hair with a cashew beak), and a Plains Indian teepee (Dan never did figure out what happened to his favorite chamois). All in the name of learning.

Kids learn better with interactive projects that engage both sides of the brain, the research shows.

But does it have to engage every horizontal surface in the house and both parents?

Yes, actually, especially when a kid like Max is in class. Thanks to his dad, Max's insect report had a bee that actually flew. In the space unit, his Milky Way spun galaxy-like when you pressed a button.

Poseidon's house took the form of cardboard wrapped in (sea) blue cellophane, with a seashell-shingled cardboard house on top. (Fire) red cellophane flamed out the windows. Plastic ponies paraded around the front yard. A week later, I was still crunching fish gravel under my feet, but I can deal with that, because, as bad as school projects can make the house look, when we roll up our sleeves and fire up the glue gun for our children, our actions say: *School matters. And you do, too.*

❋

For advice on how to create a livable home that also supports my kids' school projects, I called an expert. Montessori schools are known for creating spaces where order and learning go together. Michael Jacobson, publisher of *M: The Magazine for Montessori Families*, gave me the inside scoop:

- ***Create order.*** It's up there with godliness and cleanliness. The toughest part of achieving any goal is to not get distracted. An organized space helps kids focus on learning and not on pulling pieces together.

❋ *continues*

continued

- ***Designate a storage area for craft items.*** Make it so kids can help themselves. The area may include shelves, large bins, divided drawers, and small containers for beads, glitter, feathers, and googly eyes.
- ***Stop pretending*** the kitchen is all yours. I've surrendered an entire kitchen cupboard, a pantry shelf, and a large drawer to kids craft materials. If you think this stuff will go away if you don't make room for it, you're wrong.
- ***Store items sequentially.*** Try organizing items in the order they'll be used: paper first; then rulers, pens, and pencils; then scissors, paint, and glue.
- ***Get set.*** Have your child list what he or she needs. Then get a tray or basket and have the child pull supplies from the craft storage area, and from around the house.
- ***Dedicate a work space.*** Depending on the project, that may be the garage floor, or a table in the family room. But make it a place you won't have to clear for other family activities. "When you move a child's project to have dinner, you not only set him back but also imply that the project isn't important," says Jacobson. A Montessori rule of thumb: For shelf and workspace, allot twenty-five square feet for middle-school kids, seventeen square feet for those younger.
- ***Protect surfaces.*** Aid cleanup by cutting open large garbage bags and taping them tautly over work surfaces. They won't slide like newspapers.
- ***Create a contract with your kids.*** One nonnegotiable rule: The child puts everything back in its place. When everything has a place, this gets easier, and becomes a life-long discipline.

Such spaces help students bring schoolwork home, but what about a space that helps kids remember what to take back to school?

Back to School—Ready, Set, Blast Off!

Every fall, when my kids, along with millions of others, go back to school, my home turns from hangout pad to launchpad. "Time for school," I say cheerfully. The kids snarl, but I love back to school.

Most moms won't admit this publicly. They say, "Oh, the summer went too fast!" Baloney. They're really thinking, "Hooray! I get my life back." I picture us, a string of honest mothers, raising our arms in a giant stadium wave from California to Connecticut, because the fact is three months of having the kids home 24/7—much as we love 'em—wears. After serving as three-ring circus master, chauffeur on demand, short-order cook, sunscreen monitor, and TV plug puller, all while keeping the house from looking like a day camp, and, in my case, also working from home for a living, makes you wonder, around the third week of July, whether school will ever get here.

But when that first school bell is about to ring, I brace myself for a different challenge: getting out the door on time. At my house, this resembles a rocket launch; both acts consume 90 percent of the available energy. Leading to the blastoff, pressure builds to combustion, like an unopened soda can in a hot car.

As the year rolls along, the mayhem increases. On a typical day, we start in a rush because the kids oversleep. A lost math book needs finding. A fight breaks out over a hair appliance. A screaming match follows over a top borrowed (or stolen, depending on whose version you hear) from a sister's closet. Comments fly about somebody's bad breath, and a zit that needs emergency cover-up tactics. A classmate calls about forgotten homework. The clock chimes: four minutes to launch. One child remembers that she's supposed to bring the class snack that day. I grab a carton of stale Goldfish, which contains enough hydrogenated oil to keep the entire seventh grade hydroplaning for six months.

We drive the three minutes to the bus stop, a distance the girls could walk if they left five minutes sooner, but the fear of not making the bus is greater for me than for them. When we get there, sweat springs from my forehead as if I'm hooked to a Rain Bird sprinkler. I kiss each child good-bye. Quick as hummingbirds, they dart their chins down so my kiss lands in their hair, and they're spared the humiliation of Mom's lipstick on their faces. The bus drives off, and I issue a wistful sound that joins a collective sigh of mothers across America exhaling with toe-deep relief as their kids go back to school.

❋

To help my kids get out the door more smoothly on school days, I read up on—and test-drove—some home organizing tactics. Here's what works:

- *Set up a launchpad.* Whether a dishpan or a custom cubby, every family member should have a place near the door to land on and leave from, says Cynthia Ewer, author of *House Works* (DK Publishing). Park backpacks, school projects, coats, keys, glasses, and anything they need for school or work the next day. Otherwise, they leave an ant trail behind them as they drop belongings through the house. Have all homework printed off the computer, permission slips filled out, gym bags ready, and a sticky note for last-minute reminders. "Bring Soccer Snack!" Do anything you can before bed: lay out clothes, pack lunches, know what's for breakfast.
- *Employ a surefire wake-up.* A few years ago, I woke the girls for school with a soft voice and soothing touch. After two black eyes and a broken rib, I started poking them from a distance with a broom handle. When their cries of child abuse got to me, I traded myself in for an alarm clock with a buzzer you could hear in Puerto Rico. I station it across the room so they have to get up to turn it off. Recently, I discovered an even better alarm clock. The Clocky ($50 from www.nandahome.com) has wheels. When it sounds, the clock rolls off the nightstand and darts around the room ringing so sleepyheads have to get up and chase it, which is brilliant.
- *Have one calendar.* Every organizing professional says families must have one master calendar. I have finally adopted this as truth. For some families, having a main calendar in a common place, like the kitchen, works. I use my personal desk calendar as Central Control. If people have an activity they want to attend, they know to stick the notice on my calendar. If it doesn't get there, it doesn't happen.
- *Establish a homework station.* After school, when kids return for a crash landing, be sure they have a dedicated place to do homework. This can be their rooms, so long as other distractions, like television, aren't nearby. If kids use computers for homework, check often to see that they're not on Facebook or surfing the Web. The other day, Marissa complained that she couldn't find the Humboldt River. I glanced at her screen and said, "You're not going to find it on a Juicy Couture Web site."

And then there are those whose permanent company we really don't want. Stretching a home to accommodate out-of-town guests is one of the toughest stressors a household can endure.

42

Dear Houseguest: Please Come and Go

Unbidden guests are often welcomest
when they are gone.
—WILLIAM SHAKESPEARE

SPECIAL ALERT TO those of you unfortunate enough to live in highly desirable areas: During peak season, summer and holidays, your houseguest storm warning is Category 5. This is particularly true for those of you whose friends and family prefer free homes to paid lodging.

Brace yourselves.

I don't mean to sound ungracious. I love having company. I go into a flurry. I fuss. I clean. I cook. I get excited. I actually think this is fun—at first.

Then they arrive.

The adrenaline is still rushing, and we have this big visit fest, eating and talking until the owls go to bed. The second day carries a party afterglow. Day three, a house hangover hits. The place is a mess, and it's not just my mess. It's other people's mess. I realize how far behind I've gotten by ignoring my real life. I get crabby.

This pattern, says houseguest maven Darlene Dennis, has played out for centuries. It gave rise to that old expression that both fish and guests stink after three days, which many attribute to Benjamin Franklin, but which traces back to Cicero, as in 50 B.C.

"The feeling is long-standing and universal," says Dennis, a self-described doormat who lives in the desirable San Diego area, and has had houseguests far worse than I ever have. She has endured freeloaders who sponge with no remorse and refugees who extend their summer stays so they don't miss sharing Thanksgiving dinner. She's entertained lushes and louses and letches. Her run of rude guests caused her to write *Host or Hostage: A Guide to Surviving House Guests* (Barthur House).

When I learned of this book, I naturally had to call her. "Guests impact your time, territory, and provisions," she said. "You have to politely protect these or be miserable." Boy, was I paying attention.

For starters, be careful when you blurt out an invitation in a fit of social generosity: "Next time you're in Colorado, you'll have to stay with us!" People will take you literally.

When you get that phone call: "Guess what?! We're coming to town!" how you handle it determines whether your welcome mat turns you into a doormat.

"Lovely!" I say. "Aaach!" I think.

Wrong, says Dennis, who is more strategic. "Don't say: 'Oh, when does your plane arrive? We'll pick you up.' Instead, tell them you'll look forward to seeing them at your home and where they can rent a car." This prevents them from hijacking your car or expecting you to be a chauffeur. (Her book has a chapter titled "Hospitality Doesn't Include the Keys!") See, we're off to a better start already.

Her book has an arsenal of funny defense tactics, which I hope neither you nor I ever have to use. Like what do you do when your guest comes out to get his morning coffee wearing only his underwear? The book is also laced with grounding reminders: You are not a posh hotel or a swanky B&B, so don't try to act like one. That right there makes me breathe easier.

Here are more houseguest survival tips from Darlene Dennis to make the going—and leaving—easier.

- *Set boundaries up front.* Say, "We're so glad you can visit us. Because we are working, we can't take vacation time. But we would love to plan time to do something together on Saturday and Sunday. Meanwhile, feel free to come and go as you please."
- *Show them around.* This does you and your guests a favor. Point out where they'll find extra towels and blankets, and where food and drink are. Encourage them to help themselves (and not wait for you to wait on them). Show them how to work the television. Make them as self-sufficient as possible.
- *Stretch for that bed space.* If you don't have an official guest room, and would rather not give up (or share) your bed, look at a space-saving bed alternative, such as a pull-down Murphy bed, a futon that doubles as seating, a sofa bed, or a blow-up air mattress.
- *Provide bedroom basics.* The space your guest's use should offer privacy (even a folding screen will do), bathroom access, and, if the space has a window, shades for privacy and light control.
- *Stock them up.* Put a basket in the guest bath filled with new toothbrushes, hair brushes, a blow dryer, shampoo, toiletries, a sewing kit, and anything they could possibly rummage through your bathroom for.
- *Send them to see the sights.* Give them a stack of brochures or online literature about local attractions and recreation. Include maps, driving directions or bus routes, and a current local city magazine.
- *Put the family on notice.* I tell my family they'd better be on their best behavior or they will get the business end of my broom on their backsides, which my husband thinks sounds like fun.
- *Prepare.* Make a few good do-ahead recipes—casseroles, specialty breakfast breads, desserts—and freeze them.
- *Say welcome.* Don't go crazy, but do clean the guest's room and refresh bed linens. Add welcoming touches: fresh flowers, chocolates on the bed, and a small gift that represents your area, such as soap or honey made locally, or a cookbook of regional favorites.
- *Avoid doormat syndrome.* Ask guests to pitch in. For instance, tell them where the bakery is so when they're out they can pick up bread for dinner or muffins for breakfast. Assume they want to contribute and just need some prompting.

How Not to Be a Houseguest

We've all known house clods who don't use coasters, don't clear their dishes, leave wet towels on the floor, put their dirty shoes on the sofa, and generally act like your family. What should they do to make their presence more welcome?

Until the world's gracious hosts decide to throw in the guest towel, guests should remember that just as designing a gracious home is an art, so is living graciously in someone else's home.

I offer as a role model my friend Julia. I actually have many role models. For instance, I have always aspired to look like Marlo Thomas and write like Joan Didion—more often I achieve the reverse. But almost everything I ever learned about being a houseguest I stole from Julia. She comes bringing groceries—cheeses I've never met and wines whose names I can't pronounce. She helps cook and teaches you how to make what she's cooking. She helps clean up. She brings small gifts for the kids, usually books clairvoyantly in line with their ages and interests. She makes great conversation and can talk about touchy subjects without making anyone flinch or leave the room. She knows when to go to bed.

Not everyone is lucky enough to have Julia-type guests. Many of us endure folks who go through our mail and take all the choice magazines to their bathroom.

HOUSE RULES

Here are ten rules guests should keep in mind, so they don't get on the never-come-back list:

1. *Treat your host's home* as you would like others to treat your home—not the way you actually treat your home.
2. *A short stay* with long notice beats a long stay with short notice.
3. *Wear two accessories* at all times: antennae to pick up vibes and special glasses to read between the lines.
4. *Come bearing gifts;* leave bearing gifts.
5. *Pick up a meal.* If the hosts have been making every meal, take them out to dinner, or bring dinner in, and pay.
6. *When you're out on the town,* get something simple for the house: a bottle of wine, some great bread, cheese, or a confection.
7. *Remember* that just because you're on vacation doesn't mean your hosts are. Don't expect to be entertained 24/7.
8. *Make your bed.* Put the toilet seat down. Hang wet towels up.
9. *Don't try to change* anyone's religious or political beliefs.
10. *Assume,* even if your host tells you you're no trouble, that you are, unless you're Julia.

When work, kids, houseguests, or pets are driving you nuts, the best way to maintain your relationships is to constructively let off some steam. Having a place to work out at home can be a household's sanity saver.

43

Home Gym:
Make Room for Fitness

HAVING A HOME gym beats going to a gym for many reasons. First off, health clubs have people. People who can see you. The fact that you have to haul your lard rump to the gym probably means you're not thrilled about pulling on a pair of shorts or something spandex and shaking what your mama gave you in front of all those buff and toned gym rats. Besides, those buff and toned people aren't real, everyday people. They're models, whom the gym pays to show up to sell more memberships to people who become convinced that they, too, can look buff and toned if they join. Scientific studies have proven that exactly ninety-six hours after buying a health-club membership, people never return.

Second, there's the locker room, where you change under fluorescent lights in front of strangers. Aaach! Third, there's the inconvenience. According to a blind online survey (though I never met one that could see) conducted by Nautilus, 55 percent of those who did not have a home fitness area said they would exercise more if they did.

So, a home gym offers the best way to fight flab and avoid corporeal embarrassment: no voyeurs, no shame, no locker room ordeal, and no excuses.

The home gym downside is finding a space for it, and then getting the equipment, which may, face it, never get used. Like health club memberships, people often buy gym equipment only to find their fitness fantasies fizzle. They buy exercise contraptions, use them for a week, then turn them into a clothes rack. Some outfit home gyms with gleaming pieces of equipment, then, rather than use them, visit the plastic surgeon.

But some people actually use their home gyms, which I heartily recommend. Exercise is a great form of tension relief, so great for hectic households. (If it weren't for regular exercise, I would be living alone, a crabby hermit.) When everyone in my house is getting on my nerves, I know the problem is my nerves. The solution is a workout. In our basement gym, we have old mismatched free weights, a Lifecycle, and a treadmill, which we prefer to shaking our hubba hubba at the health club. No excuses.

❊

If getting in better shape—and in a better mood—at home is on your to-do list, here's how to surmount home gym hurdles:

Hurdle #1: Finding Space
- **Make exercise a priority.** Rank exercising up there with eating, bathing, and sleeping. You have a room for each of those, so make room for exercise, too. You can fit what you need in a space as small as eight by six feet. A spare bedroom (let that guest room do double duty) or corner of the basement is ideal. If you live in a warm climate, use the garage.
- **Create a getaway.** The space should look different from the rest of your house. Make it a getaway. Put palm trees and beach scenes on walls. If you live in the country, paint an urban scene.

Hurdle #2: Getting Equipment
- **Start with basics.** Cardio, strength, and stretching form the fitness triangle. Have equipment for each, says Wayne Westcott, author of *Get Stronger, Feel Younger* (Rodale) and consultant for Nautilus. At a minimum, invest in three items: a cardio machine (stationary bike, treadmill, or elliptical machine), a set of free weights with a flat bench, and a mat for stretching.

❊ *continues*

continued

- **Spend cardio dollars wisely.** Your biggest investment is the cardio machine. Up-right and recumbent bikes last forever, so you can buy a cheap one, says Westcott. But cheap treadmills and ellipticals break down under heavy use. If you plan to actually run on these, and not just walk, buy top of the line.

Hurdle #3: Staying Motivated

- **Make yourself comfortable.** To keep your lard rump moving, add a fan, television, sound system, a place for towels and water bottles, a large mirror (unless you hate them), and a dimmer for the lights. Make the place a no-phone zone. Then just do it.

When the kids color with a Sharpie on the sofa, the dogs have chewed through your new leather purse, or layoffs at your office mean half as many workers are doing twice as much work, you may need another kind of space to decompress, or express a primal scream. You need a sacred space to call your own.

44

Sacred Spaces:
Make Room for You

*P*AIGE SCREECHES INTO my bedroom on two wheels while I'm changing.

"Do you mind?" I say.

"No, actually," she says, then heads straight to my makeup drawer to help herself.

"Isn't anyplace sacred in this house?" I ask, echoing a line my dad used to say whenever we barged in on him.

"Nope," she says, and exits with my $10 mascara.

Ah, for that little sacred spot at home. That private corner where you can escape, rejuvenate, and focus on your inner life, which in my case has been shrink-wrapped and set on a shelf till I can get to it. But inner lives need rooms, too.

"Having a place at home where you can spend some time out of your mind is essential," said one sacred-space expert I spoke to.

"Check that box. I'm out of my mind all the time."

"You need a place you can connect to your higher self."

"Done! We have a stocked bar."

"A place you can get centered."

"Seriously, who has time to sit in the child's pose, while burning a gardenia-scented candle and writing reflective thoughts in a hand-bound journal made of pressed leaves?"

"You must make finding time for nothing a priority."

"I'll get on that."

Of course, souls matter, so we should probably feed them. *How* is a personal choice. Some people set out Tibetan singing bowls or meditation tingas. Others focus on their seven chakras, or set up shrines with Buddha figures, or altars with Lady of Fatima statues. Some pray, meditate, or practice yoga. (If my family saw me flowing from downward dog to nuclear pigeon, they'd have me committed.) Reading regenerates me. And though I have the perfect sacred place for it—a reading loft—I don't use it. When I designed it, I envisioned a place where my kids wouldn't ask me to untangle their Slinky, where my e-mails and work piles wouldn't tug at me like a leash, where I could get lost in lofty thoughts about who would be the next American idol, and, yes, read. I lined two walls of the eight-by-ten loft with bookcases, and filled them with books acquired like friends over a lifetime. I planned to curl up there regularly in a soft chair, with good light, a dog on my lap, a cup of tea, and a Russian novel.

Four years after I set the room up, I actually tried that. I found a slice of time in between making lunches, meeting deadlines, driving kids from soccer to gymnastics, getting groceries, exfoliating, paying bills, combating cellulite, pumping gas, and taking the dogs to the groomers, and just seized it. Just as I got rolling on Tolstoy's *Anna Karenina*, and was up to page 7, I heard one of my daughters calling.

"Mo-om."

I stayed silent.

"Mooo-ooom!" She raised the knell ten decibels. I thought maybe I should answer.

"She's not here!" I called back.

"Where are you?"

"Out of the country."

Next, she was in the sacred space. "What are you doing here? You're never in here."

"I'm changing that."

"Don't you have anything to do?"

"I'm doing it."

"You're still making dinner, right?"

"I'm making time for my inner life."

"I was hoping you'd make tacos."

So much for sacred.

❋

To help me better nurture my inner life, I called Riv Lynch, owner of Sacred Spaces, an organizing company in Highland Park, Illinois, who offered these practical insights. "Because we're overly scheduled, and outwardly focused on jobs and others, we need to carve out a place where we can look inward, rejuvenate, and find some solitude, or we'll go nuts." Lynch also has three kids, so she knows what she's talking about. "Sacred spaces don't have to be holy," she adds. Here are some ideas for creating one at your place.

- *Know their roots.* Sacred spaces in homes aren't a new idea. They were found in rural medieval European homes where people lived too far from communal churches to attend them. Centuries ago, Mexicans also began making altars in their homes for worship.
- *Define your purpose.* That sounds heavy, but it just means figure out how you want to chill—through yoga, meditation, prayer, reading, navel gazing, or journal writing. Then make sure the space accommodates that purpose. For instance, if you want to practice yoga, be sure you can kneel on all fours and jut your leg out without breaking a window.
- *Find your spot.* Consider creating a sequestered place in your garden, an altar in your entry, or a devotional corner in your bedroom. Wherever it is, the space should feel serene. You should not see your bill pile, your unwashed dishes, your dirty laundry, or other worldly distractions. Consider sectioning it off with a screen. (See Chapter 37 on decorating with folding screens.)
- *Make it minimal.* Include only items that support your activity. Bring in mats or pillows for meditation or yoga, and candles and religious icons for worship. Bring in any object that inspires you, such as a shell from a beach where you made a promise. If your space is for reading, have a comfortable chair, good light, and a side table. If you'll be journaling, have a small writing desk. If you want to listen to music or nature sounds, add a CD player or iPod.
- *Exclude the outside world.* Ban phones, televisions, computers, and anything work related. Now find the time to get there.

PART ✳ SEVEN

House Hygiene

Unlike the people I live with, I can't function in a messy house. I mean, what's the point of having a nicely furnished house if it looks as if the Union cavalry went through it on horseback with paintball guns? To me, a clean home is the foundation of a beautiful home. Keeping chaos and germs and stains under control requires a little science.

45

At War with the Universe:
The Science of Housekeeping

en•tro•py [en-*truh*-pee] *n*.: 1. a thermodynamic measure
of the degree of disorder in a system; entropy always increases
and available energy diminishes in a closed system, as the universe.
—*WEBSTER'S NEW WORLD DICTIONARY*

O R IN A HOME.

Many laws of physical science apply to home maintenance. Take the entropy law: The amount of available energy (that is, people willing to do work in our home) seems to continually shrink in the face of work that needs doing. Or the chaos theory: Everything in the universe is constantly moving toward a random state of chaos.

Here's another universal truth: No matter how well decorated your home, it only looks as good as the last time someone wiped, swept, organized, polished, sanitized, fluffed, plumped, and clutter busted. Forget all the fancy home design advice out there. Getting a home to look beautiful is the easy part. Keeping it looking that way requires the stamina of Lance Armstrong, the work ethic of a Puritan, and the mind-set of those who paint the Golden Gate Bridge: Once you finish, you start all over again.

"Want to see the world decomposing?" I yell to my kids, so they can hear me through their iPods and earwax.

"Sure!"

"Yeah!" They tumble down the stairs after me to see the excitement.

They arrive to see me poised at the entryway table. I dramatically drag my finger across it, leaving a streak like a meteor trail.

"Huh?" says Paige.

"That's dust," says Marissa.

"No. That, my dears, is the decomposing world. From now on, our job is to eliminate all traces of this."

"She wants us to dust," Paige mutters to Marissa.

"Call it what you want," I say. "I prefer to call it taking on the universe."

"You're gonna lose," says Marissa, with her usual knack for nailing the truth.

True, every house is at war with the universe. And every house will eventually lose the universal battle to decay, grime, wear, and weather. Put another way, doing housework is like combating aging. All you can do is wage a battle to forestall the inevitable degeneration. But wage war—and degenerate—we do. Which brings us to another rude awakening. My kids think housework is someone else's job.

Frankly, so do I. But we all have to roll up our sleeves and pitch in.

I lay down the new house cleaning rules law along with the new domestic policy. After I've gone over the rules, I lift each child's eyelids to check for consciousness. "Got it?" I ask.

"Got it," they groan.

HOUSE RULES

- ***Tidy up.*** As a consuming member of the family who contributes to the general disorder of the house, you will cheerfully pitch in because you are part of this team. (Groans.)
- ***Make your bed.*** You will make your bed every morning, and clean your room and bathroom on weekends. (Gasps.)
- ***Do your laundry.*** You will each be responsible for doing your own laundry. I will do sheets and towels. Once you start your laundry, you won't park it. You will move it through in a timely manner for the next person. (Threats to call Children's Protective Services.)
- ***Do dog duty.*** You will alternate dog-scooping duty with each other, and help in the kitchen, washing your hands between those tasks. (Argument over whose turn it is.)
- ***Claim your belongings.*** Before bed you will comb the house for your stray belongings and return them to their rightful places. Anything collected after hours will become Mom's property, to be sold at auction, donated, or possibly earned back by the original owner in exchange for more chores. (Does that include schoolbooks?)

46

Housekeepers Are
Cheaper Than Therapy

SINCE MY FIRST child was born—the moment I went from barely keeping it together to losing it altogether—I've had a steady string of helpers from Horrible Henrietta to Amazing Adriana. There was Maribel the typhoid carrier. We became a taxi service for Louisa, whose husband lost his license after a DUI conviction. The short-lived Cecelia liked to take home (and return) my nicer lingerie (creepy). Some had odd medical theories: Urine from a nursing baby is good for your skin, which explains why Alice wiped my daughter's wet diapers on her face. Others (Lucy!) were house angels. Some lasted three days, some three years. Drama aside, paid help, even if infrequent, prevents brain damage.

As any mother knows, when a baby arrives, something else goes: career, home-cooked meals, decent-looking hair, sleep, nights out, the housework, or all of the above. When I hit my child-triggered melting point, I chose to work less and to work at home. Granted, my home office lets me have flexible hours, but when I'm not writing a newspaper column or magazine article, I want to be with my kids, not scrubbing the toilet. So I pay someone to clean the house. I strongly recommend it.

Now, I know there are women who can do it all and still be a woman their husband wants to come home to, but my husband didn't marry one of those.

Whenever he complains about the cost of domestic help, or the fact that a woman he barely knows is turning his underwear right side out, I remind him that housekeepers are cheaper than therapy and a lot cheaper than divorce. Still, he likes to point out that his perfect mother raised five kids with no paid help. Yeah, but what she remembers about her kids' early years was pressing her nose against the front door to look out the peephole for her husband to come home. When he did, she turned the kids over to him and sat on the curb with a glass of wine. With all due respect, that's no way to go through life. I have a friend who's a marriage counselor. When couples with kids aren't getting along, she prescribes housekeeper therapy. Miraculously, the couples argue less, and women have more energy for, um, other stuff.

"What gets me," she says, "is when their marriages get better, they let go of the help!"

✺

One of the golden rules of Living with *Them!* is either to get them to help, or get help. I've found having a housekeeper to come in once a week, or every two weeks, is well worth the price. I'm not alone. According to Service Magic, a contractor referral network, out of the company's 500 service categories, maid service is the number-one homeowner request. Finding the right person, however, takes trial and error. For advice I called Perry Phillips, founder and executive director of the Association of Residential Cleaning Professionals. He offered these matchmaking tips:

- ***Ask friends.*** When looking for a housekeeper, ask for recommendations, then check references. This is no guarantee. What works in someone else's house may not work in yours.
- ***Seek chemistry.*** It's the most important quality a housekeeper brings. Chemistry is when you're behaving like an idiot and your help acts as if you're perfectly normal.
- ***Know what you want.*** An occasional cleaning person? Someone to help with the kids? A nanny-housekeeper combined? Will this person need to speak English or drive?
- ***Define your priorities.*** I had a friend who rethought her plan the day she found herself washing a sink full of dishes while her help played with her kids in the yard.

✸ *continues*

continued

- **Explain all you expect up front.** Adding to the task list after the person starts working raises either resentment or the price or both.
- **Agree on the work.** Ask for a list of the specific tasks they will do, and then ask to add others you want and adjust payment if necessary. Determine whether you or they will provide cleaning supplies.
- **Know you can't teach standards.** If you like your sheets tucked in with hospital corners and the help doesn't tuck at all, lower your standards, make the bed yourself, or hire someone else. As when choosing a mate, don't pick a fixer-upper. Housekeepers don't improve over time.
- **Communicate problems clearly and soon.** Don't let little things fester. If something wasn't done right, say so, or leave a note for next time.
- **Get your papers in order.** Be sure the person is working legally. Ask your accountant to set you up with the proper tax forms to file. If you use a service, be sure they insure workers. If you hire an individual, be sure your homeowner's policy covers them while they're in your home.
- **Know the pros and cons of a cleaning company.** Pro: If someone gets sick, your house still gets cleaned. Con: Though the same service will clean your house, the same people probably won't. Most services claim they do a background check, but many don't. Ask for proof.
- **When the holidays come around, tip.** If your housekeeper has been with you a while, say, almost a year or more, tip the equivalent of one day of housekeeping.
- **Have a trial run.** Tell helpers you'll try each other out a few times before committing. You'll know after two visits if they're a keeper. It's like dating.

Beyond just looking a whole lot better, a clean home is a healthier home. Still, germs happen. Here's what to do when they hit in full force.

47

Flu Season and Germ Warfare

WHERE DID I go wrong? I thought my house was clean! I thought we were clean. But when the flu took hold of our house, it clung like a London fog. We fell like dominoes. First, Marissa felt a little sick before her middle school choir performance. By the end of the evening she couldn't make the curtain call. She was backstage, a shivering mass of chills in a party dress. Two days later Dan came home from the Broncos game—all headache, sniffles, fever, and grouchiness—saying it was the longest four hours of his life. And the Broncos had won. So I knew it was bad.

In a gesture of caring, Paige and I set a ring of fire around the two of them and avoided them like the, well, you guessed it. When they neared, we made Xs with our index fingers to block their curse. Meanwhile, I became the guerrilla fighter of germ warfare. I armed myself with turbo disinfectant and sprayed it on anything that could harbor a household germ, including the dogs. I washed my hands more than Lady Macbeth. I served food and drinks with metal tongs.

No luck. Soon the four of us were sitting around the fireplace, wrapped in assorted blankets and robes, Rudolph nosed, moaning, hacking, passing the tissue box, setting a new low in family bonding. On top of the flu, Marissa got pneumonia and I got strep. We had contests: Who can go the longest without coughing or blowing? We played Who's Worse?

"I keep coughing up stuff. You didn't cough up stuff."

"I did too."

"My fever is 101."

"Mine was 102 yesterday."

"I was up all night."

"I've been up for three nights."

"Look, I'm not trying to win the who's-got-it-worst competition. I'm just saying . . . "

"Good, because I'm worse."

"Fine."

Anyone looking for sympathy won't find it. We stopped arguing for a minute while someone hacked up a pair of tonsils. The house sounded like a tuberculosis ward; coughing shook the floorboards. Next to every bed lay a tissue pile rivaling the Great Pyramid of Giza. The torrent of blowing noses sounded like a steady stream of squawking geese flying overhead. We'd gone through so much noodle soup we'd paid for a new wing on the Campbell family mansion. Someone hung a large "Quarantine" sign on our house.

"Could better house hygiene have prevented this?" I asked Ozlem Equils, M.D., a pediatric infectious disease specialist at Cedars-Sinai Medical Center, in Los Angeles.

"Household cleanliness is extremely important in reducing the spread of infections at home," she said. "But if your kid brings home something contagious, the chances that you'll get the same bug are very high, unless you're immune, no matter how hygienic you think you are."

❋

Dr. Equils suggests we all practice these home hygiene tips (besides a lot of hand washing, which is most important) to help make our homes healthier, and nip the spread of illness during cold and flu season. Prepare to be grossed out:

- *Don't confuse tidy with clean.* Often when we think of cleaning house, we think of straightening up, fluffing pillows, clearing stacks of mail. More important from a hygiene standpoint is cleaning kitchens and bathrooms. When someone in the house is sick, frequently disinfect phones, the computer, door handles, and light switches. Wash toys often with dish soap. While you're at it clean your cell phone. Think where that's been.

- *Get the right disinfectant.* A clinical study that looked at how effective different cleaning agents were against harmful bacteria and viruses found only Lysol and Clorox products killed both, said Equils. (Homemade green products using baking soda or vinegar solutions were least effective.)

- *Nuke the kitchen.* Harmful bacteria and viruses can survive and divide on surfaces all over the house, but especially in the kitchen. They can live up to twenty-four hours on a sponge. Eeyew. Clean sponges after each use by microwaving a couple of minutes, running them through the dishwasher, or saturating them with dishwashing liquid. Wipe down refrigerator handles every time you do dishes. Set grocery bags on the floor, not the counter, when unloading. And watch where you put your purse. Don't set it on the floor in a public restroom, then on your kitchen table.

- *Bathe the bath.* Once a week wipe bathrooms with disinfectant. When someone in the house is sick, put paper towels in the bathrooms for hand drying. Germs can live on a moist towel a long time. Change bathroom towels and bed linens once a week. Wash both in warm or hot water.

- *Choose hard over soft surfaces.* Next time you build or remodel, put hard floors (wood, stone, or tile) in kitchens, baths, and mudrooms at a minimum. Carpeting is difficult to clean thoroughly. In one study, salmonella bacteria were put into a carpet, and not even a commercial-strength wet cleaning process could destroy them.

- *Open the windows.* Fresh air (and clean air-vent filters) can move germs on. Sunshine is also a great disinfectant; the sun's ultraviolet rays kill many microorganisms.

Keeping the house clean takes a lot of work, energy, and, if you're lucky, cooperation. The same is true for laundry. Keeping up with it can be a career for you and your washer and dryer, which is why you need to choose these domestic partners with care.

48

Spin Cycle:
Front-Load or Top-Load?

AFTER NINETEEN YEARS of dutiful service, our washer and dryer headed for appliance heaven—a place where no one would ever again stuff them with smelly gym clothes or sandy beach towels. We saw this coming. For months, the washer was incontinent; I had to mop a puddle after every load. And the dryer would putter along for thirty minutes, poop out, rest for twenty minutes, and start up again. Then the washer went down for good, and took the dryer with her.

Two strong men hauled the old couple away and ushered in a new pair. I felt a ceremony was in order: "To think we were newlyweds when we bought the twin set," I said, running my hand under my nose to catch my sniffles. The delivery men exchanged awkward glances.

"Only you could get sentimental about old appliances," Dan said.

"They've been a big part of our lives," I said. "They raised our babies."

"Oh, for heaven's sake."

Before we got our new washer-dryer team, we saw how big a part the old pair had played. As we put off buying a new set, piles of dirty clothes grew from the laundry room floor toward the ceiling, setting a geological speed record for stalagmite formation. As pressure and laundry mounted, Dan and I approached the problem in our typical nonunified fashion: He went to the library for recent *Consumer Reports* coverage. I called my girlfriends. Together we went to the big box store. The appliance salesman homed in on the frazzled couple wearing unwashed clothes, and asked if we needed help—a loaded question if there ever was one. I was so distracted by his inch of silvery roots beneath dyed brown hair I couldn't answer. Dan took over. "We need a new washer and dryer."

"Front-load or top-load?" the man with the roots asked.

"Top-load," I said.

"Front-load," Dan said.

The salesman with the roots waited for clarification. When there wasn't any, he said, "Top-loads are cheaper and faster. Front-loads are gentler and more energy efficient."

We walked around as if in a car lot, lifting hoods, running hands across shiny metal, and went home perplexed. After more research, we decided on a front-load washer and matching dryer, for the scientific reason that I decided front-loads looked cooler. We bought them from the man with the roots.

"Would you like white or a color?" he asked, gesturing to the metallic blue, red, and silvery gray models.

"Not dyed," I said, then slapped my hand to my mouth. "I mean natural, no artificial coloring."

Dan elbowed me and said, "White. She wants white."

While the delivery men hooked up the new machines, the girls argued about who would use them first.

"I don't have any clean jeans," said Paige.

"I'm out of underwear," said Marissa.

"Well, turn them inside out and wear them twice because I'm out of socks."

"That's gross."

"We got extra tub capacity," I said. "Why don't you combine your loads?"

"No way!"

"Her clothes aren't touching mine."

As they bickered, Dan snuck in his whites.

❈

Next time your washer and dryer are heading for appliance heaven—which studies show happens on average every ten to thirteen years—consider these factors when replacing them:

- *The trend:* Front-load washers are trending up, but top-loads still outsell front-loads two to one, says Karen Cobb, spokesperson for Lowe's. The main factors driving consumer decisions and cost are capacity and energy savings.
- *Cost:* Top-loads are cheaper. Prices range from $350 to $1,000. Front-loads cost from $800 to $1,600. Dryers cost between $400 and $1,000. Most people choose the washer first, and get the matching dryer. If your set doesn't match, be sure capacity levels do.
- *Cycle time:* Top-loads finish faster. However, clothes emerging from a front-load have spun off more water so need less dryer time.
- *Energy efficiency:* Front-loads are greener. Top-loads use more water and energy. While greener is better for the planet, it could take several years before you break even costwise if you buy a front-load. Do the math. (For more green tips, see Part Nine.)
- *Performance:* I thought top-loads would get clothes cleaner because they used more water, and I didn't want to sacrifice cleanliness for efficiency. But *Consumer Reports* compared twenty front-loads and twenty-two top-loads, and the top ten front-loads cleaned better on average than the top ten top-loads.
- *Gentleness:* Since front-loaders don't have that center agitating piece, they're easier on clothes. Some of today's top-loaders don't have center agitators either, but these models cost as much as front-loaders.
- *Door position:* If you'd rather not bend over to fill your washer, get a top-load. But front-load units offer the option of stacking if space is tight.
- *Colors:* Though today's washer sets come in cool colors, white outsells colored machines two to one. Next hottest is red, followed by blue, then silver. I chose white because I'd rather not call attention to my appliances. Color also costs more.
- *Storage:* Matching drawers that slide beneath appliances are great if you're short on storage. But if you have enough, skip that option. The drawers raise the machines so high you can't use the tops as a folding surface.

❋
WAYS TO STREAMLINE THE LAUNDRY PROCESS

- *Give* a different color laundry basket to every family member.
- *Sort* laundry into white, light, bright, and dark to avoid dye transfer. Also separate items that create lint—sweatshirts, towels, flannels—from others.
- *Look* for stains to treat as you load the washer. Check pockets for lip gloss, gum, snails, felt pens, and paychecks. Close zippers and remove belts.
- *Shake* garments well when loading the dryer to give them a head start on being wrinkle free.
- *Fold* them while they're hot. The last bit of dryer heat will help smooth out garments' wrinkles.
- *Save* energy by using cold water, unless germ warfare is in order. (I sleep better if I wash my sheets in hot water.) Wash only full loads, cycle down to shorter cycles such as permanent press and delicate, and hang clothes to dry more often.

When stains fall on things that can't go in the wash, then what?

49

Stain Masters:
How a Crisis Line Saved a
Marriage and a Carpet

THE TARP WAS supposed to protect our new carpet. But when Dan yanked it back, there, soaked into the beige textured shag, lay a dark Frisbee-sized splotch in the shape of Ohio, though slightly smaller. The splotch was from the cherry-wood stain Dan had applied to some wood trim.

Experience had taught me not to panic, though I did employ the deep-breathing technique I learned in childbirth class. Experience had also taught me to keep my mouth shut, so I didn't blurt something regretful like: "Did you buy your brains in the *Penny Saver!?*"

What is it about new carpet that begs for a stain, like a new car going out of its way for its first door ding?

"I know a number," I eventually said, and started dialing. Soon a carpet expert was talking me through how to remove oil-based stain from carpet. I wrote down the instructions, and handed them to Dan.

"How did you know who to call?" he asked.

I shrugged. A woman has to keep some of her mystery. Truth was, I'd discovered this hotline years ago during another carpet catastrophe, a little incident I never told him about.

See, there was this dog . . .

Against his better judgment, Dan had promised the girls and me that we could get a dog when we moved into our last new home. We wasted no time finding our new love at the shelter. We rescued him and brought him to our new home a few hours before the movers arrived, and just twelve hours after the carpet installers had left. Next day our dearly adopted French sheepdog, a sixty-pound heart wrapped in fur, chose the middle of the living room to test our commitment.

Dan has many fine qualities, but animal lover isn't one.

That first morning in our new home, I walked down the staircase overlooking the living room and saw two paper-plate-sized mounds of wet dog excrement—one from each end—soaking into the new carpet. The dog looked nervous and guilty. But, hey, if I'd just been rescued from an untimely death, come to live with strangers on their moving day, and had a complete change of diet, I'd have GI trouble, too. I glanced upstairs to see Dan just knotting his tie and did what any woman who wanted to save both an animal and a marriage would do. I scooped what I could into a bowl, threw open the windows, and placed a large area rug over the offending patches, just as Dan came downstairs. Then I packed him off to work, and spent the next hour making desperate housewife calls.

The carpet installers told me about 1-800-4DUPONT, a number I've since tattooed on my left instep. At this Stainmaster crisis line, experts give remedies to remove just about any stain you can imagine and some you can't. (You can also get this scoop at www.stainmaster.com.) I got a recipe and repeated it three times. Alas, the stains were still bad and spreading.

Next the neighborhood fix-it man came with his heavy-duty shop vacuum. He shook his head and called his buddy who owned a carpet cleaning service. The buddy was soon on scene. Then, a miracle. In an instant one chemical compound and one heavy-duty suction device saved a carpet, a dog, a marriage. By the time Dan got home, all was well again. The dog and I never said a word.

As for the wood-stain damage, Dan and I set to work applying mineral spirits to remove it. And, once again, a miracle.

❃

Because I want my carpet to last as long as possible, I asked Ryan Hughes, territory manager for Shaw Industries, the world's largest carpet manufacturer, for some other ways to increase my new carpet's mileage:

- *Put a doormat* outside every exterior door, and an area rug inside.
- *Vacuum.* A vacuum is a carpet's best friend. The more you vacuum, the longer your carpet will last.
- *Wipe your feet,* or remove your shoes before coming inside. But don't go barefoot on your carpet. Over time, foot oils can be worse than dirty shoes.
- *Invest in a good pad.*
- *Treat stains when fresh.* The longer they sit, the greater chance they'll penetrate the fibers. New carpet cleans better than old carpet.
- *For basic stains,* scoop up anything solid, and blot liquids with a clean towel. Next mix a quarter teaspoon of dishwashing detergent with one cup of warm water. Wet the spot. Let sit five minutes, then blot more. Repeat. If this doesn't work, call a pro— fast.
- *Always blot.* Never rub. Rubbing carpet can permanently damage yarn.
- *Save scraps from installation.* If your best stain lifting methods fail, a good installer can make a patch from a large square of carpet and save the carpet, and perhaps a relationship.

When Pets Break the House Rules . . .

"Who did this?" I'm on my hands and knees growling as I clean a mess I didn't make. Oliver and Theo tuck their tails under their bellies and slink away, like teenagers caught smoking. For some un-dog-ly reason, my pampered bichon frises have forgotten their indoor manners and regressed in potty training.

It's as if they had this talk:

"See that slate floor," Theo, the lead troublemaker, starts.

"The one that looks like a patio?" replies Oliver, his ever-ready sidekick.

"Well, I say it *is* a patio."

"So who needs to go outside when there's a patio in the house?"

"My point."

And here we are.

"If I didn't love you so much . . . ," I say, as I wipe and disinfect. It's too late to scold them; besides, I never know which one did it. I tell them how I feel, though they're nowhere in sight. Like my kids, they know when to conveniently disappear, though they're listening, always listening. Call Theo and Oliver by name, and they hide behind the sofa. But run a can opener, rattle the lid to their cookie jar, or slide open the back door, and they come running like the bulls of Pamplona. Call my kids from the next room to ask them to empty the dishwasher, and they're deaf as Dalmatians, but whisper that you just bought two pints of Ben and Jerry's, and their batlike radar draws them home from two blocks away.

"Are they mad at you?" asked Sheryl Matthys, dog expert and founder of LeashesandLovers.com, when I asked her advice.

"If they are, they sure know how to hold a grudge."

"Do they need more outside time?"

"Except after 10 P.M., when they're tucked into their custom doggie beds, they're free to flip in and out the doggie door whenever their furry feet feel like it."

Dan is even more fed up with the dogs' backsliding. However, he knows better than to pick this bone with me, or he'll be the one in the doghouse. He knows how dogs rate with me, in many cases higher than people, including good husbands. Dogs don't complain about your cooking or singing. They don't care if your hair's a mess, or your breath smells like old coffee and pizza, if you're fat or skinny, or if you burp when you drink soda.

According to the Humane Society, I've got lots of canine-loving company: 39 percent of U.S. households own at least one dog, and 75 million dogs are pets. Yes, many are trouble. However, I'm sure the two-legged residents of those 39 percent households would agree with me: A house is not a home without a dog—or two.

Here's how Matthys suggests we deal with liquid pet accidents.

- ***Set the ground rules.*** To rehousebreak my boys, Matthys said to clean, clean, clean. One reason my dogs kept marking the same spots was because I was using ammonia-based cleaners. Urine smells like ammonia, and triggers dogs to mark. Duh! Best solution: one part white vinegar with three parts water. (Or buy an off-the-shelf pet deodorizer and disinfectant like Nature's Miracle or Simple Solution.) Wipe up waste. Cover the area with the solution. Let it soak in; blot.
- ***Find that spot.*** If you're not sure where the spot is, or want to be sure you got it all, shine a black light. It makes urine glow.
- ***Keep them with you.*** Until they remember their manners, keep them with you on a leash when you're home, or confined to small quarters when you're gone. Give them lots of praise when they take their business outside.

Moms of yesterday were great at making piecrust, getting stains out, and applying Band-Aids, often all at once. But one thing women of today need to do as well is fix stuff with tools. It's nice when the man of the house does this, but sometimes the upkeep is up to you. Conquer this and you can forget about the piecrust.

50

Girlfriend, You Need Some Tools

*I*N MOST HOUSEHOLDS, certain tasks fall to the man of the house. For instance, at my house, I expect Dan to carve the turkey, get up during the night when there's a funny sound, and open pickle jars. But when domestic repairs need doing, Mr. Helpful is often nowhere around.

When the toilet backs up, the garage door sticks, the door handle comes off in your hand, the vacuum breaks, or the washing machine floods, guys are usually MIA. In fact, statistics prove that the likelihood that the man of the house will be home when you need a repair is less than 10 percent. If you're after a home improvement, men become even scarcer. If I want Dan to hang a mirror, install a drapery rod, or replace the kitchen knobs, I have to compete with ESPN and his tee-off time.

Begging our men to help turns us into pathetic, sniveling, needy weaklings, which, let's face it, creates frown lines and is heck on the mascara. This is why I've taught my daughters to never, under any circumstances, be at the mercy of a man. "You always need to be able to make your own money and unclog your own toilet."

"I'm going to be a trophy wife," says Paige.

Never mind her. I encourage all women to give themselves a gift: Girlfriends, you need some tools.

Now, I'm not saying we girls have to give up our damsel-in-distress routines. I'm all for batting my eyelashes, feigning incompetence, and saying oozy things like, "How did you know how to fix that?!" and "You're so smart and strong," if I can avoid crawling into a space full of spiders, or breaking a nail, or lying under the sink in a compromising position.

But when my man's not around and I need a home repair done, I can turn into a female Hercules. And for that, I need tools, my own tools, hidden in a secret place. You need to hide them because if your family knows where they are, they'll whittle away at your stash, starting with the small screwdrivers, which they'll swipe to change the batteries in their Game Boys. I also like the idea of my own tools because I don't like to scrounge through that greasy corner of the garage hunting down a hammer. That aversion alone is why, like most women, I have hung many pictures by pounding nails in with the heel of my shoe.

So when I heard about a tool kit just for women, the Essentials Tool Kit by GreatNeck, I had to have it. All the tools in the Essentials Tool Kit, which retails for around fifty bucks, have handles molded to fit a woman's smaller hand. The tools come in a twenty-pocket zippered canvas tote, which GreatNeck claims looks like a purse. That's a stretch. It looks more like a canvas diaper bag. And that's okay, so long as it doesn't resemble a tackle box. The styling and colors—mine's pink with pink and purple tools—make it a sure bet no self-respecting man will walk off with it.

Of course, you can put together your own kit, or get this one, which includes these essentials: screwdrivers, pliers, an adjustable wrench, a level, a claw hammer, safety glasses, fasteners, steel bits, a bit driver, and sixteen hex, metric, and SAE keys, whatever the heck those are. In the extra pouches, you can add a cordless drill, a pencil, a putty knife, a flask of whiskey, a notepad, lipstick, sandpaper, and the phone number of a twenty-four-hour handyman.

But here's the downside: Once the man of the house knows you have a tool kit, next time you ask him to fix the faucet, he may very well say, "You can do it." So do. Just don't break a nail.

Once a girl has her own tools, the next thing today's woman needs is know-how. Sure, it's nice to have a handy guy around, but when he's not, every woman should know how to do these DIY basics:

- *Tell* the difference between a flathead and a Phillips screwdriver
- *Hang* a picture straight
- *Use* a cordless drill and select the right size drill bit
- *Plunge* a toilet and clear a drain
- *Check* a circuit breaker
- *Shut* off the gas and the water main
- *Know* why, when, and how to use a molly bolt
- *Assemble* a piece of furniture that comes in a box
- *Put up* a shelf
- *Hang* a window blind
- *Fix* a loose door hinge
- *Instantly change* into a helpless female the minute a partner is around who can do all that for her

Taming the Wild Kingdom

Go outside! How many thousand times did your mother holler that? How many thousand times have you hollered that? It's a universal truth that in order to create harmony inside the home, family members need to spend some time outside the home. Here's how to create a yard that gets your family members outdoors and keeps them there.

51

SOS for Desperate Landscapes

*I*F I DIDN'T know better, I'd swear the yard had been abandoned. I walk around the outside of the house with a notepad surveying the damage: Stone pavers once in the shape of a compact river have drifted into anarchy. Frozen water has cracked a hose bib so when you turn it on water sprays out like shaken champagne. The all-weather ("Great for all seasons!") outdoor rug is decomposing and moldy. Grass struggles unambitiously toward greenness. Weeds, however, thrive. Planters serve up urns of crisp-fried vegetation.

The place looks like a crack house. Only it's not. The scruffy patch of land is mine, of course. Like many people, particularly those who live in snowy climates, I'm a winter garden slacker. Come spring I must pay for my season of neglect.

Here we pause to indulge a brief fantasy: I imagine the truck from DIY Network's *Desperate Landscapes* has just pulled up. The crew hops out all handsome, hulky, and helpful. They whack weeds, spiff planters, rehab the lawn, layer in fresh mulch, and add floral flourishes. Sigh.

Then my bubble bursts. I kick through a pile of pine needles trapped in a corner of the patio and write "Help!" in the filthy film coating the outdoor barbecue. I head inside the house discouraged, with a nose full of hay fever and a yard to-do list longer than my garden rake. Then, because *Desperate Landscapes* isn't pulling up anytime soon, I call Jason Cameron, the show's brawny host, and regale him with my yard problems.

"It's definitely a cause for panic," Cameron says. "Houses all over America are in the same boat."

"And I can't stay inside by the fire with the drapes pulled anymore like I've done all winter," I say.

"Not when outdoor living beckons."

※

DIY Network's Jason Cameron offered these tips for those of us who want to rescue our yards from winter:

- **Canvas the property.** I took the right first step, he said, by walking the yard and listing the damage. However, before you do this, make sure a V-fib machine is nearby.
- **Power clean.** Look at the exterior of your house, and see if walls, windows, and screens could use a power wash. A simple hose attachment can help you reach high places and give you a spring-clean look. If it's time for fresh paint, roll it on now while the weather is mild.
- **Detail the driveway.** If yours looks run-down due to stains or cracks patch or resurface the concrete or asphalt. Add curb appeal by framing the driveway with borders of pavers, bricks, or bark chips.
- **Cut high, rake low.** Many people cut lawns too short, says Cameron. They think they will have to mow less often. But cutting grass too short kills new growth buds. Help new grass grow by deep raking lawns to dethatch dead-grass buildup. Cameron likes the Lee Valley Power Rake, which costs around $40.
- **Feed or seed?** Fall is the time to seed the lawn. Spring is the time to feed. Don't re-seed in spring unless you have a bare spot. To get the right fertilizer for your lawn and climate, bring a small lawn sample to your local garden center and ask what fertilizer the pros there recommend. Combat crabgrass by mixing preemergent herbicides in with your lawn fertilizer.
- **Create a welcome entry.** Make your porch a focal point by adding colorful flowerpots or a bench. Make sure your door has nice hardware, and is maintained. Consider painting just your door an accent color, like rich red, or pine green, if that would fit your home's architecture and neighborhood.
- **Think layers.** The best landscapes use layers: backgrounds of lawn and mulch, middle grounds of green shrubs, and foregrounds of color. Incorporate all three. However, cautions Cameron, don't put in what you won't or can't maintain. If it's too complicated, your yard will look like a desperate landscape again long before next winter.

"So how do I take the desperate out of my landscape?"

"Well, you start by rolling up your sleeves."

There's silence on the line, and I know Cameron's thinking: "You reap what you sow—slacker."

I used to think having a cleaned-up yard, with a healthy lawn, thriving plants, and a patio, was enough, until I learned about the third layer.

52

Put the Wow in Your Yard

"*I* KNOW WHAT'S missing!" I burst into the family room with news on the order of we won the lotto.

Dan raises a wary eyebrow.

"I figured out what our deck and patio need to go from furnished to fabulous!" I'm waving a copy of Kathy Peterson's book *Great Outdoor Decorating Makeovers* (Watson-Guptill).

"Oh, goody, because I've been losing sleep over that," Dan says.

"You know how accessories make an outfit, and how they're the crowning jewels on the coffee table? Well, great yards need accessories, too. Look here." I start riffling through the book's photos to prove my point.

"Why do I get the feeling this is going to cost me?"

"Without the right accessories, our yard is to a *Sunset* magazine spread what an egg is to chocolate mousse. It's got the basics but needs that *je ne sais quoi*, only now I know what!"

"How much?"

"Honey, we're missing the Wow!"

When we first moved to our current home, our yard was completely raw land. As soon as we could, we built a deck and a paver patio and celebrated. We didn't have any outdoor furniture, so we pulled chairs from the kitchen table onto the deck and propped our feet on over-turned buckets as we watched the sun set. The next year we got out-door furniture: a table, chairs, pieces for a separate seating area, and weatherproof cushions. Although I thought we were done, I had that something's-missing feeling, like I should have worn a slip.

I studied the before and after pictures in the outdoor makeover book, transformations Peterson did for less than $250, and discovered that the difference between okay and wow lay in the third layer. If layer one is the main surface—deck, patio, pool, or lawn—and layer two is the furniture, layer three includes the etcetera: potted plants, throw pillows, area rugs, painted pots, candles, and decorative lighting. That's where the magic happens.

So I called Peterson to share my ah-ha moment.

"Too many people throw patio furniture and a potted tree outside and call it a day," she said.

"They have no imagination," I said, but I was thinking, *Whew! At least I don't have a potted tree.*

❋

Here are some of Kathy Peterson's outdoor makeover tips you, too, can use:

- *Make the outdoors a continuation of your indoors.* Treat your outdoor space like a room without walls. "Connect the dots from indoors to out. Carry the color scheme through, so the two areas cohere, especially if you can see the outdoor space from inside," says Peterson.
- *Use what you have.* Raid linen closets, haul out old pillows and accessories. Bring your indoors out.
- *Protect the meek.* To shelter outdoor accessories from rain, wind, or harsh sun, get a large trunk or chest that can double as a bench or coffee table. Stash pillows, lanterns, candle holders, and throws inside, for protection and easy access.
- *Enliven plain concrete.* Paint a concrete patio to make it look tiled. First, power clean and prime the surface. Tape off would-be grout lines, then, using paint made for concrete, faux paint the rest using two tones of a similar color, say two shades of brown, or terra cotta, to get a mottled stone look.
- *Repaint tired furniture.* To add gravity to a white wicker set, Peterson suggests spray painting it black, then top that with a light coat of brown to create a marbled effect that looks expensive.
- *Use durable fabrics.* Vinyl and acrylic fabrics hold up well outdoors, as do weatherproof fabrics like Sunbrella and Taracloth. Some terrific new fabrics are now available

❋ *continues*

continued

that have sunscreen built in. If you opt for a less durable fabric like canvas, spray it with a waterproof protectant to prevent mildew and water damage.

- **Go heavy on the greenery.** Put big pots of green plants and trees on decks and patios. They add texture, color, and depth. Don't skimp.
- **Pick flowers purposely.** Select them both for their sun preference and for how their color coordinates with furniture fabrics. Shoot for one of these color schemes: high contrast (white and red geraniums against black-plaid furniture fabric), monochromatic (varying shades of one color, say, pink or purple), complementary (orange marigolds against cobalt blue seat cushions), or themed (a hydrangea-print fabric with real hydrangeas nearby). For more on combining flower colors, read on.

Skip the Deadly Learning Curve for Flowerpot Success

Little did I know that several years ago, when I began my flowerpot project, I would fuel a string of family jokes longer than a wisteria vine. The laughs begin every June when I bring home a flat of annuals from the nursery. "Call the Humane Society," the kids chime. "Mom's planting again."

"She sinks more money than a pirate ship," Dan mutters.

Har, har, har. Okay, so I had some early floral failures, but I've improved. Problem is, every time I overcome one gardening issue, another sprouts. Failure and humiliation don't deter me. So all the death isn't for nothing, let my five-year killing spree spare the lives of your annuals.

Year One

I plant flowers in five large outdoor containers. Three weeks later, the planters look like the business end of a broom, fried straw. Dan renames my planters the Jameson Botanical Cemetery.

Year Two

I hire a flowerpot expert to select and plant flowers for my five containers. I cling to her like English ivy to learn where I went wrong.

Lesson one: Pick the right plants for the exposure. If a plant says partial sun it wants no direct sun. Period. My planters get two types of sun—full and brutal. Lesson two: Water more. A lot more. In the summer, flowerpots need at least one good drink a day, sometimes two, which I totally get. With the kids home from school, I could use a couple of drinks myself.

Year Three

My flowerpot expert has run off with her sketchy boyfriend, leaving me with no choice but to try to replicate everything she did, now by myself. Fortunately, I saved all the markers from the annuals she planted the year before and have pictures. A blooming idiot could copy them. I plant proven sun survivors: marigold, vinca, geranium, and petunia. I water obsessively. The next week half my crop dies in a hailstorm. The rest dies from spider-mite infestation.

Year Four

I turn to drugs. Despite what one of my purist plant friends says—that overfertilizing hooks plants on drugs—I figure, these plants aren't driving anywhere. I pour Miracle Gro in the watering can with every watering. Flowers bloom like Fourth of July fireworks. I mix insecticide that targets mites into the potting soil. Success!

Year Five

I'm cocky enough to think I've mastered outdoor container gardening. I plant the pots, water and fertilize excessively, and watch my flowers thrive. Then, one afternoon, as I smugly kick back on my deck to enjoy my finally thriving flowers, I read an article about outdoor spaces, and suddenly need CPR. The article says that real flowerpot aficionados *design* their pots. They don't just get the exposures right and put tall plants in the back or center, short plants in the front, and cascading plants at the rim. Even I know that. They *coordinate* foliage to complement furnishings. What? I want to throw in the trowel. Now I can't sit out and enjoy the flowers. I'm too busy critiquing their color combinations.

❋

If summer flower survival is good enough for you, stop reading here before I ruin that. But, if you tend toward the obsessive—who me?—here's a crash course in advanced flowerpotting, courtesy of Steve Hill, a greenhouse manager at Arapahoe Acres Nursery, in Littleton, Colorado.

- **Combine colors with purpose.** I never used to care what color my flowers were so long as they weren't brown. However, experts plant purposeful—not random—color. When I first learned this, I wanted to crawl in a dark closet with four pounds of See's candy. Two popular schemes: monochromatic, flowers of all one color or varied shades of one color (light and dark pinks), and complementary, colors opposite each other on the color wheel (deep blue violet pansies beside orange marigolds).
- **Match styles.** The style of pot and its foliage should go together. Mexican pottery and Mexican heather; Italian pottery and Italian goat's head; French urns with lavender and herbes de Provence.
- **Vary your greens.** This isn't just good dietary advice. Sophisticated gardeners think explosive color is for amateurs, and focus on the subtlety of blended greens—lime and deep purple potato vines beside a velvety gray dusty miller. Mix not only different colors of foliage but also leaves with different shapes and textures.
- **Seek contrast.** Put glossy-leaved plants in matte pots, matte-leaved plants in glossy pots.
- **Match flora and furnishings.** The überly compulsive match the print of their outdoor fabrics to their flowers. Say you have palm fronds on your cushions; put potted palms and pots of tropical flowers around. Because my pillows have a hydrangea print, and hydrangeas would croak on my sun-soaked deck, if I want to make the ranks of advanced container gardener, I need either to buy new pillows featuring sun-tolerant florals or to import shade.

Just because your outdoor living areas now look great, that's no guarantee that those you live with will get out there and stay for a while. And isn't that the goal?

53

Outdoor Living:
Nixing the Nuisances

THOSE GLAMOROUS PICTURES of outdoor dining are yet another reminder of how short I fall on the scale of fine living. You've seen the pictures: A skinny woman with long hair and a halter top carries a tray of two martinis. A handsome man is in the background, slightly out of focus, tending the grill. A romantically lit Jacuzzi burbles. My first reaction is: "Throw that woman a burger! At her weight, if she drinks one of those martinis on an empty stomach, she'll fall straight into the hot tub!"

My next, more disturbing, reaction then hits: Would you look at the gap between this outdoor scene and my place?

Given my family and Mother Nature, a lovely, serene evening dining al fresco is about as rare as a UFO sighting.

"Let's eat outside tonight!" I cheer like a one-woman pep squad, which pretty much sums up my role around here. I hand Dan the barbecue tongs and some chicken.

The kids get wind of the idea, and the whining starts:

"It's too hot."

"Too windy."

"Too cold."

"There are too many bugs."

"There's bird doo on my chair."

I stick to the plan, knowing that wherever I put food, the family ultimately shows up.

I set the outdoor table, placing the ketchup next to the insect repellent. By the time we all sit down, the wind has knocked both over. Next, someone says grace faster than an auctioneer, after which someone bolts inside for a sweatshirt. Someone else slaps a mosquito. The wind picks up. We start pinning placemats down like a team of amateur wrestlers. A yellow jacket comes by, sees what's cooking, then goes and gets his friends. The food flash freezes. A dark cloud pulls up, opens, and empties itself. No one is talking because everyone, including the mosquitoes, is eating as fast as possible. The next night, we do it again, because I'm determined to get this right.

To see if there's a better way, I summon Jim Sweet, founder and creative director of Terrace Views, an outdoor living design firm based in Centennial, Colorado. "We want to extend the outdoor season," Sweet tells me, as he steps out onto my deck, which I quickly scan to be sure the dogs haven't done any last-minute decorating. "We want people to come outdoors sooner in the year, and stay out longer. Better, more uplifting things happen outside. What's inside? The phone, the television, the bills."

"So what's stopping us?" I ask, though I have my ideas.

"When we prepare an outdoor living design, we consider the owners' lifestyle and create spaces," he says, which is what all designers say. I write down, "create spaces," and hope someday I'll figure out what that means.

"And we explore and eliminate nuisances."

Now I am all ears. "Nuisances?"

"Like sun, wind, pests."

I perk up. "That's what's missing in those ads!"

"Ads?"

"The outdoor ads with the beautiful people never show the bees, the skin-frying sun, the noisy neighbors."

"We have so many solutions to those problems now."

I ask him to please share, so I can rise one more rung up the ladder to better living.

❋

Here are some ways Jim Sweet says we can make the outdoors more livable.

- *Design around what draws you out,* whether that's a view, a pool, a fireplace, or a rose garden.
- *Create rooms outdoors.* Use rugs, railings, lights, planters, potted trees, umbrellas, or canopies to create walls, entry points, and ceilings.
- *Add character.* People often stick furniture outside and think they're done. But it's the old wheelbarrow-turned-planter and that piece of tree trunk you hauled home from a nature walk that give space character.
- *Know the hot (and cool) trends.* People are asking for more water and fire in their yards, says Sweet. Waterfalls, bubbling rocks, fireplaces, and fire pits are trending up, replacing outdoor kitchens as the must-have feature.
- *Nix nuisances.*
  - *Sun*—To maximize the hours you can get your family out to enjoy your outdoors, sun management is key. Many varieties of umbrellas are now available, from cantilevered (to cover any angle) to commercially weighted (to stay put). Shady trees, awnings, retractable shades, pergolas, and canopies are other attractive sun-block options.
  - *Wind*—If your outdoor space gets windy, park the table closer to the house, or in a protected corner of the patio. Put up natural barriers, such as hedges, or artificial ones like Plexiglas wind blocks. Remember that wind often dies when the sun sets.
  - *Heat and cold*—Heat lamps and fireplaces or pits extend the hours you can enjoy the outdoors. Be sure heat lamps are sturdy enough so they won't blow over, or put them away when you don't need them. Water misters can feel delightful on hot afternoons.
  - *Bugs*—Citronelle candles discourage some insects. To protect yourself, find a repellent you like and use it. Some new ones last up to twenty hours.
  - *Neighbors*—Use barriers for privacy and water features and soft music to mask noise. Or just invite the neighbors over.

Sometimes the nuisances are furry.

Critter Control: We Love You, but Stay Out

"What's your worst home-remodel horror story?" came the innocent question from the audience. I steadied myself against the table. Was it the two sofas that arrived upholstered with the fabric inside out? The patio that collapsed, forming a three-foot sinkhole off the kitchen? The house we bought, then learned when the rains hit that the roof leaked like cheesecloth? Because having a stroke in front of an audience would be bad form, I quickly collected myself and picked one.

"Well, there was this possum," I began with a deep, cleansing breath. I flashed back to the first of three homes Dan and I built, in this case rebuilt. We renovated an old house in two phases, so we could live in the intact part while gutting the other. (Not a plan I'd recommend.) In the heat of July, a horrible stench overtook the site, a smell so vile that the workers—not a particularly sensitive bunch, considering they thought nothing of eating their lunch while leaning against a PortaPotty—evacuated and refused to return. Before abandoning me, one worker said, "You should find what died under your house."

"Something died?" I asked. "Like a mouse?"

"That ain't no mouse, lady."

Meanwhile, in our half home, fleas infested the carpet, and set high-jump records. Our dog took one indignant sniff and left to stay with friends.

I made some phone calls and found a thin, serious man, who pulled up and handed me his card: "Dead Under the House Animal Removal Expert."

He took a deep sniff. "Possum," he said with certainty.

"You know by the smell?" I asked. (Now there's an art.)

He slipped his pipe-cleaner body into a space suit, donned a headlamp, and wriggled under the house, which I would not have done for a lifetime supply of Manolo Blahnik pumps. Eventually, he emerged with a face full of disappointment. "I couldn't get her."

Apparently, before dying, the rodent wriggled through an unconnected drain pipe, and snuggled behind a cement foundation footing, which pipe-cleaner man couldn't get through.

"Sorry," he said. "I almost always get the carcass."

"Is it just me, or do other people have my luck?" He sprayed noxious deodorizer and flea killer around, which probably did permanent chromosome damage. As a parting gift, he handed me two coffee cans of pungent deodorant for Dan and me to park next to our heads when we slept. The bad smell lingered for weeks, but eventually the dog and workers returned, and I asked myself for not the last time: Is remodeling worth it?

❋

"**R**emodeling often invites unwanted visitors," says Bonnie Bradshaw, owner of 911 Wildlife, in Dallas, "because it creates more ways for animals to get in your house." The risk is higher in late spring and early summer when many remodel projects start and animals are looking for a nesting place. Here, according to Bradshaw, are ways to keep critters from moving in, and help them move out:

- *Know their habits.* Urban homes are ten times more likely than rural residences to be targets. "Raccoons, possums, squirrels, and skunks are omnivores. Their goal is to find the most food using the least energy." Many of these animals are nocturnal, so you never see them. They seek dark, quiet, safe places. Attics, crawl spaces, walls, and chimneys are perfect.
- *Don't invite them.* Bird feeders, pet food, and trash left out overnight look to omnivores like an open buffet. Keep pet food indoors. Put trash out in the morning, and don't keep feeders too near the house.
- *Keep up on home maintenance.* Tree branches and ivy growing onto roofs or up to decks create perfect cover. Keep them trimmed. Be sure vents, ducts, chimneys, and soffits around your house have good screen covers. Install heavy-gauge wire mesh between ground and decks. "Raccoons laugh at chicken wire," says Bradshaw.
- *Put up motion lights.* Nocturnal animals don't like light. If one goes on, they'll keep moving.
- *Respond to the call of the wild.* Sounds in the night often are the first sign that wildlife is in the house. Most people patch the hole they think the animal is using, or set out poison or traps. Those methods are mistakes. If you patch, chances are something alive is still inside, where it will die, rot, and stink. Put out poison and the same could happen. Or the poisoned animal could go away to die, then get eaten by dogs or birds, sending poison through the food chain. Traps often catch the wrong critter. Or you get the mom, then her babies cry all night. Instead, roll a tennis ball soaked with

❋ *continues*

continued

ammonia into the space. The animal won't like the smell and will move on. Cover the hole with a newspaper (not my column). Once the paper remains intact for twenty-four hours, assume the critter has moved, then patch the hole.

- ***When you're too late.*** Swarms of flies, fleas, or a bad smell indicate something died. Call a pro. (Servicemagic.com can link you to screened animal-removal experts in your area.) Experts can use a snake camera to find the animal, which beats cutting several holes in the house. They know where to look, have no qualms about crawling in dark spidery spaces, usually get the varmint, handle any offspring, deodorize, decontaminate, and dispose of the corpse. Whatever they charge is worth it.

While having wild animals living under your roof is a little too close to nature for me, I'm all for living more harmoniously with nature. Next we'll explore some greener ways to be more planet friendly at home.

PART NINE

The Future Is Green, but What If You're Yellow?

It used to be enough to have a well-maintained, beautiful, organized, hygienic home with manicured lawns and thriving planters. But today our homes must also be green. When I first heard this, I just closed my eyes and hoped that this, too, would pass like stomach cramps. Eventually, however, being greener at home made more and more sense, not only for the planet but also for my pocket. Alas, while some of the green movement is a little, uh, shall we say out there—"Get off the grid and grow your own power!" not that that isn't admirable—some ways of going greener at home really do have their place in today's homes, at least mine.

54

Twelve-Step Program for Planet Junkies

IF FRIENDS OF the planet are like flowers, then I'm a dirt clod. I have painted with toxic paint, taken long showers, left the lights burning in rooms long abandoned, and run the air-conditioning when I could have opened a window. I've done loads of laundry for only three items, used a 100-watt bulb when a 60 would suffice, driven when I could have walked, and dumped chlorine bleach straight down the drain. Now the ice caps are melting, and it's probably my fault because I'm guilty of everything. Al Gore says so.

When I came out of that blissful state of being a planet pariah, I noticed that everything around me was green. Green was all anyone in the home design and building world was talking about. Magazines launched green editions; builders hosted green conferences. I even heard talk of painting the White House green, with low-volatile organic-compound paint, of course, to form a Green House, to make amends for a certain Inconvenient Truth.

Anyway, call me late to that party, but eventually, I, too, decided to turn over a new leaf, a green leaf, an ecofriendly leaf, possibly from a bamboo tree, bamboo being an incredibly sustainable wood source, since one stalk can grow three feet in one day, like an adolescent.

First, I had to acknowledge that I was helpless in the face of my addiction to water, energy, and certain chemical substances (like paint). I knew I couldn't detox alone. I'd need a support group. First I reached out for green books and grabbed *The Earthwise Home Manual: Eco-Friendly Interior Design and Home Improvement* (Green Home Publishing), by Kristina Detjen. This clarified my crimes and deepened my resolve to get green and sober. Then I called Detjen and said I needed a twelve-step program for planet junkies. She said she would see what she could do. I also asked John Dunnihoo, general manager of West Coast Green, the country's largest residential green-building trade show, for help.

I confessed to both that I was skeptical of the whole green movement. I didn't want to slide back to the 1970s when people talked to their plants. However, I do want to do my part to preserve the planet, make a better world for my children, leave a softer footprint on the earth, and all that. Detjen and Dunnihoo both graciously accepted my skepticism. (Denial is common among planet abusers, they said.) And they took on the challenge of making me greener at home. Recognizing me for the hedonist I am, Detjen let slip that by going green I could also save some green—money, that is. Now she really had my attention.

❋

Together Kristina Detjen and John Dunnihoo offered the following green tips, which I fashioned into a twelve-step program:

TWELVE-STEP PROGRAM TO GOING GREEN AT HOME AND SAVING SOME GREEN

1. *Admit* that you are powerless over your need to consume wastefully.
2. *Give* over to the higher power of your global community. Acknowledge that only through collective effort will we restore the planet to a balanced state.
3. *Agree* to replace all lightbulbs in your home with compact fluorescent bulbs. Accept that though CFLs cost more, they last ten times longer and use one quarter of the electricity.
4. *Commit* to actually use your home's programmable thermostat the way it was intended. If you don't have one, buy one. Promise to never again run the air-conditioning when there's a cool breeze outside.

5. ***Dedicate*** yourself to only running full loads of laundry, using the coolest water possible. Don't overdry clothes, and hang them to dry more often.
6. ***Search*** for the Energy Star label when buying a new appliance. (The label is the Environmental Protection Agency's stamp of approval for energy efficiency.)
7. ***Use*** more cloth napkins and towels, and fewer paper ones.
8. ***Fully acknowledge*** the limits of our water supply. Scrape plates rather than rinse them when loading the dishwasher. Install a drip system for watering outdoor plants, and put a water-saving device (a capped jug of sand) in the toilet tank.
9. ***Choose*** paints with low or no VOCs (volatile organic compounds). Accept that they may go on runnier, but they won't hurt the planet or give you a paint hangover.
10. ***Recycle*** everything you possibly can. If you don't know how, check www.earth911.org.
11. ***Strive*** to repair, refinish, or restore furniture you have rather than buy more. Or even better, buy more antiques.
12. ***If you fall off the wagon***, get back on.

Reading so much green literature at once made me so paranoid that, for about a week, I stopped using household cleaners altogether. I looked into having the kids shrink-wrapped in nontoxic material, and the house hermetically sealed. Then finally, I found a balance. I did some investigating to separate green hype from green truths, and unearthed some sanity in the green madness.

55

Indoor Pollution:
Is It Safe to Breathe Yet?

BY ALL ACCOUNTS, I should be dead. My wood cabinets are laced
with formaldehyde, a known carcinogen. I've had a history of microwaving my food in plastic containers, which leach toxins. I've been
sleeping on—and thus inhaling—a mattress manufactured from cotton probably grown with pesticides. And I regularly trade the germs
on my kitchen counters for DNA-mutating chemicals found in cleaning supplies.

The more I read green literature, the more I think: How on earth
have I survived? How have any of us lived past our eighth birthdays? I
take a deep, cleansing breath, and remember the reassuring words Dad
used to say to Mom when she worried about us kids: "Don't worry,
dear. They'll die of something else."

I believe many green causes contain worthy truths. I also think some
are overwrought and underattributed. Take, for instance, this comment
from one well-intentioned green writer, whose scientific credential is
that she's an interior designer. About the dangers of chlorine bleach,
the kind we use in our wash, she writes, "Chlorine releases chloroform,
a probable carcinogen, into the air as you use it. As it breaks down into
the environment, chlorine creates by-products that combine with other
naturally occurring organic compounds to form organochlorines. These
compounds are believed to cause cells to mutate when they accumulate
in the food chain. This can harm DNA and cause cancer."

Holy Toledo! How did we go from getting our clothes whiter, perhaps the one thing my grandmother, mother, and I have agreed on, to mutating cells, harming DNA, and causing cancer? Thinking about this is making me dizzy and short of breath, or maybe it's my office cabinets, which are maple-veneer-covered particleboard. Formaldehyde is a binding agent in particleboard. But wait. I thought buying particleboard was more environmentally correct than getting hardwoods from the rain forests.

Confused? Me, too.

❋

Although by now you know an awful lot about me, except for maybe my birth weight and blood type (8 pounds, 0+), what you may not know is that besides writing a home design column, I'm also a health reporter. I've written for the *Los Angeles Times* since 1995. The excellent *Times* editors have trained me well to question the heck out of so-called findings from so-called experts, to look for the data, then to question that. So I called a few experts, science types, to help me separate green facts from green hysteria, and to find out what substances I really needed to worry about at home. Here's what I learned:

- *Not enough research.* Most studies on exposure to supposedly harmful chemicals have involved animals and high doses. Low doses in humans haven't been well studied, according to John Meeker, assistant professor of environmental epidemiology at the University of Michigan, and an expert on exposure assessment. In other words, scientists have had trouble finding volunteers who want to spend days with their noses stuck in beakers of formaldehyde or chlorine. Not even teenagers will do this.
- *Balance is key.* Many people believe that if a lot of a substance is potentially harmful, none is best. That's not always true. The sun causes cancer, but some is good for us, and life depends on it. Our bodies need selenium, a chemical in the sulfur family, but too much can be deadly. Find a balance between a harmless or healthy level and a toxic one.
- *Know your tolerance.* Certain people are more chemically sensitive than others, just as some people are more allergy prone. If a person has been overexposed to a toxin at work, he will be more sensitive if exposed at home, says Meeker. Parents of small children should be more vigilant. Little ones are often more sensitive and spend a lot of time on the ground.

❋ *continues*

continued

- **Formaldehyde fears.** This chemical is in everything from toothpaste to wrinkle-free fabrics, from tissues to carpet, and many wood products. Some people worry about the fumes. Chuck Frihart, a wood chemist and head of wood adhesives for the U.S. Forest Products Laboratory, in Madison, Wisconsin, confirmed that the adhesives in most pressboard, or MDF (medium density fiberboard), contain formaldehyde, too much of which is harmful. However, when natural wood degrades, it also releases formaldehyde. We've been living with aging wood for centuries. Formaldehyde levels in American wood products fall below the baseline for concern. (Anything under one part per million is considered safe. Over two ppm and people can experience a sore throat and stinging eyes.) Ironically, the wood from exotic trees from rain forests, which some people choose over manufactured wood products, often naturally releases harsher toxins to protect the tree against insect infestation.
- **Open the windows.** The best solution for indoor pollution is fresh air. If you've just gotten new carpet, or cabinets, or a new computer, which all release fumes, leave the windows open. Rates drop off fast, says Frihart. In one week they drop to half. In another week the level halves again. If you're painting or installing drywall, insulation, or carpet, wear a mask.
- **Cut back on chemical cleansers.** Some ecofriendly experts suggest using vinegar mixed with water as a cleaning agent. I tried it, but didn't like having a kitchen that smelled like salad dressing. Plus, it left a dull finish. (I later learned it's ineffective against germs. See Chapter 47.) I prefer diluting my regular cleaning chemicals (Windex and 409) with water.
- **Beware of scams.** Lack of clear scientific evidence drives many people to pay more for products they believe are safer. If you don't mind paying extra, and you like the green-labeled product, then buy it. But be leery of marketing from companies who stand to profit from paranoia. When you hear a claim, carefully consider the source. Be green, but be smart.
- **Focus on the positive.** You'll probably die of something else.

Another way we can leave a lighter footstep on the planet, and save money, is to buy less, and be smarter, more conservative consumers. Replacing quantity with quality, which we've discussed, is one way we can live simpler, and better. And we've all heard the green expression "Reuse, recycle, restore." Turns out that philosophy proves good for the planet, our homes, and our mental health. Some people have made reusing what would otherwise be trash into an art. We can all take some inspiration from this re-creative artist.

56

New Uses for Old Stuff

I DON'T KNOW about you, but when I see a smashed hubcap, I see junk. Steve Dodds sees art. Dodds, an architect, is the author of *Re-Creative: 50 Projects for Turning Found Items into Contemporary Design* (Penguin).

"Take a piece of metal from a junkyard, clean it, mount it on a white board, hang it on a bare wall in a Manhattan loft, and hit it with an art light. It can look great," he insists.

Clearly, some people have vision I lack.

His gift lies in seeing new ways to use stuff most of us throw out. When his sister-in-law sat on a lampshade and crushed it, instead of sending it to the trash pile, he recovered it with spent subway tickets, and gave the shade a new, more interesting veneer, and a second life.

Empty dog food cans? Dodds stripped the labels, connected a row of five cans to a metal rod using thick elastic ponytail holders, and attached the rod with pushpins to a bulletin board above his desk. The result: a multitasking pencil holder. Old vinyl records? He slipped them inside a T-shirt, ironed them till they could bend like sticks of gum, removed them, and then curved them around a cardboard tube so they looked like Js. He stacked four bent records, spreading them several inches apart, connected them together with grommets, and hung them on the wall using a nail inserted through the top record's spindle hole, and voilà—a mail rack.

"Sure, you can buy a new mail rack or lampshade," he said, "but it's cheaper in the long run to make something unique that expresses your life. Plus you have a story behind it more interesting than 'I bought it at Pottery Barn.'"

I try to imagine what would happen if I started repurposing in my home:

"Honey, look at our new living room art!"

"That looks like my steering wheel. That is my steering wheel!"

"And those silk ties you never wear? I wove them into this crib blanket."

"My ties! What crib?!"

One rule, says Dodds: Don't repurpose stuff you're using. Only stuff you're not.

So Dodds and I played a game. I threw at him pieces of common trash—well, not literally—to see what he would make of them:

- **Plastic water bottle**—Collect a bunch of caps. Wire them together to create a doormat, or a purse. Then, cover the bottle with fun fabric and attach a rope hook, for a hanging flower vase.
- **Wine corks**—Wrap seventy-five or so (that's some party) in a tight circle with a strip of bent wood, like walnut. Secure the ends of the wood and make a trivet.
- **Wire coat hangers**—Cut the ends off, so you have lots of straight pieces of wire. Stick them into a predrilled board so all the ends stand up, and use it to store files.

While I'm definitely motivated to repurpose more and buy less new, you won't catch me dead with a bottle-cap purse.

Here's how Steve Dodds says you, too, can be re-creative:

- ***Think laterally, not literally.*** That is, look at things not for what they are but for their elemental properties. Take a door: When architects see a door, they don't see a door. They see a big, flat, lightweight, sturdy plane. This is why there probably isn't an architect in America who hasn't once laid a door across two file cabinets and made a desk.
- ***Find a new function*** for little-used things. This is how the top to Dodds's wok became a fruit bowl. He turned the lid upside down, placed it on a stand, and filled it with fruit.
- ***Amplify trash with repetition.*** This can give an otherwise ordinary object more impact. Ask what you would do if you had two of something, four, ten, or a hundred, like Andy Warhol did when he contemplated Campbell's soup labels.
- ***Don't buy new.*** Everything you need is already made. If people would buy more home decor from flea markets, garage sales, and antique stores instead of from the mall, they'd do the planet a favor and have more fun. When we redistribute instead of buy new, we save not only the planet's resources but also all the costs of advertising, packaging, shipping, and distributing. (See more of his ideas on www.stevedodds.com.)

While some people, like Dodds, see new uses for everyday items, others see how nature has solved problems we grapple with daily. Those observations have evolved into greener answers.

57

Biomimicry:
Looking to Nature to
Solve Problems at Home

A NEW SCIENCE called biomimicry is impacting home design. It involves imitating nature. While that's a lovely idea, for the past fifteen years, I've been trying to get my family to *stop* imitating nature. As designers extol the virtues of bringing the outdoors in, I'm crying, "Leave the outdoors out!"

What's also weird about looking to nature to improve home design is that for so long we've done the opposite. Our species began at one with the elements. Then mankind got into caves because some prehistoric woman said if her guy wanted any action he'd better find a bearskin and a windbreak. We evolved to mud huts, log cabins, and production houses with plumbing and Betty Crocker. For a while, we devolved, and women stopped shaving their armpits, but thank goodness the gene pool corrected that. And now we've made a U-turn and found another path that looks to Mother Earth for answers.

The large brain behind biomimicry belongs to Janine Benyus, founder of the Biomimicry Institute in Missoula, Montana, and author of *Biomimicry: Innovation Inspired by Nature* (HarperCollins), a serious science book first published in 1997. Interior designers took more than ten years to catch on because it's taken them all these years to get through the book.

Biologist Benyus has traveled the world studying nature to learn not about it but from it. She asks questions like: How come nature can make a substance as durable as an abalone shell in a cold solution using only seawater, while humans burn heat energy to make ceramics, which are only half as strong? Or why can 80 million locusts occupy one square kilometer and not collide with each other, while people have 3.6 million car collisions a year? Locusts obviously have better blinkers.

But heck, Benyus didn't have to go gallivanting off to the Galapagos for her research. She could have learned all about wildlife at my house. We mimic biology daily: We grow our own mold forests. Everyone's as sensitive as a sea anemone. My daughters can make purple and green eye shadow from the scum in their sinks. My husband insists the holes in his underwear create a perfect drafting system. When I'm not looking, a symbiotic system cleans our dishes: My kids put dirty plates on the floor. The dogs lick them clean. The girls put them away. My sighs let off so much pressure they mimic a whale's blowhole.

We are the world.

Still, Benyus is on to something. After biomimicry got its, uh, sea legs, architects, designers, and engineers began looking for ways to apply nature to design. A paint company, Lotusan, studied the lotus flower to learn how it repels dirt and stays clean without soap. It copied the self-cleaning principles at work on the plant's surface and engineered a paint that repels dirt. A fabric company analyzed morpho butterflies and peacocks to figure out the source behind their vibrant coloring. Neither the scales on the butterfly wings nor those on peacock feathers have any pigment. Their color comes from the way layers of their surface materials refract and reflect light. Today Teijin Fibers, of Japan, makes dye-free colored fabrics using the same method.

As Benyus puts it, nature's been solving design problems for 3.8 billion years. "Organisms in nature have figured out how to do what they do while taking care of the place that will care for their offspring. They build soil, clean water and air, mix the cocktail of gases we need to live, and do it all while having great sex." No wonder people started paying attention.

Though Benyus's examples are mind-bending, you don't have to be a Mensa member to apply some of nature's principles at home.

- *Follow the light.* Life depends on sunlight. Capitalize on sun exposure in your home by maximizing south-facing windows to bring in natural light and heat. When rays get too intense, pull the shades, just as a leaf turns or a flower folds.
- *Seek balance.* Nature rewards cooperation and depends on connections. Species that endure are in harmony with their environment and each other. Mix your furnishings so that patterns, textures, shapes, sizes, and colors depend on each other for success. Work for harmony, not dominance.
- *Choose sustainable furniture.* Pick sturdy, well-made pieces with good lines. Maintain and repair them as needed to conserve natural resources and make investments last.
- *Think locally.* When choosing a color or design scheme, draw from the nature in your region. Using local materials will help your home look as if it belongs. Match outdoor paint to colors in your surrounding landscape. Save shipping, keep resources in your community, and support your ecosystem by hiring local contractors and craftspeople.
- *Waste not, want not.* Break the store-to-landfill cycle. When a household item has exceeded its useful life, think of other ways to use it. (See previous chapter.) Reclaim that old chest and use it as an end table. Turn that stained tablecloth into pillows or a valance. Nature wastes nothing. When a sea critter discards a shell, a hermit crab moves in. The shell home gets handed down until it ultimately becomes sand, which is almost the state my home is in.

Now let's peek at some new technologies that are already making homes smarter, safer, greener, and, thankfully, more user friendly.

58

Brave New House

IF I COULD pick a time in history to live, I would plant myself somewhere after the invention of matches but before the remote control. The arrival of the remote marks the point where houses got so smart they started to make me look bad.

An incident in my neighborhood reminded me of how humbling my smart house is. A woman's new car was stolen out of her driveway. I'm not a detective, but I suspect the fact that she left the keys in the unlocked car, which was so new it did not yet have license plates, might have tempted this fate. The brazen act tripped widespread hysteria. You'd have thought Jack the Ripper was in town. Neighbors sent frantic e-mails: Close your garage! Don't leave keys in your car! Set your alarms!

Set the alarm? I stopped setting the alarm long ago because I kept setting it off. Ever since, I've suffered acute code freeze. I remember all my PIN and password codes at all times *except* when I have to punch them in correctly. On the house alarm, a little green light blinks for thirty seconds, to let me punch in my code. Pressure mounts: Is it star plus my anniversary? My anniversary plus star? Or is it pound first? Or my birthday plus enter? The last four numbers of my Social? Aaach! The light's red. Wah! wah! wah! The alarm sounds. The dogs bolt. Next thing two handsome officers are at my front door, which is as good as my fantasy life gets.

The security system is just one source of techno intimidation. The theater system with its six remotes is another. My family has issued a restraining order forbidding me to touch it. My smoke detector is so sensitive that the local fire department knows every time I burn toast, which is embarrassingly often. Even our basement is wired for extra-terrestrial communication. One freezing night the basement tele-phoned our security service, which called and woke me at 3 A.M. to tell me my pipes were on the brink of bursting. I grabbed a robe and stumbled downstairs to the freezing basement to turn on the remote-control fireplace to heat the space.

I stared blearily at the remote, trying to remember the installer's "it's-so-easy" demonstration. To program the heat sensor, adjust the flame height, set the fan, and create the mood you want, just click, click, click. But how do you turn it on? Remembering high school trigonometry would be easier. I yearned for a coal stove.

Of course, not everyone's technically challenged. Dan and the kids share techy genes I don't, and make a sport of my shortcoming. Dan recently brought me a new cell phone, though my old one, which my family called "the brick," and I had been getting along fine. "This one's much cooler," he said, handing me something as substantial as a graham cracker. "It takes pictures and has GPS."

"You can take pictures when you get lost," Marissa chirps.

"Just show me how to place a call."

Now every time it rings, Dan and the kids watch the entertain-ment as I frisk myself and then empty my purse. By then the caller's into voice mail.

"I live to watch you do this," Dan says.

This is just one more matter I will need to bring up with the thera-pist I'm surely headed for.

If you, too, are a low-tech person in a high-tech world, here's good news: The trend in home technology is toward being more user friendly, says Mike Holmes, chair of Home Technology Alliance for the National Association of Home Builders (NAHB) and a custom builder in Reno, Nevada. I'll click to that. The bad news? Houses will keep getting smarter. Here's a sampling of the smart-home technology he says is here and coming soon to a home near you:

- *Start dinner from your office.* You will be able to control anything that has an on/off switch from your computer or iPhone. From your office or on your way home, you will someday turn on lights, heat the Jacuzzi, and start the oven.
- *Getting greener.* You'll see more high-efficiency furnaces and air conditioners, tankless water heaters, multiroom programmable thermostats, water-saving devices, and energy-efficient windows.
- *Tomorrow's house.* By 2015, according to the NAHB, many if not most homes will have these smart technologies: monitored burglar, fire, and toxic-gas alarm systems; fiber-optic networks; multiroom video and audio; and sensor-operated faucets.
- *The power of light control.* Many homes already have remote-control window treatments, which raise and lower motorized shades or open blinds to save on heating and cooling bills. Remotes also turn lights on and off, and dim them. Eventually, computers will let you program your lights and window treatments to operate at certain times.
- *More candid camera.* As closed-circuit televisions enter more homes, you will be able to see who's at your door or by the pool from the television in your bedroom, or from your office.
- *So long, remotes.* Touch-screen menus will replace keypads. Remotes will go away. (Hooray!) Wires will disappear, as more home gadgets go wireless. You will no longer need to remember your alarm code or your door key. (This can't happen soon enough.) Entry systems will read your fingerprint, retina, facial features, or voice. In other words, soon houses will be so smart they will make people like me look brilliant.

Final Thought:
Going Home

Home is so sad. It stays as it was left,
Shaped to the comfort of the last to go
As if to win them back.
—PHILIP LARKIN, BRITISH POET

I'M SITTING IN the living room of the home my dear parents, now in their eighties, have lived in since I was four. It's a single-story California ranch house. There's not a window in it I haven't crawled through. When I visit, I feel like Alice in the rabbit hole. Everything seems to have shrunk, as if I'm seeing it from an airplane. As someone who left to make her own family home somewhere else, I certainly do see this once-upon-a-time home from a new perspective. I can't look at it without judgment and sentiment and humble pride.

Much of the house, for better or worse, is still original. My parents have always been more interested in tending to sick members of their congregation with prayers and Jell-O salad than in decorating, and who can argue with that?

So this day when Mom asked, "If you were going to redo this living room, where would you start?" I caught the question as if it were a hot potato.

My first thought, "I would take the place back to the studs," but I know better than to say that. I start softly: "It would be messy, but I'd start by scraping the cottage-cheese coating off your ceilings and make them smooth."

"What's wrong with the ceiling?"

"Most people think cottage-cheese ceilings are out," I say. "They prefer smooth ceilings."

"I don't find them objectionable. Your father and I recently had them resprayed."

"1987," Dad says from a nearby chair, where he pretends to be dozing.

"Then leave them," I say, even though looking at them reminds me of those women at community pools who are all cellulite and no tan.

I try to change subjects, but Mom keeps going: "What else?"

"Well, maybe we could paint the walls something besides white."

"What's wrong with white?" she asks, then looks toward the window. "And I suppose you would throw out the drapes."

"Well," I search for a delicate answer while I survey the drapes, ivory damask over sheers, which were fine when new but now look like the balloons from last week's party, "when did you get them?"

"Wasn't that long ago," she says.

"1972," Dad says, eyes still closed.

"I've always liked these drapes," she says.

"They do go with the walls," I say, which is the nicest true thing I can think of.

I'm not bothered that my parents don't mind my decorating advice. Just because I write a nationally syndicated home design column doesn't cancel out the fact that they scared the bogeyman out from under my bed. And while the room for improvement here is great and obvious, part of me likes this house just the way it is.

I park my suitcase in the guest room, my old room. It has the same yellow-flowered wallpaper, with matching bedspread, curtains, and lampshade, it had when I was a girl. From the window, I can still see straight into the neighbor's kitchen, a vantage that gave me quite an education. In the closet is a box containing all the dresses I wore to school dances, and their corresponding flashbacks. I don't know why Mom saved them.

Later, as I'm helping her put together a big family dinner, which she still does with enviable ease, I see her head out the side door to the garage.

"Where are you going?" I ask.

"To get the stemware."

"In the garage?"

"No room for it inside."

I think, "Maybe if you purged one kitchen cabinet of all the fifty-cent flower vases you've amassed over four decades, you'd have room," but I stifle my urge to redecorate and reorganize. I appreciate that my parents have created a home that works, and that is beautiful in its worn-in way. As I watch them go through the routine they've perfected after sixty years of marriage, a routine where Dad gathers the laundry and Mom runs the washing machine, where he slices the bananas and she pours the cereal, I see how comfortable they are with where and how they live. They've arrived to a place we can only hope to arrive.

For all the advice dished out here, advice aimed at bridging the gap between real and ideal home life, what ultimately matters most is that our homes support, nurture, and sustain the lives within. That they create an environment where families can love and laugh and learn, make memories and build character. If a home can do that with beauty and order, that's even better.

As I watch my girls hang out in the same big backyard I played in, climb the same trees, and stand where I helped my brother (now an architect) build underground forts, I hope this time capsule of my childhood builds a bridge between my youth and theirs. I also hope that someday, they will get, like I'm finally getting, the essence of home.

These are the days.

Acknowledgments

I AM NOT an interior designer who also writes. I am a writer who has her nose pressed to the glass of that beautiful, elusive world of design. And I want in. For those who have cracked their windows, who have let me into their worlds and shared their views on living better, more beautifully, and more graciously, I am grateful, and so are my readers.

To each of my newspaper editors who continue to carry my column despite budget cuts, shrinking sections, and pressure from the top, I have heard from a reliable source that you each have a special place in heaven with all-down bedding.

Because writers, and I speak for myself, can be wayward and rudderless, I thank all those who have shepherded me, and corralled my instincts and musings into this book. *House of Havoc* would not have found its way between covers without my personal angel and agent, Faye Bender, and several wonderful editors: Wendy Francis, who helped me focus this book when I felt as if I were arm wrestling an octopus; Renée Sedliar, who so gracefully and deftly stepped in and offered a well-calibrated eye and a sure hand; Erica Truxler and Cisca Schreefel, who did an awful lot of heavy lifting behind the scenes. Finally, I'm indebted to Matthew Lore for selecting my voice from among a surely raucous chorus, and declaring, before I even knew, "She's got more than one book in her." I feel so lucky. For bringing my work into the limelight, I thank the talented publicity team at Perseus, including Lissa Warren, Kate Burke, and Diane Mancher.

If it weren't for Susan Beane, Tracy Beckman, and Stephanie Abarbanel, and their friendship, support, editorial opinions, and free therapy, I would require heavy medication. I am certain I cannot adequately express my appreciation for my parents, Neal and Nancy Jameson, who continue to teach me by their loving, tolerant, and morally centered example.

Finally, I am grateful for my long-suffering husband and children, who put up with a lot of crummy dinners while I'm on deadline, and I'm always on deadline, and who provide an endless stream of material and madness, havoc and humor, love and life.

Index